The Making of Modern Anglo-Jewry

JEWISH SOCIETY AND CULTURE

General Editor DAVID SORKIN

FORTHCOMING

Tony Kushner *The Jews in Post-War Britain*
Frances Malino *Zalkind Hourwitz: A Jew in the French Revolution*
Peter Pulzer *Jews and the German State 1848–1939*

Jewish Communities of the Modern World

Todd Endelman *The Jews of England*
Paula Hyman *The Jews of France*
Aron Rodrigue & Esther Benbassa *The Jews of Turkey*
David Sorkin *The Jews of Germany*
Norman Stillman *The Jews of North Africa*
Steven J. Zipperstein *The Jews of Russia*

The Making of
Modern Anglo-Jewry

Edited by
David Cesarani

Basil Blackwell

THE UNIVERSITY OF TOLEDO LIBRARIES

Copyright © Basil Blackwell Ltd 1990

First published 1990

Basil Blackwell Ltd
108 Cowley Road, Oxford, OX4 1JF, UK

Basil Blackwell, Inc.
3 Cambridge Center
Cambridge, Massachusetts 02142, USA

All rights reserved. Except for the quotation of short passages for the purposes of
criticism and review, no part of this publication may be reproduced, stored in a
retrieval system, or transmitted, in any form or by any means, electronic,
mechanical, photocopying, recording or otherwise, without the prior permission of the
publisher.

Except in the United States of America, this book is sold subject to the condition
that it shall not, by way of trade or otherwise, be lent, re-sold, hired out, or
otherwise circulated without the publisher's prior consent in any form of binding or
cover other than that in which it is published and without a similar condition
including this condition being imposed on the subsequent purchaser.

British Library Cataloguing in Publication Data
A CIP catalogue record for this book is available
from the British Library.

Library of Congress Cataloging in Publication Data
The making of modern Anglo-Jewry / edited by David Cesarani.
    p.   cm.
Includes index.
ISBN 0-631-16776-5
    1. Jews—Great Britain.   2. Great Britain—Ethnic relations.
I. Cesarani, David.
DS135.E5M25   1989   89-31794
941'.004924—dc20   CIP

Typeset in 10 on 11½pt Ehrhardt
by Footnote Graphics, Warminster, Wilts
Printed in Great Britain by
Billing & Sons Ltd, Worcester

DS
135
'E5M25
1990

Contents

Part IV: Politics

Acknowledgements

Six of the essays in this volume are based on papers that were delivered at conferences in Leeds between 1986–7. The first, 'Jews in British Cities: Immigration and Settlement 1815–1915' took place on 4–5 May 1986 and the second, 'Jews in Britain in Peace and Wartime, 1914–1945' on 10 May 1987. The conferences were held under the auspices of the Department of Adult and Continuing Education, University of Leeds. I would like to thank Diane Jacks and Marilyn Moreland of the Department for their efforts and organizational skills. I was fortunate to be the first Montague Burton Fellow in Jewish Studies at the University of Leeds, based in the School of History, from 1983 to 1986, and I would also like to express my deep gratitude to the benefactors who made the Fellowship, and the conferences, possible.

David Sorkin, the editor of the series Jewish History and Culture, gave this project enormous encouragement and was the source of much sound advice. I would like to thank David Sorkin, Bryan Cheyette and Tony Kushner for their comments on my own contributions and their generous assistance in the preparation of the book. My special thanks go to Dawn for her help and constant support. This book is dedicated to Henry and Joyce Cesarani.

David Cesarani,
The Wiener Library, London

List of Abbreviations

AAC	Academic Assistance Council
AJA	Anglo-Jewish Association
AJFS	Association of Jewish Friendly Societies
AJTMP	Amalgamated Jewish Tailors', Machiners' and Pressers' Trade Union
AST	Amalgamated Society of Tailors
AYZS	Association of Young Zionist Societies
BDA	Board of Deputies Archive
BOD	Board of Deputies Minutes
BSP	British Socialist Party
BUF	British Union of Fascists
CBF	Central British Fund for German Jewry
CGJ	Council for German Jewry
CP	Communist Party
CZA	Central Zionist Archive, Jerusalem
ELA	*East London Advertiser*
ELO	*East London Observer*
EZF	English Zionist Federation
FSA	Federation of Synagogues Archive
GJAC	German Jewish Aid Committee
GLRO	Greater London Record Office
HC Debs	Hansard, House of Commons Debates Fifth Series
ILP	Independent Labour Party
JC	*Jewish Chronicle*
JFC	Joint Foreign Committee
JHSE	Jewish Historical Society of England
JLB	Jewish Lads' Brigade
JPC	Jewish People's Council against Fascism and Anti-Semitism

JPSA	Jewish Publication Society of America
JRC	Jewish Refugees Committee
JSR	*Jewish Standard and Recorder*
JTS	Jews' Temporary Shelter
JW	*Jewish World*
MCN	*Manchester City News*
MG	*Manchester Guardian*
MHA	Manchester Hebrew Association
MZA	Manchester Zionist Association
NAFTA	National Amalgamated Furnishing Trades Association
NUTGW	National Union of Tailors and Garment Workers
NUWM	National Unemployed Workers Movement
ORT	Society for the Promotion of Trades and Agriculture among Jews
SDF	Social Democratic Federation
ULTTU	United Ladies' Tailors' Trade Union
USA	United Synagogue Archive
WA	Weizmann Archive, Rehovoth, Israel
WJC	World Jewish Congress
YZ	*Young Zionist*
ZF	English Zionist Federation/Zionist Federation of Great Britain and Ireland (after 1930)
ZFEC	Zionist Federation Executive Committee
ZR	*Zionist Review*

List of Contributors

Bill Williams is the author of *The Making of Manchester Jewry 1740–1875* (Manchester, 1976), *Manchester Jewry A Pictorial History 1788–1988* (Manchester, 1988) and numerous articles on the Jews of Manchester. He is a founder of the Manchester Jewish Museum.

Anne J. Kershen completed an M.Phil. at Warwick University on trade unionism amongst clothing workers of London and Leeds. While curator of the London Museum of Jewish Life, 1988–9, she edited *Off the Peg* (1988), a history of the women's wholesale clothing industry. She is currently writing the official history of Reform Jewry in Britain.

Rickie Burman trained as an anthropologist. She has written on Jewish women's history and women in Judaism in *Oral History* and other publications. She is currently curator of the London Museum of Jewish Life.

Rosalyn Livshin wrote her M.Ed. thesis at Manchester University on 'Aspects of the Acculturation of the Children of Immigrant Jews in Manchester, 1890–1930'. She is currently working on the development of multicultural curricula for schools.

Bryan Cheyette holds a British Academy Post-doctoral Fellowship in the School of English, University of Leeds. He is currently completing a book entitled *Jewish Representations in English Literature* and is working on a comparative study of British- and American-Jewish literature. He is the literary editor of the *Jewish Quarterly* and a regular contributor to the *Times Literary Supplement*.

David Cesarani is Director of Studies at the Wiener Library, London. He has published articles on the inter-war history of Anglo-Jewry in *The London Journal, Journal of Contemporary History* and various collections of essays. He is currently writing a history of the *Jewish Chronicle* newspaper and is completing a study of the Zionist Movement in England, 1917–1939.

Elaine R. Smith is completing her doctoral thesis on 'East End Jews in Politics: 1918–1939: A Study in Class and Ethnicity', at the University of Leicester. She has published in the *Jewish Quarterly* and has contributed a chapter on 'Jewish Responses to Antisemitism and Fascism in the Inter-war East End', in T. Kushner and K. Lunn (eds), *Traditions of Intolerance* (Manchester, 1989).

Louise London is working on a doctoral thesis on 'British Immigration Control Procedures and Jewish Refugees, 1933–1951', at Queen Mary College, University of London. Before this she was a practising solicitor, specializing in immigration cases. She has written many reviews and articles on immigrants, minorities and the law.

Tony Kushner is James Parkes Fellow in the Department of History, University of Southampton. He is the author of *The Persistence of Prejudice: Antisemitism in British Society During the Second World War* (Manchester, 1989) and co-editor, with Kenneth Lunn, of *Traditions of Intolerance. Historical perspectives on fascism and race discourse in Britain* (Manchester, 1989).

1
Introduction

David Cesarani

Until quite recently Anglo-Jewish history and culture has been one of the most neglected areas in the study of modern Jewish life. Sandwiched between the rich heritage of Eastern and Central European Jewry before World War II and the massive Jewish presence in North America, Anglo-Jewry has appeared numerically insignificant and overshadowed by the Jewish learning and prodigious economic, social and cultural energies of these Jewish super-populations. Its political affairs have seemed pygmy-like, apart from moments when Jewish world history and Anglo-Jewish history have intersected, as in 1917 with the Balfour Declaration. Within the fields of modern Jewish studies, the specificity of the Anglo-Jewish experience has been undermined by constant reference to paradigms drawn from the Jewish experience in Eastern and Central Europe or the Americas.[1] These essays represent an attempt to break with this practice and to write on Anglo-Jewish life in its own terms and within its specific context.

The period covered by this volume, broadly 1870–1945, also reflects the relative paucity of published research on modern Anglo-Jewry. There has certainly been nothing to compare with the major studies of American, French or German Jewry in the late nineteenth and, in a far more pronounced manner, the twentieth centuries.[2] This is not because Anglo-Jewry is undeserving of

---

[1] For a critique of the use of such inappropriate models, see T. Endelman, 'The Englishness of Jewish Modernity in England', in ed. J. Katz, *Towards Modernity: The European Model* (New Brunswick, 1987), pp. 225–46, and pp. 225–8 and 242–5 in particular.

[2] See for example, J. Gurock, *When Harlem Was Jewish* (New York, 1979), D. Dash Moore, *At Home in America: Second Generation New York Jews*, (New York, 1981); D. Weinberg, *A Community on Trial: The Jews of Paris in the 1930s* (Chicago, 1977), P. Hyman, *From Dreyfus to Vichy: The Remaking of French Jewry, 1906–1939* (New York, 1979); D. Neiwyk, *The Jews in Weimar Germany* (Baton Rouge, 1980).

study or because the material is lacking. Although Jews in Britain were spared occupation and persecution, their history did not go into suspended animation between 1933 and 1945, and cannot be said to have lacked immediacy and urgency. If this collection does nothing else, it proves that there is a super-abundance of subjects for research and a vast amount of untapped material on Anglo-Jewry since 1900. Rather, the lacunae have stemmed from a tradition of self-deprecation and a lack of collective self-esteem.

The study of Anglo-Jewry has been hobbled by an apologetic tendency that has taken two successive forms. The first mode of apologetics was the product of Anglo-Jewry's particular route to modernity and the conditions under which Jews in Britain gained emancipation in the mid-nineteenth century. Jews were accepted not for who and what they were, but according to terms set by the English majority and cast in the liberal rhetoric of toleration and universalism. Accordingly, Jewish historical research devoted itself to showing that Jews had earned and continued to deserve full civic equality. Research stressed the duration of Jewish settlement in Britain and the contribution of Jews to the 'host' society. Studies concentrated on the earliest generations of settlers and rendered hagiographic accounts of the institutions they created; Jewish economic, political and cultural activity was described largely in terms of the struggle for acceptance, the justice of Jewish claims and the extent to which Jews fulfilled the conditions of the emancipation bargain by becoming worthy British citizens.[3]

The second form of apologetics was a by-product of the 'Zionist revolution'. The historians and social scientists who fashioned Jewish history and social analysis to support the Zionist project did so to the detriment of Jews who remained in the Diaspora. The 'lessons' of history 'proved' the inevitability of assimilation, enervation or annihilation. A viable, healthy and authentic Jewish life was considered to be possible only in Israel; Jewish populations in the Diaspora were treated like curios and thereby marginalized.[4]

[3] This mode reached its apogee in Cecil Roth's *A History of the Jews in England* (Oxford, 1941). Although it was written in 1941, Roth's narrative effectively ceases with Jewish emancipation in 1858. Four pages sum up the period 1858–1905, comprised in a large part by Roth's eulogization of English society. The apologetic tone and complete absence of critical scrutiny of the stormy years after 1858 can be judged from this elegant and typical passage (p. 270, 1978 edn): 'The alembic of English tolerance has operated now on the newer arrivals as well. Their sons have taken part in English life, contributed to English achievement, striven for England's betterment, shed their blood in England's wars. In this happy land they have attained a measure of freedom ... which has been the case in scarcely any other.'

[4] See M. Marrus, 'European Jewry and the Politics of Assimilation: Assessment and Reassessment', *Journal of Modern History*, 49: 1 (1977), pp. 89–109, for a corrective view. Although Marrus deals explicitly only with the tragic interpretation of modern European Jewish history, this historiographic mode is typical of most studies influenced by Zionist assumptions. For a critique from a different angle, see D. Biale, *Power and Powerlessness in Jewish History* (New York, 1987), pp. 5–6. Recent scholarship has gone a long way towards redressing the balance through empirical studies which are not overdetermined by assumptions about the inexorability of assimilation or of powerlessness leading to destruction; see, for example, Hyman, *From Dreyfus to Vichy*, M. Rozenblit, *The Jews of Vienna, 1867–1914: Assimilation and Identity* (Albany, NY, 1983), D. Sorkin, *The Transformation of German Jewry, 1780–1840* (Oxford, 1987), H. Kieval, *The Making of Czech Jewry, 1870–1918* (Oxford, 1988). S. Zipperstein, 'Jewish Historiography and the Modern City: Recent Writing on European Jewry', *Jewish History*, 2:1 (Spring 1987), pp. 73–88, links the demographic and sociological investigations which supplied the data and conceptual framework for many Jewish studies to the Zionist commitment of their authors.

During the last decade, however, Diaspora Jewry has enjoyed something of a revival. This has found a partial expression in the excavation of its own roots and their evaluation in a new light – that of the continuity of Jewish life in Diaspora countries. The sense of belonging and endurance has provoked a re-examination of the trajectories of Jewish history, society and culture, while the example of other ethnic minorities struggling for acceptance and respect has been an inspiration and a model. This volume is a part of a regenerated awareness of history and rootedness, which, albeit complex and often problematic, reflects all the tensions and contradictions that come from being a minority ethnic group in a society that is notoriously ambivalent towards immigrants.[5]

I

Prior to the 1960s, Anglo-Jewish studies were almost entirely the preserve of gifted amateurs or part-time historians who combined busy professional lives with research and writing.[6] Cecil Roth was the doyen and virtually sole exponent of professional Jewish studies in Britain.[7] The monopoly position of enthusiasts in the Jewish Historical Society of England, clustered around Roth, remained virtually unbroken until the welcome intrusion of the American-born and trained Jewish historian Lloyd Gartner. His study *The Jewish Immigrant in England*, published in 1960, catapulted modern Anglo-Jewish history onto a new level of accomplishment and vastly broadened its scope.[8]

Over the succeeding quarter of a century a variety of historians and social scientists added to the literature on Anglo-Jewry in the modern period. The immigrant milieu was further investigated by William Fishman, in *East End Jewish Radicals, 1875–1914*, which paid particular attention to anarchist politics in East London and Jerry White's *The Rothschild Buildings: Life in An East End Tenement Block 1887–1920*, which tackled questions of culture, community, class and gender.[9] Immigrants in a non-London setting were dealt with from different perspectives by Bill Williams in *The Making of Manchester Jewry, 1740–1875* and Joe Buckman in *Immigrants and the Class Struggle: The Jewish*

---

[5] For a useful recent overview of Britain's ambivalence towards immigrants and immigrant society, See. C. Holmes, *John Bull's Island: Immigration and British Society, 1871–1971* (London, 1988).

[6] For a convenient overview of the development of Anglo-Jewish history writing and the role of the JHSE, see L. P. Gartner, 'A Quarter Century of Anglo-Jewish Historiography', *Jewish Social Studies*, 48: 2, p. 106.

[7] On Roth and his work, L. P. Gartner, 'Jewish Historiography in the United States and Britain', in eds S. Zipperstein and A. Rapaport-Albert, *Jewish History: Essays in Honour of Chimen Abramsky* (London, 1988), p. 207. For an in-depth and admiring account of Roth's work, see L. P. Gartner, 'Cecil Roth, Historian of Anglo-Jewry', in eds D. Noy and I. Ben-Ami, *Studies in the Cultural Life of the Jews in England* (Jerusalem, 1975), pp. 69–86.

[8] L. P. Gartner, *The Jewish Immigrant in England* (London and Detroit, 1960).

[9] W. J. Fishman, *East End Jewish Radicals, 1875–1914* (London, 1975), J. White, *The Rothschild Buildings: Life in an East End Tenement Block, 1887–1920* (London, 1980).

Immigrant in Leeds, 1880–1914.[10] Aubrey Newman in *The United Synagogue, 1870–1970* chronicled one of the most important of the central institutions of metropolitan Jewry.[11] The immigrant economy was dissected by Buckman, on Leeds, and Harold Pollins, whose *Economic History of the Jews in England*, included the immigrants in a sweeping survey of the economic activity of the whole Jewish population.[12] Early studies of the responses to Jewish immigration by John Garrard and Bernard Gainer were added to by monographs on anti-semitism in Britain by Colin Holmes, *Anti-Semitism in British Society, 1876–1939*, and Gizela Lebzelter, *Political Anti-Semitism in England, 1918–1939*.[13] Immigrant politics and Jewish reactions to anti-alien feeling were covered by Fishman and Buckman, while Geoffrey Alderman, in *The Jewish Community in British Politics*, described the political behaviour of immigrants and natives within the context of British political trends.[14] Internal Jewish politics received virtually the first serious, scholarly treatment by Stuart Cohen in *English Zionists and British Jews: The Communal Politics of Anglo-Jewry, 1895–1920*, while in a number of articles Gideon Shimoni carried the investigation through to the 1940s.[15] Debate about the treatment of the Jewish refugee crisis in the 1930s and 1940s was opened up by A. J. Sherman's *Island Refuge: Britain and Refugees from the Third Reich, 1933–1939*, and developed by Bernard Wasserstein in *Britain and the Jews of Europe, 1939–1945*,[16]

This innovative and sophisticated work nevertheless left a number of significant gaps in the study of Anglo-Jewish life and skirted questions that were central to historiographical and cultural debates taking place elsewhere. Most research concentrated on the history of Jewish men and adults to the exclusion of women and the young. It often assumed the existence of a Jewish 'community', with little attempt to define the nature of this elusive social concept. In fact, the notion of community is extremely problematic and its careless usage promotes a false impression of homogeneity, shared values and

[10] B. Williams, *The Making of Manchester Jewry, 1740–1850*, (Manchester, 1976) and J. Buckman, *Immigrants and the Class Struggle: The Jewish Immigrant in Leeds, 1880–1914* (Manchester, 1983).

[11] A. Newman, *The United Synagogue, 1870–1970* (London, 1977).

[12] H. Pollins, *Economic History of the Jews in England* (London, 1982).

[13] J. Garrard, *The English and Immigration, 1880–1910* (London, 1971), B. Gainer, *The Alien Invasion: The Origins of the Aliens Act of 1905* (London, 1972), C. Holmes, *Anti-Semitism in British Society, 1876–1939* (London, 1979), G. Lebzelter, *Political Anti-Semitism in England, 1918–1939* (London, 1978).

[14] G. Alderman, *The Jewish Community in British Politics* (Oxford, 1982). See also his *London Jewry and London Politics, 1889–1986* (London, 1989).

[15] S. Cohen, *English Zionists and British Jews: The Communal Politics of Anglo-Jewry, 1895–1920* (Princeton, NY, 1982); G. Shimoni, 'Selig Brodetsky and the Ascendancy of Zionism in Anglo-Jewry (1939–1945), *Jewish Journal of Sociology*, 22: 2 (1980), pp. 125–61, 'From Anti-Zionism to Non-Zionism in Anglo-Jewry, 1917–1937', *Jewish Journal of Sociology*, 28: 1 (1986), pp. 19–47, 'The Non-Zionists in Anglo-Jewry, 1937–1948', *Jewish Journal of Sociology*, 28: 2 (1986), pp. 89–115, 'Poale Zion: A Zionist Transplant in Britain (1905–1945), in ed. P. Medding, *Studies in Contemporary Jewry*, vol. 2 (Bloomington, Ind., 1986), pp. 227–69.

[16] A. J. Sherman, *Island Refuge: Britain and Refugees from the Third Reich, 1933–1939* (London, 1973) and B. Wasserstein, *Britain and the Jews of Europe, 1939–1945* (Oxford, 1979). For a comprehensive review of the recent literature on Anglo-Jewry, see Gartner, 'A Quarter Century of Anglo-Jewish Historiography' pp. 105–26.

accepted sources of authority for a social collectivity in which none of these things actually obtained. In particular, there was a reluctance to consider class allegiances in juxtaposition with the 'communal unity' which the identification of class called into question. And it was often communal history, charting the institutions established by the elite and operating with their definitions of Jewish identity as primarily denominational rather than ethnic. When the religious self-definition of British Jews was exposed to questioning, this was from a Zionistic standpoint. The issues of anti-semitism in British society and related questions of culture were overshadowed by continental models and subtly marginalized, if not entirely dismissed. Moreover, such work was overwhelmingly centred upon London Jewry and, for the most part, on the communal institutions created by the Anglo-Jewish elite.[17]

While gratefully acknowledging the debt that is owed to previous researchers, the essays in this book are intended to fill some of the lacunae, to redress the balance in favour of the still neglected areas of the Anglo-Jewish experience and to offer a critique of some of the assumptions which have underpinned existing studies. The following sections of this introduction aim to give the reader a guide to the specific points which the essays alight upon, the common elements running through the individual contributions and the authors' shared background which gives the collection a thematic unity despite the divergence of subject matter.

II

Jewish ethnicity is a central concern of these essays. Anne Kershen examines the ways in which ethnicity modified relations between Jewish employers and employees in the tailoring trades in London and Leeds. The customary antagonism between capital and labour was mediated by kinship, religion and communal ties. She also shows that English antagonism towards Jewish immigrants both impelled Jewish workers towards greater involvement with the wider trade union movement and frustrated complete unity with it. Kershen rejects the treatment of Jewish workers' struggles and experiences in isolation from the rest of the British working class; yet she also questions the notion that Jews were just members of that class and that Jewishness was an irrelevant factor in determining their behaviour.[18]

As Geoff Dench has argued, the extent to which minorities are tolerated in an open society is circumscribed by the preferences of the majority which, although it might cloak these predilections in the guise of universalism, is itself

---

[17] Some notable exceptions are Fishman, *East End Jewish Radicals*, Buckman, *Immigrants and the Class Struggle*, White, *The Rothschild Buildings*, and Williams, *The Making of Manchester Jewry*.

[18] For the two extremes of this argument, see Gartner, *The Jewish Immigrant in England* and Buckman, *Immigrants and the Class Struggle*. For one of the best discussions of the problematic, see D. Feldman, 'There Was an Englishman an Irishman and a Jew ... Immigrants and Minorities in Britain', *Historical Journal* (March, 1983), pp. 183–96.

effectively indulging in a form of ethnic communalism.[19] Bryan Cheyette illustrates the double bind which this imposed upon Jewish novelists in England in the nineteenth century. They are shown as torn between a desire to condemn clannishness and Jewish particularity and the urge to represent the Jews in terms of the dominant values of Victorian England.

In his study of the 'alrightniks', Bill Williams examines the intersection between class and ethnicity, showing how cultural links could unite well-off immigrants with their poorer brethren in opposition to the Anglicization policy of Manchester's native Jewish elite. Yet the immigrant parvenus shared the elite's hostility to the trade unionism and socialism that flourished amongst the immigrant workers. Eventually, the immigrants who had 'made it' entered into the ranks of the social elite, but not until both had modified their policy and behaviour. The process of negotiation and concession tellingly illustrates the subtle way in which ethnicity plays into class formation.

Ethnicity modified the experience of Jewish women and children, too. Rickie Burman disputes the ethnic stereotype of the Jewish woman as homemaker and demonstrates the extent to which they were participants in the immigrant economy. There were particular niches reserved for women, particularly widows, according to traditions imported from Eastern Europe. Jewish women were also able to draw upon supporting networks of kin and *landsleit*, immigrants from the same town or region, in hard times. In another piece of research drawing upon the Jewish experience in Manchester, Rosalyn Livshin scrutinizes the means by which the Anglo-Jewish establishment sought through the education system to eradicate the obvious manifestations of Jewish ethnicity amongst the children of East European immigrants. The policy of Anglicization led to the opening of a tragic chasm between immigrant Jews and their children, but did not accomplish the desired degree of integration. Young Jews found themselves cut off from their parents and still at odds with the surrounding society.

The politics of this deracinated generation are the focus of the essays by David Cesarani and Elaine Smith. In the received version of internal Jewish politics after 1917, change is usually ascribed to the 'rise of the immigrants' and the 'triumph of Zionism'. David Cesarani challenges this view to argue that the inter-war years are marked by a struggle for power between sections of the Jewish middle class rather than any insurgency by the 'immigrant masses'. This interpretation breaks with traditional diplomatic and Palestine-centred accounts of Zionism to argue that Jewish nationalism in England is more usefully understood as the vehicle for middle-class Jewish ethnicity. In the East End, the ethnicity of immigrant and British-born Jewish workers took a quite opposed form, propelling many Jews into the communist movement and Labour Party politics. Elaine Smith draws out the influence of Jewish ethnicity on political leadership, party allegiance and the definition of issues in East London politics.

The impact of animosity towards the Jews in Britain is another central and

[19] G. Dench, *Minorities in the Open Society: Prisoners of Ambivalence* (London, 1986), pp. 3–4.

unifying theme of this volume. As Elaine Smith shows, hostility towards the Jews was crucial in the definition of a 'Jewish politics' in East London. However, in the work of previous historians anti-semitism has consistently been marginalized and restricted to upper-class drawing rooms or slightly lunatic fringe groups. Tony Kushner challenges the complacent view of anti-semitism in British society. Such was the strength of anti-semitism that the state was put on the defensive by it and repeatedly capitulated to 'anti-alien' panics, of which Jews were the prime victims. While anti-semitism was considered acceptable, the Jews were deemed virtually unassimilable. Tony Kushner shows that this warped the Jews' employment profile, distorted their participation in politics and led them to establish separate social facilities. Intolerance generated a constant pressure to erase all that was distinctively and visibly 'Jewish' – defined as such by the majority ethnic group, but internalized and frequently elaborated by Jews themselves – in political, economic, cultural and social activity.

The readiness to receive refugees from Germany in the 1930s was another casualty of anti-Jewish animosity and the resultant Jewish defensiveness. Louise London shows that British immigration policy was largely determined by the fear that mass Jewish immigration would aggravate anti-Jewish sentiment in the country. Thus the normal criteria of alien controls were applied at a time when the principle of asylum or emergency measures directed towards rescue could have saved thousands of Jews trying to flee Nazi persecution. Her research also reveals that English Jews were just as worried by the prospect of a massive influx of assorted Jews and colluded with the government in the selection of those whose assimilation would be fast or who were suitable for re-emigration according to age or qualifications.[20]

Several of the other studies bear out Kushner's thesis that anti-semitism had a powerful, warping effect on Jewish thought and behaviour. The pressure to assimilate and the intolerance of Jewish difference underlies the work of Livshin and Cheyette. Bill Williams and Anne Kershen argue that anti-alienism played a major part in determining elite policies towards Jewish workers, while they were themselves motivated and victimized by its incidence. Jews in Britain have tended to play down the extent and oppressiveness of prejudice in their country, both out of an apologetic tradition and in view of the incomparably more terrible fate of Jews on the European mainland. Yet, while it is true that anti-semitism in Britain claimed few victims through direct physical violence, it wreaked a terrible effect on the psychology and self-expression of generations of Jewish immigrants and their children. Indirectly, it was responsible for consigning many European Jews to their doom and inhibiting efforts at rescue during the Holocaust. Taken cumulatively, these essays document the extent to which the state, society and culture in Britain operated a discourse about Jews that was exclusive and oppressive, that eventuated in and legitimated discrimination and that was so pervasive and well-entrenched that it resisted self-questioning even

[20] The important new study by E. Black, *The Social Politics of Anglo-Jewry, 1880–1920* (Oxford, 1989), chs 9, 10, provides material that is highly suggestive of comparisons between these two periods and the continuities of Anglo-Jewish attitudes towards immigration.

in the face of Nazi persecution of the Jews during World War II and the revelations made in its aftermath.[21]

III

Despite the umbrella use of the term Anglo-Jewish history to describe the contents of this book, the contributors come from a variety of disciplines and bring to their subject matter different methodologies and vocabularies. Background and training has also influenced choice of subject. Rosalyn Livshin's work is situated in the field of education studies in which she is particularly concerned with the education of ethnic minorities. Rickie Burman trained as an anthropologist and has been involved extensively in researching and writing women's history. Bryan Cheyette's work on the representation of Jews in English literature forms part of a broad concern with literary and cultural studies. Louise London practised immigration law for many years and brings to her research a nuts-and-bolts knowledge of immigration procedures as well as an acute sensitivity to the experience of the immigrants. Commitment to a Jewish subject is common to all these contributors, but the reader will be aware of differences of approach and language. This reflects a conscious intention to work in an interdisciplinary framework and a belief in the need to introduce a plurality of perspectives into the field of Anglo-Jewish studies.

This breadth of experience, academic background and interests led the authors of these essays to explore areas that have been persistently neglected in Anglo-Jewish history. In particular, questions of class, gender, childhood and culture that have been probed in other fields here receive attention for almost the first time. As Rickie Burman points out, accounts of immigration and settlement have been assembled largely from the perspective of men: women and children have been all but written out of Jewish history. Part of this has been due to the absence of traditional sources for historical research which would illuminate the position of Jewish women and for this reason oral history has been essential in the recovery of women's history. Rickie Burman's work on Jewish women in the economy uses oral history techniques that have been honed in general history to open up a formerly closed area of the Anglo-Jewish past.

Oral history plays a major role in the chapter by Rosalyn Livshin. The reconstruction of childhood and the experience of education has relied upon unorthodox sources, yet it has grown as a distinct field in general historical studies. Rosalyn Livshin brings to the experience of Jews in Manchester a problematic which has existed for some time in the history of education with regard to ethnic minority needs and aspirations. Her work goes beyond narrowly focused, laudatory accounts of communal education to examine the assumptions which underlay and determined its operation.

The marginalization of women and children in Jewish history may be

[21] See T. Kushner, *The Persistence of Prejudice* (Manchester, 1989).

explicable in terms of a male- and adult-centred view of the world stemming from Jewish religious and social traditions, but the peripheralization of culture is harder to account for. Yet, there has been in Anglo-Jewish history writing a systematic denigration of cultural achievements.[22] It has become a received wisdom that Anglo-Jewry has made no distinctive cultural contribution within the spheres of Jewish learning or letters. Yet culture is narrowly defined as a continuation of traditional Jewish scholarship. Cultural creativity in music, the arts and literature of the wider society is taken as an expression of non-Jewish interests, even a rejection of Jewish society. The 'Jewishness' of these cultural producers is reduced to the origins of the artist or identifiable 'Jewish' themes. Yet, as Bryan Cheyette demonstrates, a sophisticated analysis of texts, using techniques drawn from recent literary theory and cultural studies, can tease out practices of self-effacement or self-assertion which are derived directly from the situation of the author as a member of a Jewish minority. The 'Jewish' content of these novels is highly problematic (which may be why it has remained unexplored), but it cannot be extruded from either English culture or Jewish creativity.

IV

The last decade has seen a burgeoning interest in the study of Anglo-Jewry and a rapid expansion in the numbers of young, professionally trained scholars who have selected the Jews in Britain as their main field of research. The work which is presented here, with the obvious exception of Bill Williams, represents part of the output of this new generation.[23] With E. H. Carr's well-known dictum in mind – 'Study the historian before you begin to study the facts' – some explanation of the origins of this interest and the form it has taken may help a reading of the final products.[24]

The authors of these essays combine a professional training with a determination to apply this to the study of Anglo-Jewish history and culture. Three of them research and teach aspects of modern Jewish studies; three others are deeply involved in the collection of Jewish archival material and running Jewish museums in Britain; one is a graduate student whose work is concerned heavily

---

[22] See, for example, L. P. Gartner, 'Emancipation, Social Change and Communal Reconstruction in Anglo-Jewry, 1789–1881,' *Proceedings of the American Academy for Jewish Research*, 54, (1987), pp. 113, 116.

[23] For important work by other historians whose research challenges the established version or fills major holes in the historiography, see M. Levene, 'Jewish Diplomacy at War and Peace: A Study of Lucien Wolf, 1914–1919', D. Phil, thesis (Oxford, 1981); D. Feldman, 'Immigrants and Workers: Englishmen and Jews: Jewish Immigration to the East End of London, 1880–1906', Ph.D. thesis, (Cambridge, 1985); S. Kadish, 'Bolsheviks and British Jews: The Anglo-Jewish Community, Britain and the Russian Revolution', D. Phil, thesis, (Oxford, 1987). See also, M. Schmool, 'Register of Social Research on the Anglo-Jewish Community 1987–1988,' *Jewish Journal of Sociology*, 30: 1 (1988), pp. 37–50 and A. Newman, 'Research Newsletter', Research Committee of the Jewish Historical Society of England, Autumn 1987.

[24] E. H. Carr, *What is History* (London, 1972), p. 23.

with Anglo-Jewish history. Their work is the product of scholarly commitment and sits alongside a practical contribution to the production and dissemination of Anglo-Jewish historical and cultural studies. Several are, or have been, based in non-London Jewish centres, which is reflected in their fields of inquiry.

All but two of the contributors were connected with the informal Jewish history group which met intermittently from 1981 onwards. The group crystallized around Bill Williams, then head of the Manchester Studies Unit at Manchester Polytechnic, and debate circulated around issues of class, community, gender and culture. Those who participated in these meetings shared an awareness of Britain's problematic record as a host for immigrants from the New Commonwealth and Pakistan and had witnessed the dynamism of racism along with neo-Fascism in this country during the 1970s. The optimistic, liberal panaceas and the received wisdom concerning British 'tolerance' looked increasingly suspect in the light of appeals to popular xenophobia by leading politicians and the role of the state in the evolution and implementation of racist policies. Yet the post-war settlers in British cities displayed a marked resilience and contested the assumptions of assimilationism in the cause of a genuinely multi-cultural society.

The possibility that Britain might be moving towards a multi-ethnic society provoked questions about the fate of Jewish culture in England and the reasons why Anglo-Jewry was mired in self-effacement and apologetics. In their political behaviour the official communal organizations were insistent that Anglo-Jewry was only a denominational group in spite of all evidence to the contrary – such as its voting behaviour and its commitment to Israel and Soviet Jewry – and the enticements which multi-culturalism now offered to a more confident, assertive ethnic Jewish identity. This concern with the specific trajectory of Anglo-Jewish society was reinforced for some by misgivings about trends in Israel and a concomitant questioning of Israel-centred interpretations of Jewish history. In particular, this led to a determination to rebut the systematic denigration of Diaspora Jewry; Anglo-Jewry came to be evaluated in its own terms and not treated as a shard on the scrap-heap of Jewish history.

This preoccupation with the specificities of Anglo-Jewish history and culture married with the desire to integrate Anglo-Jewish studies into general historical and cultural studies by utilizing their methodologies, criteria and, above all, the same broad scope and perspective. Anglo-Jewish history and cultural studies had to be liberated from the trammels of a narrowly Jewish national history, overdetermined by assumptions about assimilation and decline, or an equally restrictive denominational, 'communal' focus in which the behaviour of Jews within their own communities was assumed to be autonomous from their surroundings, inherently different and resistant to the modes of inquiry common to general historical, cultural or sociological studies.

Yet, at the same time, this interest in context promoted an awareness of the extent to which Jews in Britain had been the subjects of exclusion in the form of prejudice and state-managed or condoned discrimination. The investigation of Anglo-Jewry's place in British society also revealed its apartness. Consciousness of this induced an inquiry into the complex and uncomfortable questions of anti-Jewish hostility, the fissures between Jews and non-Jews as well as the unifying factors. Class, community, gender and culture all became intensely problematic points of juncture between the Jewish experience and British history and culture.

These essays are an attempt to explore this difficult and subtle legacy. They are united by common themes and a shared project: to rescue and assert the specificity of the Anglo-Jewish experience and at the same time to reconnect Anglo-Jewry with British history and locate it within British culture. The contributions are based on original research and are frequently parts of work in progress, tentative explorations of new ground. It is hoped that they will help in the definition of an agenda for future work, stimulate debate and lead more researchers towards the study of the Jews in Britain.

PART I
Class and Community

2

'East and West': Class and Community in Manchester Jewry, 1850–1914

Bill Williams

The aim of this essay is to use Manchester evidence to suggest a new perspective on 'the confrontation between East and West': the confrontation brought about in the late nineteenth century by the arrival in the emancipated and culturally assimilated Jewish communities of Western Europe of large numbers of immigrants from the besieged centres of Jewish life in Eastern Europe. In particular, I want to question a line of argument which explains this confrontation, and the tensions which accompanied it, either solely or essentially in cultural terms, as a simple collision between two contrasting patterns of Jewish life. This is the argument pursued by Jacob Katz when he seeks to define the moment at which the patterns of Eastern and Western Jewish culture began to diverge,[1] and it is the prevailing opinion of Anglo-Jewish historiography. Even those who accept a social dimension speak only of the sharp distinction between a hard-pressed working-class immigrant group and a comfortable native bourgeoisie.[2]

While not wishing to deny the existence or the importance of a 'clash of cultures' or to underestimate the social distance which initially separated Anglo-Jewry from the immigrant newcomers, a crucial element is missing. What the argument lacks is a more precise sense of the social context in which the clash took place, and, in particular, an appreciation of the social divisions prevalent in the late nineteenth-century Jewish communities of both East and West. This essay argues that the nature of the culture-clash and of its effects on Western Jewry, both immediate and permanent, were deeply influenced by

---

[1] Jacob Katz, 'Vom Ghetto zum Zionismus, Gegenseitige Beeinflussung von Ost und West', *Bulletin of the Leo Baeck Institute*, 64 (1983), pp. 3–14.

[2] Lloyd Gartner, *The Jewish Immigrant in England, 1870–1914* (2nd edn; London, 1973), pp. 49–56; Harold Pollins, *Economic History of the Jews in England* (London, 1982), pp. 130–141.

social divisions within each of the communities which came into collision. The notion of a clash between two socially homogeneous communities, each bound by a distinctive pattern of culture, should be replaced by one which takes into account the way in which cultural interchange is mediated through class structures and influenced by social change.

While there are several ways of attempting this, most as yet untried, the one chosen here is to focus on the role of a social group rarely taken into account by historians of Anglo-Jewry: a *nouveaux riches* of entrepreneurs in commerce and the workshop trades within the Eastern European immigrant community itself. Emphasis is placed on the status and ambition of the immigrant parvenu and on his relationship with the Eastern European working class on the one hand and with the Anglo-Jewish middle class on the other. The immigrant parvenu's role can be seen as deeply ambiguous. On the one hand, he looks back to the distinctive values and aspirations of the immigrant masses out of which he has risen and with which he remains in close contact; on the other, he looks forward to a status both within the Jewish community and in the wider Manchester society which befits his economic success. Out of this ambiguity arise the particular ways in which the cultural patterns of Eastern Europe were integrated into the institutional structure and general outlook of the long-settled Anglo-Jewish community. In this interpretation, the Eastern European *alrightnik* becomes the less than selfless mediator between East and West.[3]

I

Although immigration from Eastern Europe carried the Jewish population of Manchester from rather less than 10,000 in 1875 to at least 30,000 in 1914,[4] we should resist the temptation of seeing the later 1870s or the early 1880s as the dividing line between, on the one side, an Anglicized middle-class community of chiefly German, Dutch and Sephardi origin and, on the other, a community increasingly dominated by the arrival, settlement and concerns of an Eastern European working class. If Anglo-Jewry badly needs revision, this is surely one of the most important ways, for in spite of the pioneering work of Rollin,[5] Eastern European settlement and its impact are still largely regarded,

---

[3] Irving Howe, *World of Our Fathers* (New York, 1976) pp. 137–41 discusses the emergence of a 'fiercely energetic and ambitious' Eastern European bourgeoisie on New York's East Side. Howe tells how the journalist Abraham Cahan coined the term 'alrightnik' to describe this group. In the absence of any other appropriate word, I have used it to describe the emerging Eastern European bourgeoisie of nineteenth-century Manchester.

[4] There are no absolutely reliable figures for Manchester's Jewish population in any period. According to the Chief Constable's report for 1891 there were then 15,000–16,000 Jews in Manchester, at least 70 per cent of them Russian immigrants. Max Hesse, *On the Effective Use of Charitable Loans to the Poor* (Manchester Statistical Society, 1901) uses school records to produce an estimate of 24,300. The *Jewish Year Book* for 1920 gives 32,000.

[5] A. R. Rollin, 'Russo-Jewish Immigrants in England before 1881', *Transactions of the Jewish Historical Society of England*, 21 (1962–7), pp. 24–56.

or at any rate widely interpreted, as a phenomenon of 1875–1914.[6] In reality, Eastern European settlement in Manchester must be located in an earlier period: on a small but still significant scale in the 1840s, which saw the completion of an efficient and relatively cheap passenger service by rail and sea between western Russia and Liverpool, and on a larger scale in the 1860s, when the dislocations of the American Civil War persuaded many intending transmigrants to seek their fortunes in Britain.[7] By 1875, the eve of the so-called 'era of mass immigration', families of Eastern European origin already made up between a half and two-thirds of Manchester's Jewish population.

The distinctive social, economic and religious patterns associated with Eastern European settlement were also well-established by 1875. Concentrations of Eastern European working-class settlers had already taken shape in Red Bank and Strangeways, densely populated districts of poor but cheap and available housing on the northern edge of the city, immediately to the south of the semi-rural suburbs occupied by the established Jewish middle class. Eastern European workers – men and women – were already concentrated, by choice and perhaps by discrimination,[8] in a narrow range of workshop trades, chiefly tailoring, cap-making, cabinet-making and waterproof-garment making, as distinct from Manchester's staple industries – textiles and engineering – as they were from the occupations of the older-established Jewish community. These 'immigrant trades' already occupied the distinctive role in the Manchester economy so vividly described by Joseph Buckman in his study of Leeds Jewry:[9] they were made up largely of small sub-contracting workshops on the vulnerable periphery of an industrial and distributing network serving a growing mass market for cheap clothing and furniture. Fierce competition between workshop masters had combined with the weak bargaining power of 'greener' labour to produce the long hours, low pay and cramped working conditions often summarized as 'sweating'. Finally, the typical religious expressions of Eastern European settlement – orthodox *chevroth*, societies which combined religious worship with study, social interchange and mutual aid, and guided by rabbis especially imported from Eastern Europe, were already proliferating in the 'immigrant districts'. The fifteen to twenty which existed in the mid-1870s included three which were to occupy a central position in the religious life of a later period – the Chevra Torah (1865), the Cracow Chevra (1869) and the Chevra Walkawishk (1871) – along with their immigrant Russian rabbis, Elia Tumin, Mendel Dagutski and Susman Cohen. Alienated by the cold decorum, elitism, and dubious observances of the four older-established synagogues, and the English rhetoric of their ministers, immigrant *landsleit* had created an

[6] Gartner, *Jewish Immigrant*, pp. 24–56; Pollins, *Economic History of Jews*, pp. 130–41.

[7] The account given here of developments up to 1875 is based on Bill Williams, *The Making of Manchester Jewry, 1740–1875* (Manchester, 1976), unless otherwise stated.

[8] Oral evidence of a later period suggests that occupational choice was produced by more than discrimination; previous experience in Eastern Europe and the influence of social networks in Manchester were also important.

[9] Joseph Buckman, *Immigrants and the Class Struggle: the Jewish Immigrant in Leeds, 1880–1914* (Manchester, 1983), chs 1 and 2.

alternative religious network characterized by religious warmth, Talmudic scholarship, strict observance and a social life in which Yiddish served as the lingua franca.

In a word, Eastern European settlers of the mid-nineteenth century had kept away, either by choice or by necessity, from the residential districts, occupations and synagogues of established Anglo-Jewry, so that alongside an older Jewish community of German, Dutch and Sephardi retailers, cotton merchants and professional men, residing in suburban villas, integrated into the social, political and cultural life of the Manchester bourgeoisie, and worshipping in four impressive suburban synagogues, one of them Reform, there existed by 1875 a proletariat of Eastern European origin, Yiddish-speaking, living in slums, working in sweatshops and worshipping in *chevroth*.[10]

But if the community of the early 1870s was sharply divided between an Anglicized bourgeoisie and an Eastern European working class, it was characterized also by more subtle divisions within Eastern European Jewry itself, divisions not simply along the lines of nationality, region of origin or religious preference (although all these existed), but even more in terms of differing degrees of success in the search for economic betterment and social respectability in Manchester. In particular, I would like to focus on those Eastern Europeans, a minority, who by dint of enterprise and luck had risen fairly rapidly, usually from a base of poverty, to entrepreneurial positions in retailing, travelling commerce and the workshop trades: a brash *petit bourgeoisie* of successful masters in the tailoring, cap-making, waterproofing and furniture industries; fent dealers, rag merchants and wholesale drapers in the lower reaches of the Manchester textile trade; in retailing particularly jewellers, opticians, pawnbrokers, clothiers, money-lenders, Scotch drapers and stall-holders in the thriving world of Lancashire's public markets. The British cap-making and waterproofing industries, which had been attracting Jewish enterprise since the 1840s, were by the 1870s becoming centred in Manchester, where they were dominated by Jewish entrepreneurs. In cap-making, a key role was being played by Russian and Polish immigrants of the mid-nineteenth century like Louis Cobe, Nathan Hope and Mark Steinhart; in waterproofing by families from the Cracow Chevra like the Mandlebergs, the Rothbands, the Kestenbergs and the Weiners; in fent-dealing by immigrants from Brody on the Russo-Austrian border. Of shopkeepers, the most successful in these early years was Wolf (later William) Aronsberg, a Russian immigrant to Britain in the 1830s who, after a disastrous beginning in Liverpool, founded a large-scale enterprise in Manchester selling optical goods and mathematical instruments.[11]

---

[10] There was also a 'native poor', chiefly of street hawkers, but not one large enough to have a significant impact on the history of the period.

[11] A brief biography of William Aronsberg appears in *Manchester Faces and Places*, 2 (1890), pp. 5–7, which erroneously places his arrival in England in 1850. Aronsberg became well known during the 1870s for his conspicuous charity, chiefly to non-Jewish causes. He became a JP in 1876. In 1893, however, he became involved in a breach of promise case, which he lost. He became bankrupt and took refuge from scandal in Corfu, although retaining the loyalty of the immigrant *chevroth*, whose members sent him a testimonial now preserved in the Archive Department of Manchester Central Library.

What we have, then, in the Manchester of 1875, is neither a community numerically dominated by an established middle class of German, Dutch or Sephardi origin, nor one sharply divided between an older elite and a new Eastern European working class. What we have is a highly tesselated and exceptionally mobile social scene, with Eastern Europeans already at every stage of economic improvement.

Moving from a social to a political perspective, however, it becomes clear that whatever economic and social progress sections of the Eastern European community had made by 1875, and however great the numerical predominance of Eastern Europeans in the general Jewish population, power in the community continued to reside with members of the older middle-class elite. It was they who had laid the basis of Jewish communal life in Manchester in the late eighteenth and early nineteenth centuries: they who had created the community's first educational and philanthropic institutions – a Hebrew Philanthropic Society in 1826, a Jews' School in 1841; they who had won a degree of acceptance and respect from a suspicious and often hostile Manchester society; they who had led the local movement for Jewish emancipation between 1838 and 1858, organizing within the community into a Manchester Hebrew Association and exerting pressure on local and national government to support the Jewish cause. It was they, too, who had responded to the earliest waves of immigration from Eastern Europe, instituting systems of relief designed specifically for the immigrant poor: at first a charity based within the synagogue, but which had evolved by 1867 into a distinct communal body, the Manchester Jewish Board of Guardians.

Symptoms of friction were already visible in the workings of this charity: indications of the profound shock experienced by emancipated Jewry on this first encounter with the children of the shtetl. Its best efforts were directed towards keeping the immigrants on the move, either forward to the United States or back to Hamburg. For those who, in spite of such discouragement, chose to remain, material welfare became the vehicle for social and cultural objectives. So, for example, relief was denied to familes who refused to send their children to the Jews' School, where the speaking of Yiddish was not tolerated, even in the playground, and for a time to anyone who belonged to what was described as a 'clandestine society', that is to one of the early *chevroth*.[12] This latter was not simply an attack on immigrant religious independence, but still more on an institution which was perceived, then and later, as the bastion of a foreign culture. That is, the communal leadership was already committed by the mid-1870s to an intense and single-minded pressure towards the Anglicization of the Eastern European poor: an Anglicization which meant not simply the adoption of the English language and integration into the Manchester economy, but also the breakdown of the cultural forms, styles and values (other than the practice of Judaism itself) with which the immigrants arrived and their

---

[12] *Manchester Jewish Board of Guardians, 1st Annual Report* (1867–8) (Manchester 1868), *6th Annual Report* (1872–3), *8th Annual Report* (1874–5).

replacement by forms of cultural expression, manners and customs dictated by middle-class notions of English respectability.

While not wishing to attempt a full analysis here,[13] I would argue that the elite's attachment to Anglicization was not simply a matter of cultural preference, but more particularly a function of the way in which the earliest Jewish residents had achieved acceptance and status in Manchester society. This acceptance was essentially conditional: the outcome of an informal contract worked out in the arena of public discourse during the struggle for emancipation. It was a contract through which Jewish settlers received acceptance in return for cultural integration, or, to put it another way, cultural assimilation was seen as 'proof' that Jews 'deserved well' of their fellow citizens. Implicit in the contract was an obligation on the Jewish middle class to ensure that future Jewish settlers (and, for that matter, the existing Jewish poor) took the same path to integration: an obligation, that is, to ensure that the image of the Jewish community at least approximated to the ideal set by the native bourgeoisie. In a sense, emancipation was marked by an alliance of convenience between the middle-class elites of the minority and majority societies in which the minority elite took on a social mission towards the 'foreign poor' similar to that pursued by the native elite towards the native working class. And the Jewish elite adopted this role because they perceived their status to depend upon it.

II

In the period after 1875, as immigration from Eastern Europe gathered pace and found new sources in Austria-Hungary and Romania, what took place was not so much a 'transformation'[14] as an intensification of earlier developments. Side by side with an expansion of the immigrant community, which had perhaps tripled in size by 1914, was continuing social diversification within it, reflected in the development on the ground of new immigrant residential concentrations, like Hightown and Higher Broughton, between the older immigrant slums and the suburbs of the Anglicized elite.[15] In particular, the nascent Eastern European middle class received a continuous flow of new recruits, a few arriving with capital and business or professional skills, most achieving modest

[13] A fuller analysis is attempted in Bill Williams, 'The Anti-Semitism of Tolerance', in eds A.J. Kidd and K.W. Roberts, *City, Class and Culture: Studies of Social Policy and Cultural Production in Victorian Manchester* (Manchester, 1985), pp.74–102.

[14] Pollins, *Economic History of Jews*, pp.130–41.

[15] Jeremy Hodge, 'Hightown Jewry 1881–1939: A Methodological Essay in the Study of Residential Patterns in the Jewish Community in Manchester', BA Honours dissertation, University of Manchester, 1979. An anti-alien account, 'Jewish Invasion of an English Suburb', appears in *Manchester City News*, 17 January 1891. The first indication of Jewish settlement in Higher Broughton is a scheme for the opening of a synagogue in the area (Committee Minutes of the Manchester Great Synagogue, 30 December 1894, 20 January 1895).

economic success by enterprise in Manchester.[16] On the other side, in the face of increasing immigration, and as the outlines of a separate immigrant Jewish life became ever more distinct, the strategies of Anglicization, still orchestrated primarily by the older elite, became more wide-ranging and more intense. The history of the Jewish community in this period may be seen as a dynamic interrelationship between the three main social elements in communal life – the established middle class, the immigrant mass and the alrightniks.

One of the most impressive features of communal development after 1875 was the creation by the Anglicized elite of a vast network of educational, social, philanthropic and cultural organizations intended to serve almost every aspect of immigrant need.[17] A handful were perhaps truly altruistic: most served also as a means of modifying immigrant social and cultural behaviour. For although each had a specific object defined in its title – the Jewish Working Men's Club, the Jewish Lads' Brigade, the Jewish Soup Kitchen, the Jewish Ladies' Visiting Association and so on – behind them all lay an underlying, and often explicit, pressure for Anglicization, a drive to 'iron out the ghetto bend', to use the words of the *Jewish Chronicle*, 'to facilitate the transformation of Polish into English Jews'.[18] So while the Jewish Working Men's Club had on paper the bland aim of providing 'amusement for the members as well as instruction',[19] one of its founders described it in 1888 as an institution designed 'principally to Anglicise the foreign poor'.[20] Those who founded the club a year earlier had set out to organize it 'on a similar basis to that of the club in London',[21] where the aim was to 'neutralise ... un-English habits and thoughts, intensified and encouraged as they are by the Hebroth' and to render the immigrant 'more amenable to English ideas and less opposed to English culture'.[22] Essentially, it sought to move immigrants away from Yiddish culture (and, it may be said, away from such immigrant vices as gambling and socialism) towards an interest in the respectable pastimes of working-class England, from billiards and table-tennis to opera, debating, amateur dramatics and brass bands.[23] In so doing, it played a seminal role in the cultural transformation of immigrants.[24] Even a revamped Jewish Board of Guardians, still an organization offering in theory only material

[16] Although not typical, the best-known examples are Ephraim Sieff and Michael Marks (Israel Sieff, *Memoirs* (London, 1970), pp. 6–13; Goronwy Rees, *St Michael: A History of Marks and Spencer* (London, 1969), pp. 1–11).

[17] For a brief account of Jewish welfare in London in this period, Gartner, *Jewish Immigrant*, pp. 162–65. Gartner's judgement is that Jewish charitable effort towards the immigrants was 'extensive and generous'.

[18] *JC*, 12 August 1881.

[19] *MCN*, 7 February 1891.

[20] *JC*, 28 September 1888.

[21] *JC*, 18 February 1887.

[22] *JC*, 16 February 1883.

[23] For the growing range of activity in the Jewish Working Men's Club, *JC*, 2 September, 14 August, 4 November 1887, 9 March 1888, 1 March 1889, 23 January, 13 March 1891.

[24] After 1890, cultural activities which had begun within the club gradually assumed the shape of separate organizations which became part of the fabric of communal life. So the important Jewish Literary Society movement in Manchester began as a club activity (*The Jewish Literary Annual* (Union of Jewish Literary Societies, London, 1903), p. 33).

support, was described by its secretary in 1894 as having 'Anglicisation' as the first amongst its objectives.[25] The material relief offered by other charities was more often than not either made conditional on modifications of social behaviour or accompanied by what were, in effect, Anglicizing devices – visits, social gatherings, outings, the offer of 'useful advice' and so on.[26] In most there was the further expectation that the immigrant poor would derive benefit from the simple fact of contact with the Anglicized rich. So the Monday Evening Social Gatherings for immigrant women and girls, inaugurated by the Jewish Ladies' Visiting Association in 1899, were seen as providing 'the means of uniting the wealthier and poorer classes of the Jewish Community in social intercourse'.[27]

All these organizations operated over a wide social gulf: they were founded, financed and managed by an elite of Anglicized and well-to-do families, to serve the immigrant poor. Often, too, over a wide religious gulf, for families from the Reform Synagogue, although constituting perhaps less than 2 per cent of the total Jewish population, played key roles on all their management committees. In charity, therefore, immigrants faced the added humiliation of investigation by those whom they scarcely identified as Jewish. The social bias of these institutions – their role as the instruments of Anglo-Jewish middle-class self-interest and control – is reflected in their names, derived most often from movements founded by the middle-class of the wider society to shape working-class life. So the Jewish Working Men's Club derived from the Working Men's Club movement which was evolving in English urban society to offer 'rational recreation' as an alternative to vicious street pursuits and radical politics,[28] the Jewish Lads' Brigade from the Church Lads' Brigade, which sought to inculcate notions of patriotism, discipline and obedience in the children of the Christian poor.[29] A characteristic of elite Jewish strategies as a whole was the adaptation of institutions from outside the community to serve communal needs. The aims of such institutions reflected the preconceptions of English middle-class society rather than Jewish precept. So the investigative techniques of the Jewish Board of Guardians, and the distinction it made between the deserving and the undeserving poor, derived not from Jewish tradition but from the harsh doctrines which informed the English Poor Law.[30]

[25] *MCN*, 13 January 1894.

[26] For examples, see *The Manchester Jewish Ladies Visiting Association: A Record of Half a Century's Work amongst the Jewish Poor, 1884–1934* (Manchester, 1934). Also the minutes of the Jewish Ladies' Visiting Association, the Jews' School Ladies Clothing Society and the Soup Kitchen for the Jewish Poor of Manchester, all in the Archive Department, Manchester Central Library.

[27] *JC*, 5 July 1889.

[28] Peter Bailey, *Leisure and Class in Victorian England: Rational Recreation and the Contest for Control, 1830–1885* (London, 1978).

[29] The aim of the Jewish Lads' Brigade, adapted from that of the Church Lads' Brigade, was 'to instill into the rising generation from its earliest youth, habits of orderliness, cleanliness and honour, so that in learning to respect themselves they will do credit to their community'. The annual reports of the Manchester JLB are in Manchester Central Library.

[30] Williams, *Manchester Jewry*, p. 287; Miriam Steiner, 'Philanthropic Activity and Organisation in the Manchester Jewish Community, 1867–1914', MA dissertation, University of Manchester, 1974, ch. 2.

In Anglo-Jewish philanthropy it is possible to detect a modicum of disinterested benevolence, a protective and supportive sympathy, a desire to help immigrant co-religionists integrate comfortably and quickly into Manchester society and so escape the hostility, anti-semitic or xenophobic, of a wider society.[31] But the new agencies were more evidently the instruments of class control in a communal setting, designed to protect the status of the communal elite at the expense of the culture of the communal poor.

But, of course, the image of a simple confrontation between an Anglicized elite and an immigrant mass leaves out of account the third major social element in Manchester Jewish society, the Eastern European *nouveaux riches*. Often cold-shouldered in the first instance by the major synagogues, and particularly by the oldest and most prestigious, the Great Synagogue, the 'Englisher Shul', and barred by the preference of Anglicized subscribers and managers from positions of leadership in such bodies as the Jews' School and the Jewish Board of Guardians, the ambitious parvenu had at first to convert his economic success into power and status within the immigrant community, with which, at all events, he had the most immediate cultural links and ties of sympathy.

This he did most frequently as the patron and financial backer of an immigrant religious organization. More often than not it was he who enabled a struggling *chevra* – one of the many 'bedroom *chevras*', as they were slightingly called by the elite[32] – to rent larger premises, perhaps a vacated shop or a defunct Christian church rendered redundant by the northward advance of Jewish settlement, as a more impressive place of worship and who paid the passage, and perhaps part of the salary, of a suitably learned rabbi from Eastern Europe. From the mid-1880s, under this kind of impetus, some of the earlier *chevroth* evolved, by expansion and amalgamation, into major synagogues under alrightnik control. Such was the New Synagogue and Beth Hamedrath, created in 1889 by bringing together a group of Polish and Russian *chevroth* in a new building financed by the Russian immigrant optician William Aronsberg, who became its secular mentor and Life President.[33] Such also was the Holy Law Beth Aaron Congregation, the successor of the Chevra Torah, which in 1901 assumed its final shape in a former Presbyterian chapel through the patronage of the Russian immigrant money-lender Samuel Aaron Claff.[34] It is symptomatic of the coming together of immigrant aspiration and alrightnik ambition that the synagogue bore Claff's middle name and that it was more popularly known in the community as 'Claff's Shul'.[35] Equally symbolically, it stood on Bank View, an eminence overlooking the major immigrant district, Red Bank.

[31] For a discussion of the extent of anti-semitism and anti-alienism in Manchester, Williams, 'Anti-Semitism of Toleration', pp. 78–90.

[32] *JC*, 3 April 1896.

[33] *JC*, 26 October 1888 to 20 September 1889.

[34] *JC*, 12 April 1901; ed. Michael Fidler, *The Holy Law Congregation: One Hundred Years, 1865–1965* (Manchester, 1965), pp. 8–12.

[35] Taped interview with Mrs Marjorie Smith (Samuel Claff's daughter) in the Manchester Jewish Museum.

So did the new Central Synagogue, the former Chevra Walkawishk, which moved in 1894 from a house in Fernie Street, Red Bank, to an impressive Congregational chapel on Cheetham Hill Road, one of the two main arteries running northwards through the 'Jewish Quarter'.[36] The North Manchester Synagogue, opened on the second artery, Bury New Road, in 1891 was the successor of a Brodyer Chevra and represented the culmination of the ambitions of a group of Galician fent dealers, shopkeepers and textile warehousemen.[37] The more affluent immigrant retailers and cotton dealers who founded the prestigious Higher Broughton Synagogue in 1907 included the rag-dealer Ephraim Sieff, Michael Marks, founder of Marks and Spencer, and the calico printer and cotton manufacturer Sam Finburgh.[38] There are many more examples. The religious history of Manchester Jewry from the 1890s to World War I was marked not only by the foundation of new immigrant synagogues, but by a procession of emerging *chevroth* awaiting recognition and support.[39]

The immigrant parvenu was also behind a number of new communal bodies which reflected the distinctive standards and patterns of immigrant religious observance: the Talmud Torah (1879),[40] the Manchester Yeshivah (1910)[41] and the Manchester Burial Society of Polish Jews Limited (1877), which sought to free immigrants from dependence on the burial grounds (and therefore from the influence) of the older synagogues.[42] In these contexts, the alrightnik may be seen as giving impressive shape and some permanence to the separate religious styles of Eastern Europe.

In much the same way, it was the alrightniks who created an alternative network of charities – quite distinct from those of the elite – which offered the immigrant poor a more open-handed material support. The aims of these Benevolent Societies, as they were called, conflicted with those of the elite charities and sometimes negated them: so there were no preconditions of social or cultural change, no deterrent regulations such as the Board of Guardians' rule that only one relief payment could be made during the first six months of an immigrant's stay in Manchester.[43] They were also firmly rooted, not in mean-minded English middle-class notions of charity, but in a more generous traditional Judaism, so that, for example, they prided themselves on 'secret

---

[36] *JC*, 21 September 1894, 19 October 1894, 1 February 1895; *The Manchester Central Synagogue: A Centenary Brochure* (Manchester, 1971).

[37] *JC*, 11 December 1891, 21 October 1892, 3 March 1893.

[38] *Higher Broughton Synagogue: The First Fifty Years 1907–1957* (Manchester, 1957), p. 26.

[39] In the *Jewish Year Book* for 1912, the Manchester entry lists 25 synagogues, of which 19 are recognizable as new immigrant foundations, and 14 'minor synagogues' (that is, *chevroth*); *Manchester United Synagogue and Beth Hamidrash Hagodol: Golden Jubilee Brochure, 1904–1954* (Manchester, 1954).

[40] I. W. Slotki, *Seventy Years of Hebrew Education, 1880–1950* (Manchester, 1950), p. 9.

[41] *Manchester Talmudical College, 40th Anniversary Souvenir Report* (Manchester, 1951).

[42] The minute books of the Manchester Burial Society of Polish Jews Limited from 1901 are in the Archive Department, Manchester Central Library.

[43] Minutes of a Public Meeting of 27 January 1908 in the minute books of the Manchester Russian Jews Benevolent Society in the Archive Department, Manchester Central Library.

charity' based on Talmudic precept.[44] The names of applicants were not recorded in the minute books, the recommendation of one of the committee being deemed sufficient to authorize a payment. The Benevolent Societies grew out of the more informal support offered by immigrant settlers to newly arriving *landsleit*:[45] in a sense, they represented an alternative to the charitable functions of the *chevroth*.[46] The first in time was the Cracow Benevolent Society, an adjunct of the Cracow Chevra, founded in 1869.[47] A Romanian Benevolent Society was first founded in the early 1880s and, after early difficulties, recreated in 1900,[48] an Austro-Hungarian Benevolent Society in 1901.[49] The largest was the Russian Jews Benevolent Society, founded in 1904 by members of the Bardichever Chevra, led by the Russian immigrant insurance agent Eli Fox, and backed by one of Manchester's most famous immigrant rabbis, Mendel Dagutski.[50] Their importance in their earliest days can be overrated. The Russian Jews Benevolent Society began operations with £4 cash-in-hand and during its first five years had sometimes to suspend relief through lack of funds.[51] But in the longer term they became an important and permanent part of communal life. What they show is a philanthropic drive distinct from that of the elite, and what they again represent is the alrightnik giving expression to distinctive immigrant values.

It was the alrightniks, too, who promoted the myriad lodges of the Jewish Friendly Society movement, the first of which can be traced back in Manchester to the 1860s, but which flowered particularly between 1890 and World War I. A few had explicit Zionist leanings; one – the Jewish Workers' Circle Friendly Society, of which a Manchester Circle was founded in 1911[52] – was Socialist in orientation; and a handful were independent. Most belonged to one of the great national 'Orders' – Achei Brith, B'nai B'rith, the Grand Order of Israel, the Order Shield of David or the Ancient Order of Hebrew Druids. Modelled on similar organizations in the wider society, the Jewish Friendly Society lodge was primarily a mechanism for insurance: in return for small weekly payments, it offered sickness, burial and shiva benefits and sometimes a small annual dividend. The lodges were attractive to immigrant workers in part because they offered an alternative to the charity of the Jewish Board of Guardians. Otherwise, in the absence of specialist studies and substantial records, their precise place in Anglo-Jewish history remains problematic. In a sense, they have the characteristics of a secularized *chevra*, offering not only insurance but a social life for their members, although one most usually

---

[44] David Friedman, *The Manchester Jewish Benevolent Society: A Comprehensive History of the Creation and Development of this Institution* (Manchester, 1952), p. 5.

[45] The Russian Jews Benevolent Society agreed to 'take over' an informal group organized by Rabbi Dagutski (Minutes, 18 June 1905).

[46] Friedman, *Manchester Jewish Benevolent Society*, pp. 4–5.

[47] Asher Myers, *Jewish Directory for 1874* (London, 1874), p. 376.

[48] *JC*, 15 March 1888, 12 January and 17 August 1900.

[49] *JC*, 29 March 1901.

[50] Russian Jews Benevolent Society, Minutes, 30 May 1905.

[51] Ibid., 28 May 1905, 26 January 1907.

[52] The earliest membership book of the Manchester Circle is in the Greater Manchester Archives.

conducted in English rather than Yiddish.[53] It may be that they mark an important point of transition for immigrants undergoing acculturation through informal as well as formal processes. With their glittering regalia, formal hierarchies and punctilious ceremonial, they also offered a degree of status both to the alrightniks and, perhaps particularly, to a worker-aristocracy evolving in immigrant society and centred on Hightown. In that sense, they are another sign of social differentiation within the immigrant milieu, offering ambitious members, according to the *Jewish Chronicle*, a way 'to be bowed to for one moment a week on average'.[54] They suggest that immigrant workers shared the ambiguity of their alrightnik betters – looking back to Eastern Europe and forward to a place in English society – and that the alrightnik was prepared to take both aspirations under his wing. It may be that they appealed to the alrightniks, too, as an alternative to trade unions: certainly when the workers of the Provincial Waterproof Company in Strangeways came together in 1922 to form the Provincial Independent Tontine Society, it was under the Life Presidency of their employer in a trade notorious for its trade union militance.[55]

Finally, it was the alrightniks who shaped the infant Zionist movement in Manchester in the late 1880s and early 1890s, lending their support to the most distinctive form of immigrant political expression. Entrepreneurs in the cap-making, cabinet-making and tailoring industries like Mark Doniger, Louis Cobe, Louis Ellison and Joseph Taylor were prominent during the 1880s in movements to promote the colonization of Palestine which culminated in the foundation of a Manchester 'tent' of Chovevei Zion in 1890.[56] But the key figure was Joseph Massel, a Russian immigrant Hebraist and poet, who established a successful Hebrew and English printing works in Cheetham Hill around 1889 and who seven years later founded the first successful Herzlian Zionist organization, Dorshei Zion.[57] The story of Manchester Zionism is too complex and many-sided and too intertwined with the national and international progress of Zionism to be told here. Sufficient to say that the alrightniks constituted its backbone in the years before 1914. Samuel Claff, of 'Claff's Shul', was one of Manchester's delegates to the sixth Zionist Congress in Basle in 1903 together with Israel Yoffey, rabbi of the Central Synagogue, who did much to promote the Mirzachi movement in Manchester.[58] The members of

---

[53] Minute books of most of Manchester's Friendly Society lodges have not been preserved or, at any rate, located. A number of commemorative brochures give only a flavour of their round of social activities: *Souvenir Programme to celebrate the 25th Anniversary of the Manchester Hebrew Tontine Society* (Manchester, 1924); *Souvenir of the Golden Jubilee of the Reverend J. H. Valentine Lodge and Samuel Finburgh Lodge of the Grand Order of Israel and Shield of David* (Manchester, 1952); *Golden Jubilee of the Dr Moses Gaster Lodge of B'nai Brith* (Manchester, 1962). Also the minutes of the Provincial Independent Tontine Society (founded 1922) preserved by the society.

[54] *JC*, 8 September 1905.

[55] Provincial Independent Tontine Society, Minutes, 4 December 1922.

[56] *JC*, 14 September 1885, 28 November 1890.

[57] *JC*, 14 August 1896.

[58] Photograph of Manchester delegates to the sixth Zionist Congress in the Manchester Jewish Museum; *Report of the First Mizrachi Conference in the United Kingdom held at the Grosvenor Hotel, Manchester on December 28 and 29 1918* (London 1919).

Aronsberg's New Synagogue, who included Massel, were particularly active, and it is perhaps no coincidence that when Dorshei Zion came together with a number of smaller Zionist bodies in 1902 to create the Manchester Zionist Association (MZA), its first headquarters were directly opposite the gates of the synagogue.[59] Most of the elite held aloof: in 1902 Charles Dreyfus, president of the MZA, 'regretted that up to the present the leaders of the community and the Jewish ministers had not given Zionism that support they ought to have done'.[60] Before Weizmann's arrival in Manchester in 1904, and notwithstanding his gloomy view of the state of Manchester Zionism at that time,[61] the movement was already safely afloat on alrightnik patronage.

III

One effect of all this activity was to bring the alrightniks and the institutions they controlled into conflict with the older elite. Such conflict took many forms: tension between Zionism and the assimilatory international politics of the Anglo-Jewish Association, tension between the Jewish Board of Guardians and its satellites and the 'indiscriminate charity' dispensed by the Benevolent Societies, tension between the older orthodox synagogues, with their allegiance to the Chief Rabbi in London, and the *chevroth* (and the new synagogues arising out of them), with their different styles and standards, looking back to Eastern Europe for their inspiration.[62]

A rare head-on collision occurred in 1900, when a plan was first mooted for the creation of a Jewish Hospital in Manchester.[63] In brief, the scheme was promoted by alrightniks, amongst whom Samuel Claff and Joseph Taylor were prominent, to provide the immigrant poor with hospital treatment in an environment in which they felt at ease (that is, surrounded by Yiddish-speaking *landsleit*) and in which their need for strictly kosher food could be adequately met. The scheme ran into immediate opposition from Dr Berendt Salomon, minister of the Englisher Shul, and from that synagogue's young president, Nathan Laski,[64] and the bulk of the elite. This was partly on the grounds that it might be seen by non-Jewish society as a move towards exclusivity, partly because it might actually consolidate immigrant separatism (a hostile correspondent to the *Jewish Chronicle* spoke of 'the creation of a Jewish Hospital

[59] *MCN*, 13 September 1902.

[60] *MCN*, 13 September 1902.

[61] Chaim Weizmann, *Trial and Error* (London, 1950), pp. 135–6.

[62] Tension between established synagogues and newly emerging immigrant congregations often took the form of complaints about the 'unnecessary proliferation' of places of worship: *JC*, 19 October 1894, 25 January and 1 February 1895.

[63] *JC*, 9 February 1900. The story unfolds in reports and letters in *JC*, 1900–1905. The alrightniks sought the patronage of Charles Dreyfus, founder of Clayton Aniline Dye Works, a Conservative City Councillor and prominent Zionist: Dreyfus was from Alsace.

[64] Nathan Laski's family migrated from Russia to Middlesbrough when he was an infant. Educated in England, he began work in the warehouse of a Manchester shipping firm before setting up in business as a cotton merchant on his own account: *JC*, 8 June 1906.

Ghetto'),[65] partly because, arising as it did out of immigrant concerns, it was said to lack the kind of financial support which supposedly only the elite could provide. The highly symbolic counter-proposal of the elite was for a Jewish Ward in the Manchester Royal Infirmary. A battle of words raged fiercely for four years and it is perhaps symptomatic of the growing power and confidence of the Eastern European *nouveaux riches* that in 1904 the new hospital was built, although not without the conciliatory gestures of naming it the Victoria Memorial Manchester Jewish Hospital and opening its doors to non-Jewish patients.[66] In the last resort, the hospital was financed in its early days partly by alrightnik donations and fund-raising enterprise, partly by weekly house-to-house collections, particularly in the Hightown district.[67]

Less clear-cut was a running battle surrounding control of communal *shechita*. It is important not to trivialize disputes surrounding *shechita* as storms in the communal tea-cup, involving only clashes of personality and temperament. It is necessary to take them seriously as symptoms of deep social and religious conflict. Chiefly they arose out of the attempts of one or more *chevroth*, with alrightnik backing and the support of at least one immigrant rabbi, to establish a system of *shechita* independent of that of the Englisher Shul, which from the early nineteenth century had exercised overall control and collected all the revenue.[68] For a *chevra*, an independent *shechita* had many advantages. It served, first of all, as a barometer of orthodoxy. A move by a *chevra* to establish its own system advertised its dissent from the lax standards of the older-established community and its determination to enforce a higher degree of traditional observance. But there were also more concrete benefits. *Shechita* brought revenue in the form of butchers' fees which might make it possible for a *chevra* to rent larger premises or employ a more prestigious rabbi. So a separate *shechita* brought a *chevra* not only a high repute for orthodoxy, but also a financial mechanism which might secure its permanent independence from the older synagogues and from the London Chief Rabbinate. It was a means by which the religious styles and standards of Eastern Europe might possibly be maintained in an English setting.

For the Great Synagogue, on the other hand, secession on the issue of *shechita* was an unqualified disaster. It meant loss of revenue and, if unchecked, loss of religious prestige. It seemed calculated to strengthen the *chevroth* as islands of foreign culture and to underwrite a traditional religious outlook viewed by many of the elite as a compound of superstitions.[69] All the verbal guns of the Great Synagogue were brought to bear on the offending *chevra*, and if local artillery proved insufficient, the Chief Rabbi was called in to declare *treife* meat sold under the independent system or to bring into question the

---

[65] *JC*, 28 September 1900.
[66] *Annual Report of the Manchester Jewish Hospital, 1905* (Manchester 1906).
[67] A record of the sums collected from each house is appended to each annual report.
[68] For the beginning of this control, Williams, *Manchester Jewry*, p. 53.
[69] For example, Great Synagogue, Minutes of the General Committee, 28 February 1886.

qualifications of an immigrant rabbi or *shochet*.[70] A bitter war of posters was waged on the walls of Cheetham Hill, and amongst the few which have survived are two issued by Israel Yoffey, of the Central Synagogue, which declare the Chief Rabbi himself *treife* and proclaim that only the learned rabbis of Eastern Europe are to be taken seriously as religious authorities.[71] The Chief Rabbi's intervention often made sufficient impact to bring a recalcitrant *chevra* to heel, if only because butchers licensed by a rebel *chevra* were now threatened with the loss of a wider market, immigrant *shochetim* with a narrowing of the field for their enterprise. But in the ending of *shechita* disputes, most often in the Great Synagogue's favour, it is possible to detect a reluctance on the part of the alrightniks and the immigrant rabbinate to make a last-ditch stand against a religious and secular establishment they were anxious, in the last resort, to join. Disputes such as these were frequent between the 1870s and World War I, as each newly arising *chevra* (and some established immigrant synagogues), backed by the alrightniks, sought in turn to underwrite its autonomy.[72]

If conflict, however muted, was the norm, there was one area, at least, in which alrightnik ambition and elite preconception found common cause. This was in relation to a Jewish trade union and socialist movement which took off in Manchester with a series of five strikes in the workshop trades between 1889 and 1891.[73] By 1891 a high proportion of Jewish workers in all the immigrant trades were organized into unions and there existed in Strangeways an International Working Men's Educational Club, its rules printed in Yiddish and dedicated to the spread of revolutionary Socialism. The strength of this early movement can be overstated: some of the early unions were weak and ephemeral, the International Working Men's Educational Club short-lived. What it achieved, however, was a permanent socialist and trade union presence within the immigrant milieu, emerging now as a successful strike, now as a workers' cooperative, now as a new socialist formation,[74] a presence sufficiently visible and militant for 'extreme socialism' to be seized upon by fanatical anti-aliens as one of the evil importations of the Eastern European.[75] Some can, in fact, be traced back to the socialist movement in Russia; most represented the impact on immigrant workers of the new Unionism and the Socialist Revival,

[70] For example, Great Synagogue, Letter Book, Isaac Asher Isaac to the Chief Rabbi, 2 January, 13 January, 14 January, 30 January 1880.
[71] Posters in the collection of the Manchester Jewish Museum.
[72] I. W. Slotki, *History of the Manchester Shechita Board, 1892–1952* (Manchester, 1954) lists the disputes after 1892, although without exploring their deeper implications; other disputes are reflected in the minute books of the Great Synagogue.
[73] Bill Williams, 'The Beginnings of Jewish Trade Unionism in Manchester, 1889–1891', in ed. Kenneth Lunn, *Hosts, Immigrants and Minorities: the Responses to Newcomers in British Society, 1870–1914* (London, 1980), pp. 263–307.
[75] For examples of trade union activity and worker's cooperatives, *JC*, 1 January 1904, 3 August 1906, 11 October 1907, *MG*, 2 August 1907 to 3 September 1907, 22 August and 24 August, 1910, *The Waterproofer: Official Organ of the Waterproof Garment Makers' Trade Union*, Vol. 1, Numbers 3, 4 and 5. A Jewish Social Democratic Association supported an SDF candidate in the North-West Manchester election of 1908, a Cheetham Clarion Fellowship was founded in 1905, with a Jewish secretary.
[75] *MCN*, 13 February 1892, 12 August 1893.

both of which had a high profile in Manchester. In Red Bank, Strangeways and Lower Broughton, the centres of working-class Jewry, social contact with working-class England (for these districts were never exclusively Jewish) and involvement in the English labour movement were mechanisms of acculturation with a cumulative effect as important as the Anglicizing institutions of the elite.

The attitude of the elite towards immigrant trade unionism was at first cautious rather than hostile, for they, after all, as cotton merchants, shopkeepers and professional men, were not the immediate targets of worker demands, while the fact of immigrant trade unionism might also be used to counter the anti-alien charge that Jewish workers were undercutting the wages of their native brothers. Typical of early elite attitudes was the belief that immigrant trade unionism was to be tolerated provided it took a respectable English form: the form, that is, of peaceful collective bargaining conducted in the English language and free from the taint of socialism.[76] At the same time, the Jewish Working Men's Club, the elite's answer to the 'international' club, was expected to draw the immigrants away from socialist preoccupations towards more harmless pastimes: talking politics was forbidden – except, that is, to speakers willing to condemn socialism.[77] Dr Salomon of the Englisher Shul told members in 1889 that socialism was an opinion 'subversive of religion, of government, of the family, and all that which their holy faith told them to hold dear'.[78] Dr Hermann Adler, on a visit to Manchester in the same year, visited the club and spoke to its members of the 'pestilential opinions' of East End socialists.[79] Socialists were, as the *Jewish Chronicle* told its Manchester readers, 'un-Jewish Jews'.[80] With this verdict the alrightniks could readily concur, for it was in the workshop trades that a socialist-informed trade unionism made itself felt. In whatever other ways the alrightnik might pose as the champion of immigrant causes, in the workshop trades he was the exploiter of immigrant labour, for here the battles between masters and men were between alrightnik masters and immigrant men. However the alrightnik might lend his prestige and give his money to an immigrant *chevra*, it is worth keeping in mind that it was often money derived from the 'sweating' of greener labour. In socialism, the elite and the alrightniks perceived a common enemy.

During the 1890s a majority of alrightniks with the right to vote probably yielded to Nathan Laski's call to Manchester's Jewish citizens to rally behind the Liberals as the party of Jewish Emancipation and Free Trade, but early in the twentieth century a number were drawn elsewhere by economic self-interest, particularly after the intervention of Winston Churchill, then Liberal MP for North-West Manchester, in the cap-makers' strike of 1907 to enforce a settlement on the masters.[81] In 1908, when Churchill was defeated in his

[76] *MG*, 15 April and 7 July 1890.
[77] Earliest rule book (nd., but probably 1890s) in the Manchester Jewish Museum.
[78] *JC*, 29 March 1889.
[79] *JC*, 25 March 1889.
[80] *JC*, 3 July 1891.
[81] For the cap-makers' strike, *MG*, 2 August 1907–3 September 1907.

attempt to retain the seat, the three leading immigrant cap-manufacturers, Mark Doniger, Nathaniel Jacobson and Samuel Lizar, together with water-proofing entrepreneurs like Jacob Weinberg and Louis Pavion, the calico printer Sam Finburgh, and perhaps others, were the unlikely bedfellows of elite mercantile families like the Henriques, the Samsons and the Garsons in the Conservative Party of Joynson-Hicks.[82]

This was only an extreme example of the forces which were drawing the alrightniks as a whole towards a closer association with the elite. For although the alrightniks may have begun by sharing the cultural inclinations of the immigrant masses, and however much this may have brought them into conflict with the elite, their desire for status both in English society and within the Jewish community drew them ever closer to the institutions and outlook of the established middle class. And however much they might first have hoped to further distinctive immigrant institutions and to float their ambitions on immigrant causes, they were drawn by events towards cultural concession and compromise. Nor, as the example of the Friendly Societies suggests, did this cut them off from the immigrant masses as sharply as might have been expected, for the masses, too, were being drawn as much by informal influences as by the strategies of the elite towards social and cultural integration.

IV

It was out of the social chemistry of these and other triangular encounters – between the elite, the alrightniks and the immigrant masses – that a 'new community' was created and a new communal leadership forged. So, for example, although it is true that in the battles over *shechita* no *chevra* or immigrant synagogue won lasting autonomy, important concessions were won from the elite, if only to ensure their overall control. Most notable were the setting up in 1892 of a communal Shechita Board, on which immigrant rabbis were represented as supervisors and alrightniks as members,[83] and in 1902 of a Beth Din on which Eastern European rabbis like Yoffey and Dagutski sat in judgement alongside Dr Salomon of the Great Synagogue. It was as representatives of their synagogues on the Shechita Board, which by the later 1890s had evolved into a more general clearing-house for communal prob-lems,[84] that alrightniks like Claff and Finburgh began to play a wider role in the direction of communal affairs, and often, too, from the nature of their new position, in opposition to immigrant separatism.[85] The Shechita Board and the Beth Din also mark the way in which the distinctive standards and styles of the

[82] *MG*, 22 April 1908; *Manchester Courier*, 21 and 22 April 1908; taped interview with Leon Lizar (son of Samuel Lizar) in the Manchester Jewish Museum.

[83] *JC*, 27 May 1892. The founding of the Board did not end disputes: to achieve independence, immigrant congregations had now to rebel against the Board's control.

[84] *JC*, 8 May 1896.

[85] For the rebellions which members of the Board, including, for example, Samuel Claff, had to face, see Slotki, *Manchester Shechita Board*, *passim*; *JC*, 13, 20 and 27 November 1896.

immigrants were drawn into the mainstream of the community, in a watered-down version, perhaps, but moving the whole orthodox community towards stricter observance.

Concession was one way in which the elite coped with challenge. Another was co-option, in the way that Susman Cohen of the Central Synagogue, the most articulate and fiery of Manchester's immigrant rabbis who had once led the whole immigrant community through the streets of Cheetham in protest against a ruling of the Chief Rabbi, was in 1897 elevated to the Beth Din of that same Chief Rabbi in London.[86] A farewell testimonial in the form of an illuminated address was signed by members of the elite as well as by the alrightniks, with Nathan Laski acting as secretary.[87] The way was also opened, if only slowly and with circumspection, for alrightniks to enter into the management of institutions founded by the elite, an opening they were only too ready to accept. From the other side, new immigrant institutions which clearly fulfilled some permanent need or which commanded popular support – the Jewish Hospital, the Jewish Temporary Shelter, the Home for Aged and Infirm Jews, the Benevolent Societies, the Talmud Torah, the Yeshivah and Zionism, particularly after it had been rendered respectable by British government backing in 1917 – attracted elite support and sometimes fell under elite tutelage: so Nathan Laski, the implacable opponent of the Jewish Hospital, had by the 1920s become its president.

None of these changes was sudden. The acceptance of immigrant institutions and aspirations into the permanent fabric of communal life, the movement of alrightniks into positions of management within the community, the varied processes of immigrant acculturation all began in the 1870s and continued into the 1920s. Throughout the period, the blurring of the distinction between an older elite and immigrant *nouveaux riches* was a very gradual, sometimes almost imperceptible process. Such broad categories also fail to do justice to the more complex differentiation within both or to their more intricate social and political interrelationship. None the less, these bold lines seem justified by the need to emphasize the crucial importance of social division in this period. For this is surely how the confrontation between East and West really happened: a confrontation between cultures, certainly, but in class-divided societies in which cultural differences acquired social weight. And a confrontation resolved not by overall victory or defeat, still less by some impersonal process of 'transformation', but by piecemeal bargaining at every level, by negotiation, concession, compromise. And in this negotiation the alrightniks played a central role, mediating on cultural issues between the immigrant masses and the elite, a mediation deeply coloured by their social ambitions. Alliances of convenience

[86] *JC*, 5 November 1897, which opposes his appointment on the grounds that he could not speak English and 'had never taken the trouble to learn it... He has his being in a Polish environment from which it is impossible for him to emancipate himself.'

[87] The testimonial is in the possession of the family of the late Mr David Goldberg, a descendant of Susman Cohen.

drew the alrightniks and the elite together. As a result, the community of 1920 was already a complex amalgam of East and West, its leadership – its new elite – now drawn as much from the immigrant as from the native bourgeoisie: now only the socialists were excluded.

3
Trade Unionism amongst the Jewish Tailoring Workers of London and Leeds, 1872–1915

Anne J. Kershen

Within the last twenty years historians have begun to pay increasing attention to the processes of acculturation, Anglicization and assimilation undergone by Eastern European immigrants who arrived in England during the last half of the nineteenth century. Following the appearance of Lloyd Gartner's seminal work *The Jewish Immigrant in England*[1] a number of historians went on to investigate the social, economic and political conditions under which alien communities developed in major cities such as London, Leeds and Manchester.[2] With the exception of Gartner there is general agreement that the evolution and organization of the immigrant Jewish proletariat took place within the wider framework of the English labour movement,[3] even though for reasons of work organization and language independent Jewish trade unions emerged in the

[1] L. Gartner, *The Jewish Immigrant in England 1870–1914* (London, 1960).
[2] The growth of anti-alienism and the response of English society is examined in B. Gainer, *The Alien Invasion* (London, 1972), J. A. Garrard, *The English and Immigration 1880–1910) (London, 1971)* and C. Holmes, *Anti-Semitism in British Society 1876–1939* (London, 1979). W. J. Fishman reveals the Jewish involvement with the radicals and anarchists of London's East End in *East End Jewish Radicals 1870–1914* (London, 1975); and the interaction of Jewish and English trade unionists in Manchester and Leeds is described in Bill Williams, 'The Beginnings of Jewish Trade Unionism in Manchester', in ed. K. Lunn, *Hosts, Immigrants and Minorities* (London, 1980) and J. Buckman, *Immigrants and the Class Struggle* (Manchester, 1983).
[3] In his book *The Jewish Immigrant in England*, Professor Gartner makes no reference to the Jewish branches of the Amalgamated Society of Tailors, the first of which was opened in 1883. Nor does he reveal the direct links that existed between English and Jewish socialists and trade unionists, especially in Leeds. Most particularly, under the heading 'The climactic year of 1889' (p. 122) Gartner omits any reference to the growth of 'new unionism', the wave of strikes that swept through London involving Jew and non-Jew alike and the shared platforms of London dockers and Jewish tailors during the strikes of 1889 and 1912.

latter part of the nineteenth century and the early years of the twentieth. The interaction of Jewish and English socialists and trade unionists from the 1870s onwards is a factor in any examination of Jewish trade union regional strengths and weaknesses and was one of the determinants of their success or failure. An investigation into the Jewish tailoring trade unions of London and Leeds, the two major centres for the production of tailored garments, provides an opportunity to look at the immigrant Jewish proletariat in the context of their assimilation with the host work force and labour movement and, in addition, to consider their reaction to communal nexus and class division within the ghetto.

During the years covered by this essay the clothing trade dominated the Jewish trade union movement. This is not surprising when it is remembered that tailoring was the occupation most favoured by the Eastern European immigrant. The 1901 Decennial Census revealed that almost 35 per cent of the capital's Eastern European population was employed in some branch of the trade – the second most popular trade being boot-making, which occupied some 10 per cent of the London Jewish work force.[4] In Leeds the ratio of Eastern European tailors to total Jewish population was even greater than that recorded in the capital. By 1901, 6,204, or 41.36 per cent, of the city's 15,000-strong Jewish community were reportedly engaged in the production of tailored garments.[5]

Two major factors were instrumental in determining the form and fate of the Jewish tailoring trade unions founded in Leeds and London between 1872 and 1915. Firstly, those which were the result of organizational problems inherent in the industrial structure of the two cities; and secondly, those which related directly to the ethnicity of the alien work force. The separations between the two were not always distinct. There was a grey area, particularly in the capital, where ethnicity and the complex infrastructure of the tailoring trade combined to weaken the formation and direction of Jewish tailoring unions. The key points in the foundation and duration of the tailoring trade unions of London and Leeds were:

1　the structure, nature and growth of industry and markets;
2　the intellectual, social and communal nexus and divisions that existed within the Eastern European community;
3　the interaction of English and Jewish trade unionists and labour activists;
4　the role of Anglo-Jewry; and finally,
5　the efficiency, availability and stability of trade union leaders.

By expanding on the above factors I intend to illustrate how they affected the course of tailoring trade unionism in the two cities. How in Leeds, by 1915, a single Jewish tailoring union, the Amalgamated Jewish Tailors', Machiners' and Pressers' Trade Union (AJTMP), had enjoyed an unbroken existence of twenty-two years and had by 1915 a Leeds membership of 1,500 which

---

[4] *Decennial Census 1901*, Parliamentary Papers 1904, CVII (London, 1904).
[5] Ibid, and *Jewish Chronicle*, 12 June 1908.

represented approximately 23 per cent of the city's Jewish tailoring work force.[6] And how in London these same factors were responsible for the rise and fall of some fifty different Jewish tailors' unions over a period of forty-three years. By 1915 only three major Jewish tailors' unions remained in the capital. Together they represented 20 per cent of the Jewish tailoring work force.[7] A comparison of the numbers of unionized English and Jewish tailoring workers in the metropolis helps destroy the myth that the organization of Jewish labour was invariably weaker and less successful than its English counterpart. Of the 64,993 occupied tailors in London (male and female),[8] 8,310, or approximately 13 per cent, were organized, and of those 5,634 were Jewish and 2,676 English.[9] Therefore by the outbreak of World War I some 65 per cent of the organized tailoring work force of London was Jewish, though in total it represented only 30 per cent of the whole.

A key feature in the origin and development of any trade union is the environment and structure of the industry it represents. A comparison of the London and Leeds tailoring industries' origins, infrastructure and consumer markets highlights how influential a point this was in trade union formation and survival. The London tailoring trade was marked by its variegated nature, separated as it was by divisions of skill, location and diversity of consumer outlets. Manufacture was concentrated in two specific areas of production, the West End and the East End. As the centre of finance, politics and the court, London created a natural market for high-class bespoke garments. Immigrant tailors were not employed at the very highest level of craft tailoring. But in tailors' shops that had sprung up around the periphery of Savile Row second-class bespoke garments were sold. While some of these were made up on shop premises by English journeymen tailors, others were produced by outworkers employed in the workshops of Soho, where by the late 1890s a small number of immigrant Eastern European Jews could be found at work. Their number remained small and it was not until 1903 that the first West End Jewish tailors' union was formed as the West End branch of the craft-based Amalgamated Society of Tailors.[10]

Increasingly during the latter years of the nineteenth century bespoke merchants sent work out to the cost-effective East End, where levels of skill and the quality of finished garments produced varied even within individual workshops. The area along the eastern perimeter of the City of London had been associated with the sale of second-hand clothes since Tudor times. During the first half of the nineteenth century second-hand gave way to new slop and shoddy

[6] Leeds Amalgamated Jewish Tailors' Machiners' and Pressers' Trade Union Annual Report, 1915. Archives of the National Union of Tailors and Garment Workers, London N.1.

[7] Amalgamated Society of Tailors Annual Reports, 1914–15, Archives of the National Union of Tailors and Garment Workers. Scottish Operative Tailors' and Tailoresses' Association, Ballot for Amalgamation, 1914, Archives of NUTGW.

[8] *Decennial Census 1911*, Parliamentary Papers 1913, LXXVIII (London, 1913).

[9] Amalgamated Society of Tailors Annual Reports, 1914–15, and Scottish Operative Tailors' and Tailoresses' Association, Ballot for Amalgamation, 1914.

[10] Amalgamated Society of Tailors Annual Report, 1903. Archives of NUTGW.

garments. In 1830 H. Hyam opened a shop in the East End to sell slop clothes. Several years later E. Moses opened his 'humble warehouse' at 154 Minories. By 1846 the warehouse had been transformed into the vast emporium 'to which custom came from all over the metropolis' to purchase clothes which ranged in price from 8/6 for a ready-made suit to as much as three or four guineas for a bespoke garment.[11] By the mid-nineteenth century the cheaper sector of the tailoring industry was well established. It catered for white-collar workers, artisans and that section of the emergent working class that wanted to be seen dressed in newly made clothes however poor and shoddy.

The feasibility of the wholesale supply of garments which were of rough material and manufacture resulted from three main factors: (1) the earlier industrial revolution; (2) by the early 1830s, the availability of 'shoddy',[12] and (3) the increased use of sub-divisional tailoring. Contrary to popular belief the system of sub-divisional tailoring, the sector of the industry synonymous with 'sweating', preceded both the arrival of the mechanical sewing machine in 1851 and the mass 'alien invasion' of the early 1880s. It was developed in the late 1820s by journeymen tailors who initially employed their wives and daughters to assist in the production of clothes by making buttonholes and sewing on buttons. The economic viability of the system rapidly became apparent and it soon spread beyond the nexus of the family, eventually mushrooming into a complex and sophisticated method of production. The sub-divisional tailoring workshops of London's East End were mainly small-scale and situated in a variety of unsuitable or insanitary locations such as back rooms, attics, workshops built onto the backs of existing buildings and in multi-occupancies converted from large single residences. In 1888 Beatrice Potter revealed that in the East End of London there were over 900 tailoring workshops in which fewer than ten hands were employed and only 42 in which over 25 were at work.[13] This ratio continued well into the twentieth century. Conditions were reportedly 'filthy with foul atmosphere and neglected occupants'.[14] Jewish tailors were exploited both materially and physically; sub-divisional work paid the lowest wages and created the worst conditions. For while the most fortunate of East End tailors earned as much as £1 10s. per week, as late as 1906 others with less skill averaged as little as 11s. 6d. a week, often working fourteen to eighteen hours a day.[15]

Sweating, the subjection of poorly paid labour to excessively long hours and insanitary conditions,[16] was not restricted to the capital's tailoring industry. It was a feature of other consumer trades such as footwear, furniture, furriery as

---

[11] E. Moses, *The Past, the Present and the Future* (London, 1846).

[12] Shoddy was produced by adding a small amount of new wool to a quantity of shredded rags; this resulted in a very cheap cloth of inferior quality.

[13] C. Booth, *London Life and Labour*, vol. 4 (London, 1892), p. 67.

[14] *Children's Employment Commission Second Report 1864*, Parliamentary Papers 1864, XXII, p. 67, (London, 1864).

[15] S. B. Dobbs, *The Clothing Workers of England* (London, 1928), p. 108.

[16] For detailed analysis of the sweating system in London see: D. Bythell, *The Sweated Trades* (London, 1978); G. Stedman Jones, *Outcast London* (London, 1984 edn) pp. 106–10; and J. A. Smiechen, *Sweated Industries and Sweated Labour* (New York, 1984).

well as lesser industries such as cap- and stick-making – trades which were stimulated by the emergence of new groups of consumers from the middle class and upper strata of the working class. These trades were not inhibited by the capital's inability to expand industrially, but were reinforced by the economic advantages of sub-divisional production, a labour pool composed of casual workers and a growing number of semi-skilled and unskilled Eastern European immigrants.

The tailoring workers of London served a multiplicity of small-scale bespoke and ready-to-wear retail outlets, a number of glass-fronted emporiums such as those of E. Moses and Co., together with the discreet bespoke establishments of Mayfair. In addition to home industry, London's sub-divisional tailors made up the cheapest quality linen trousers for export to the 'Kaffirs' of South Africa. It was an industrial structure which encouraged a mode of production based on the continuing use of small-scale units, a system dominated by a multitude of manufacturers, middlemen and masters controlling a complex chain of production.

London trade was not comparable to that of Leeds, where the wholesale production of ready-made tailored menswear accounted for at least 75 per cent of the city's clothing industry.[17] The wholesale manufacture of tailored garments began in Leeds in 1856 when John Barran opened a small factory in Alfred Street equipped with three sewing machines and employing six cutters and twenty female hands.[18] It was possibly the fact that Barran was aware of the growing number of artisans and white-collar workers 'eager and able to afford to act as guinea pigs for new ranges and styles' that encouraged him to advance production methods through the introduction of innovatory technology.[19] His invention of the bandknife facilitated the cutting-out of up to one hundred layers of cloth in a single move. In order to accommodate this velocity John Barran sought the economically viable assistance of sub-contracted labour. Having been refused by local English journeymen tailors who were concerned to retain their image as the aristocrats of the trade and at the same time inhibit the expansion of what appeared as a new and threatening branch of industry,[20] John Barran turned to a local German/Jewish master tailor, Herman Friend.[21] Friend agreed to produce jackets and coats in his small workshop using sub-divisional methods while Barran's factory operatives, nearly all female, produced the trousers and vests. This laid down a structural pattern which was to be emulated by the majority of wholesale clothiers in Leeds: a system of separation yet interdependence. Barran and the other Leeds wholesale clothing manufacturers could not, as did the merchants of London, wait for trade to come to them. The man in the street, the drapery store owner and the overseas buyer did not go to Leeds looking for clothes but were encouraged to place

[17] *Report of the Truck Committee 1906*, Parliamentary Papers 1908, LIX, qq 5888 (London, 1908).

[18] *Yorkshire Post*, 4 May 1905.

[19] *Leeds Mercury*, 25 August 1888.

[20] *Royal Commission on Alien Immigration 1903*, Parliamentary Papers 1903, X, qq 15144 (London, 1903).

[21] J. Thomas, 'A History of the Leeds Clothing Industry', *Yorkshire Bulletin of Economic and Social Research*, Occasional Papers no. 1, (Leeds, 1955) p. 19.

orders by travelling salesmen employed to seek out and open up new markets. Accordingly, future trade could be estimated, labour requirements and styles pre-determined and the destructive effects of seasonality to some degree reduced; factors which encouraged the utilization of large-scale production units, both factories and workshops.

As the Leeds wholesale clothing factories expanded so did the alien tailoring workshops. In the 1870s these had been small, containing on average six to eight machines and ten to twelve hands.[22] In the early 1870s as demand and industry expanded, a number of semi-skilled and skilled hands were recruited from Eastern Europe by a Leeds-based master tailor, Moyshe Goodman.[23] By the close of the decade, as the flow of indigent immigrants increased, further recruitment became unnecessary. Significantly, as the volume of workers and workshop sizes grew and the sub-divisional system extended further, the overall level of skill declined. By the end of the nineteenth century the average Leeds Jewish tailor's workshop housed between twenty-five and thirty-five hands,[24] while there were a number in which sixty, eighty and even one hundred worked side by side, day by day, seasonality and the economy permitting.[25] This is not to deny the existence of small, even 'bedroom' workshops: it has to be emphasized that large and medium-sized Jewish workshops operated alongside small ones. Though size of production unit was a key factor in the successful unionization of sub-divisional labour, it had little bearing on working environment. Leeds tailor's machiner Joseph Finn revealed the fiendish conditions Jewish tailoring workers were forced to endure,[26] while David Lubelski, a workshop master, confirmed in his evidence to the 1888 House of Lords Select Committee on Sweating that 'hands were forced to live and work in wretched conditions.'[27] A reporter from the *Lancet* exposed the constant danger from infection in even the largest Leeds Jewish tailoring workshops: 'Floors were rarely cleaned' and 'the revolting state of the water closets resulted in an appalling stench.'[28] Contemporary evidence confirms that, irrespective of size, all but a small number of the Jewish tailoring workshops of Leeds were as insanitary as their counterparts in London's East End. In Leeds, as in the metropolis, tailoring was not the only sweated trade. Slipper-making, cabinet-making and brush-making providing other examples of worker exploitation.[29]

In both cities a hierarchically structured work force served in the tailoring workshops. The machiner was the aristocrat of the workshop, the presser the strong man who, with the adept application of his iron, could improve the fit

[22] *Lancet*, 9 June 1888, p. 1146.
[23] Information supplied by Dr G. Raisman.
[24] *Leeds Express*, 25 May 1894.
[25] *JC*, 4 February 1898.
[26] Letter from Joseph Finn to A. R. Rollin dated 27 October 1943: Rollin Collection, Modern Record Centre, University of Warwick.
[27] *House of Lords Select Committee on the Sweating System 1889*, Parliamentary Papers 1889, XIV, Evidence of D. Lubelski (London, 1889).
[28] *Lancet*, 9 June 1888, p. 1147.
[29] For conditions in the Leeds alien slipper-making industry see Buckman, *Immigrants and the Class Struggle*, pp. 125–51.

and shape of the garment. The tailor, in the sub-divisional workshop, was responsible for basting-out and basting-under and as such ranked below the other two. The lowest on the rung were the sub-contracted workers, the under-pressers and plain machiners. Lacking experience or skill, and often 'greeners' as well, they were paid and employed by the more experienced machiners and pressers. This internal division of work had repercussions in both London and Leeds. In the capital in 1904 a short-lived and ineffectual Anti-Sub-Contracting Trade Union was founded.[30] Two years later the Leeds Amalgamated Jewish Tailors', Machiners' and Pressers' Union threatened to deny membership to those who practised workshop sub-contracting.[31] But in spite of its divisive effect on worker unity neither in London nor Leeds was the thorn of workshop sub-contracting eradicated. It was not until the 1930s, and the introduction of government legislation making employers responsible for their workers' holiday pay, that the system was abandoned.

The sub-divisional system of production undermined unity within the tailoring work force. In Leeds during the 1880s the parallel existence of separate unions for Jewish tailors, machiners and pressers manifested the divisions. By 1893 evidence that the separations had been overcome was provided by the formation of the Amalgamated Leeds Jewish Tailors', Machiners' and Pressers' Trade Union. Divisions in the capital covered a far wider spectrum, a major split emerging in 1880 with the birth of the mantle trade.[32] By the end of the decade the production of mantles had become an important part of the London tailoring industry, sustaining still further the use of small workshops and introducing its own fissions of craft and quality. Mantle-making reinforced still further the separations that existed amongst the Jewish tailoring workers in the metropolis. Between 1880 and 1910 unions were not only founded for ladies' and gents' tailors, but in addition for machiners, pressers, plain machiners, under-pressers, waistcoat makers, military tailors, trouser makers, as well as those that represented religious and political differences.

The foregoing outline of the structure and growth of the Leeds and London tailoring industries highlights their differences. The development of Leeds industry encouraged a form of unit expansion which resulted in large numbers of workers being employed by one employer under one roof. This was facilitated by the ready availability of premises suitable for use as large workshops at rents which were 44 per cent less than those in the capital.[33] In London restricted space and exorbitant rents meant large workshops were the exception rather than the rule. However, it is significant that the spatial and economic constrictions that inhibited unit expansion in the metropolis provided the basis for the tailoring trade's continued viability.

Within small-scale units of production, where master and hand worked side

[30] *JC*, 14 October 1904.

[31] Minute Book of the Leeds Amalgamated Tailors', Machiners' and Pressers' Trade Union, 1905–7. Archives of the National Union of Tailors and Garment Workers.

[32] *Royal Commission on Alien Immigration 1903*, Parliamentary Papers 1903, X, qq 18968.

[33] *Labour Gazette*, May 1908.

by side, class division did not always override communal ties. Within the synagogue, the confines of the ghetto and even the workshop, bonds of religion and kin at times held fast. The working Jewish tailor, machiner or presser adopted an identity in keeping with the occasion: exploited hand, consoling mourner, or even employee inviting his employer to celebrate a son's barmitzvah or a daughter's wedding. Class division was at times blurred by the nexus of community. Small-scale workshop relations weakened trade union affiliation. Jewish trade unionist Joseph Finn told the Royal Commission on Alien Immigration in 1903 that 'intimacy between masters and men' was a factor in weakening trade union organization amongst the tailoring workers of London's East End.[34] In many instances that 'intimacy' was the result of kinship: brothers, brothers-in-law, uncles and cousins provided employment for, and exploited, their newly arrived indigent relatives. In the larger workshop the social and economic distance between employer and work force facilitated organization. Evidence from the Minute Book of the Leeds AJTMP indicates that in large Jewish workshops, such as that of Benjamin Joseph,[35] union membership was widespread while in the smaller units support for trade unions was weak and volatile. Evidence from other industries, other countries and other periods of history confirms that in the case of small-scale units of production with enforced personal contact between employer and employee trade union support was, and continues to be, difficult to encourage and hard to retain. This was true in the boot and shoe industry in the later years of the nineteenth century,[36] the early stages of organization amongst the print workers of New Delhi,[37] the London mantle-making trade during the 1930s,[38] and, even today, in the small immigrant-run tailoring sweatshops of the Midlands and London's East End.[39]

In both Leeds and London industrial structure and communal nexus affected organizational homogeneity and survival. In London, in the late nineteenth century, the intellectual and ideological differences that were manifest within the Eastern European community further damaged attempts at trade union organization. In the 1870s and 1880s London provided a refuge for Jewish intellectuals escaping from Eastern Europe. They arrived in the capital with their ideals and the belief that they could lead the Jewish proletariat to socialism through combination. The first to try was Louis Smith, who arrived in London in 1872 via the Paris Commune of 1871.[40] Smith preached that combination

[34] *Royal Commission on Alien Immigration 1903*, Parliamentary Papers 1903, X, qq 20271.
[35] Minute Book of the Leeds Amalgamated Jewish Tailors', Machiners' and Pressers' Trade Union 1905–7.
[36] A. Fox, *A History of the National Union of Boot & Shoe Operatives* (London, 1958), pp. 27 and 135.
[37] F. Munson, *Indian Trade Unions* (London, 1970), p. 36.
[38] Information from Mr Mick Mindel, officer of the London Ladies' Tailors' Trade Union from 1936 until its amalgamation with the National Union of Tailors and Garment Workers in 1938.
[39] Information Office of the National Union of Tailors and Garment Workers, London, November 1986.
[40] A. R. Rollin, 'Russo-Jewish Immigration into England before 1881', *Transactions of the Jewish Historical Society*, London, 21 (1968).

was a means of overcoming the excesses of the capitalist employer. His view of trade unionism differed from that of contemporary English trade unionists, who in the 1870s saw combination as a means of preserving craft qualities and ensuring good working conditions and a high level of income for their members. Shortly after his arrival Smith founded the Lithuanian Tailors' Union in Whitechapel.[41] This union, though attracting an initial membership of seventy-two, collapsed within weeks as a result of its founder's idealism, its members' naivety and the capitalist employers' duplicity.[42] Louis Smith, disillusioned, left for America. He had not understood that the indigent alien tailors of London's East End preferred bread today to jam tomorrow.

Four years later, in 1876, a second London Jewish tailors' union was founded, this time as an offshoot of the Hebrew Socialist Union.[43] The impetus came from a Lithuanian, Aaron Liberman, the founding father of Jewish socialism. The description of the events surrounding the rise and fall of the short-lived tailors' union which appear in the *Polishe Yidel* in August 1884 spotlight the differences between the Jews from Lithuania and those from the region of Galicia. The 'Litvaks' considered the Galicians their intellectual inferiors, while they in turn were eyed with suspicion by their more illiterate co-religionists. This was emphasized by the paper's reference to the 'problems' Liberman and his associates had in persuading the Jewish tailors of the East End to attend a peoples' assembly: 'What was this problem? The Litvaks wore brille (Yiddish for glasses). Everyone had a different opinion about the brille (as Liberman's group was nicknamed). One said they were missionaries, others said that they were almost entirely simple murderers who carried loaded rifles in their trouser pockets. Everyone was in doubt about the little Litvaks.'[44] Ridiculing the glasses emphasized the intellectual distance between the two groups and stressed the workers' lack of confidence in the ability of those early socialists to improve their condition of work. Even so, together with English representatives of local craft unions, several hundred Jewish immigrant workers attended the assembly which took place on the 26 August. At the meeting the call for the formation of a tailors' union was immediately approved and by mid-September membership numbered nearly 300.[45] But by the end of November personal and methodological differences over ideological issues as opposed to pragmatic solutions to the everyday problems of the workshop exasperated an increasingly dissatisfied and volatile rank and file. Discontent exploded at what proved to be the last meeting of the union. A fight broke out between the socialists and the more religious members. Liberman was assaulted, his glasses were smashed, and he was forced to take cover under a table until the police

[41] Ibid.
[42] *Polishe Yidel*, 8 August 1884.
[43] For details of the Hebrew Socialist Union see Fishman, *East End Jewish Radicals*, pp. 103–24, and N. Levin, 'While Messiah Tarried', *Jewish Socialist Movements 1871–1917* (New York, 1977), p. 43.
[44] *Polishe Yidel*, 22 August 1884.
[45] Notes of A. R. Rollin, Rollin Collection, Modern Record Centre, University of Warwick.

arrived and restored peace. The final straw came when the treasurer absconded with the union's funds.[46]

In 1883 Isaac Stone, a Jewish Socialist and a tailor by trade, tried once again to overcome the problems inherent in the organization of the alien tailoring work force of London's East End.[47] However, the union he founded collapsed within months. Disillusioned and despondent, Stone published his views on contemporary trade unionism in the first edition of the socialist Yiddish newspaper, the *Arbeiter Fraint*. He thought that the dual role of the union – as a body that organized strikes in order to improve the condition of the workers and as a friendly society which provided benefits at times of strikes or illness – was 'damaging and useless'. Under the existing capitalist system the best the worker could hope for from a strong trade union was to keep his family from starving. Stone wrote: 'Trade unions alone cannot end the wretched life of the worker, ... they lead workers off the right road with their belief in self-help ... we socialists say that the role of the union should not be only to make strikes but completely to rebuild society.'[48]

Unions had to be harnessed to the movement to overthrow capitalism, but if members were concerned only with immediate goals this would never happen. Once again, ideology was in opposition to the workers' desire for a rapid amelioration of conditions of employment. The inability of those early intellectual Jewish radical refugees to capture and maintain the support of the Jewish working class was largely due to their reluctance to acknowledge that the exploited worker regarded the provision of food, warmth and clothing for his family and himself as more imperative than devotion to socialist dogma. As Professor Fishman illustrates in his book on East End Jewish radicals, the popularity and success of men such as Rudolf Rocker was not only due to their political ideology and charisma but to their open recognition of the proletariat's need for immediate and tangible ameliorations.[49] Even though in the years that followed socialist ideology remained very much a part of trade unionism, dogma was never again permitted to dominate.

Unlike the earliest Jewish tailoring trade unions in London, the first Leeds Jewish tailors' society originated in workshop conditions and local English organization. In the 1870s the Leylands ghetto attracted no radical intellectual refugees seeking to rescue and convert the downtrodden and exploited proletariat. Instead, the foundation of the Leeds Jewish Working Tailors' Society[50] in 1876 has been attributed to the workers' own desire to oppose exploitation. Writing in 1899, the secretary of the Leeds Amalgamated Jewish Tailors', Machiners' and Pressers' Trade Union told how those early tailoring hands experienced irregular working hours and a working day often in excess of

[46] *Polishe Yidel*, 22 August 1884.
[47] Ibid., 28 August 1884.
[48] *Arbeiter·Fraint*, 15 July 1885.
[49] Fishman, *East End Jewish Radicals*, pp. 229–302.
[50] *Report of the Chief Inspector of Friendly Societies 1876*, Parliamentary Papers 1877, LXXVII, (London 1877).

seventeen hours. This set the men 'thinking about trade unionism'.[51] The nature of the Leeds Jewish tailoring colony created a need for interaction with English trimmings merchants and English tailors whose society's headquarters was very close by. Such an association was not called for in the more self-contained and longer-established tailoring ghetto of Whitechapel. The proximity of the indigenous tailoring community and the form and development of the Jewish tailors' society suggests the influence of the local English tailors and their 'new model' union. The Leeds branch of the Amalgamated Society of Tailors (AST) refused alien membership. But it would have encouraged and welcomed the formation of a Jewish tailors' union whose stated intention, to increase wages and reduce hours, was an attempt to bring the alien workman in line with his English counterpart. Therefore the foundation of that first Jewish tailors' society in Leeds can be seen as the outcome of the alien's desire for personal protection and improvement, fashioned after the model of an English trade society through the influence of local craft unions.

The history of the Leeds Jewish tailors' union for the remainder of the 1870s, and during the following decade, underlines the absence of foreign influence and the interaction between the Jewish and English trade unionists and socialists of Leeds. In 1884 the tailors' society and the newly founded pressers' and machiners' societies affiliated to Leeds Trades Council.[52] The link between English and Jewish socialists and trade unionists was strengthened in 1885 when Joseph Finn, a member of the machiners' society, became the sole Jewish founder member of the Leeds branch of the Socialist League.[53] In that same year, the year of the first and successful Leeds Jewish tailors' strike, an English socialist and trade unionist, boot-maker James Sweeney, forged another link when he became secretary of the Jewish Tailors' Society.[54] Though the Jewish tailors' membership of the Trades Council lapsed between 1886 and 1893,[55] contact between local Jewish and English socialists grew stronger. Their common political and ideological bond helped to overcome ethnic differences and enabled members of the Socialist League such as Tom Maguire, Tom Paylor and James Sweeney to direct the second, albeit unsuccessful, Leeds Jewish tailors' strike in 1888.[56]

The strike of 1888 exposed political and religious fissures amongst the Jewish tailoring trade unionists of Leeds. Those divisions led to the ultimate collapse of their three tailoring societies. They were also the differences which English socialists such as Maguire and Sweeney fought hard to overcome in order to unite all the opposed and exploited proletariat of Leeds and the West Riding, irrespective of race, religion or skill. For a short while, during the explosion of

---

[51] *Trade Unionist*, July 1899, p. 449.
[52] Leeds Trades Council Annual Report, 1884, Leeds City Archives.
[53] Socialist League Foundation Certificate, February 1885, Leeds City Archives.
[54] *Leeds Daily News*, 13 May 1885.
[55] Leeds Trades Council Annual Reports, 1884, Leeds City Archives.
[56] For detailed accounts of the Leeds Jewish tailors' strike of 1888 see: *Leeds Evening News, Yorkshire Post*, and *Arbeiter Fraint* May and June 1888 and Buckman, *Immigrants and the Class Struggle*, pp. 75–80.

'new unionism', they succeeded. In 1889 the Leeds branch of the Gasworkers' and General Labourers' Union was formed.[57] By 1890 the organized Jewish tailors, machiners and pressers of Leeds had become the Jewish tailors' branch of that general union.[58] The peak membership of 2,000, almost 50 per cent of the alien tailoring work force of the city, was never equalled again in the years leading to 1915. But as the Jewish tailors of Leeds had reflected the national euphoria of 'new unionism' so they reflected its demise eighteen months later. The ideological rift between parliamentarians and anarchists that was weakening the cause of socialism nationally was the catalyst that led to the collapse of the Jewish Tailors' branch of the Leeds Gasworkers' and General Labourers' Union.[59] The situation was further aggravated by the breakdown in relations between the English executive of the Gasworkers and a number of Jewish trade unionists. The latter complained about the union's officers' excessive drinking and bureaucracy and departed the union.[60] Although that first conjunction of Jewish and English trade unionists ended in failure, it nevertheless had set a precedent, even whilst highlighting the problems of inter-ethnic organization. The lessons were well learnt and when the Jewish tailoring workers of Leeds reorganized in 1893 as the Amalgamated Jewish Tailors', Machiners' and Pressers' Trade Union their leaders, conscious of the need for cooperation, gradually developed a working relationship with the Amalgamated Union of Clothing Operatives, the union founded and based in Leeds for those employed in the wholesale clothing factories. It was a relationship which, twenty-two years later, led to those two Leeds clothing unions, one Jewish, one English, amalgamating and providing the power behind the first national clothing workers' union, the United Garment Workers' Trade Union.[61]

Unlike the Leeds branch of the Socialist League, to quote E. P. Thompson, 'the active Leaguers of London were a poor bunch,'[62] and it was mainly the Social Democrats who were involved in organizing the capital's exploited. But even though English socialists such as James MacDonald and Charles Mowbray, both tailors and members of the Amalgamated Society of Tailors, provided the nexus between the alien tailors and the English labour movement during the climactic years of the late 1880s and early 1890s, neither they nor their Jewish counterparts succeeded in creating a fusion of interests as had occurred in Leeds. There was a level of cooperation, as exemplified by the

[57] E. P. Thompson, 'A Homage to Tom Maguire' in eds A. Briggs and J. Saville, *Essays in Labour History* (London, 1966), p. 296.

[58] *Yorkshire Factory Times*, 9 May 1890.

[59] Ibid., 29 August 1890.

[60] *Arbeiter Fraint*, 11 December 1891.

[61] The United Garment Workers' Trade Union was founded in July 1915 following the amalgamation of six independent tailoring trade unions. These were the Amalgamated Union of Clothing Operatives, the Amalgamated Jewish Tailors', Machiners' and Pressers' Trade Union, both Leeds-based; the London Society of Tailors and Tailoresses, the London and Provincial Clothiers' Cutters' Trade Union, the London Jewish Tailors' Union and the Manchester Waterproof Garment Workers' Union. (The Manchester union seceded from the national union shortly after its formation.)

[62] E. P. Thompson, *William Morris* (New York, 1976 ed), p. 533.

striking dockers and striking tailors both in 1889 and again in 1912.[63] But the first, though ultimately unsuccessful, fusion of Jewish and English tailoring unions did not take place in London until 1906.

At the turn of the century political and economic events taking place on the broader national canvas were becoming of as much concern to the alien as they were to the English trade unionist. The depression in the industry which followed the end of the Boer War caused a slackening of trade and unemployment. The Taff Vale judgement had exposed the vulnerability of all trade unions, large or small, English or alien. In addition, anti-alienism in the overt form of organizations such as the British Brothers' League and the government-sponsored Royal Commission on Aliens unnerved an already unsettled London Jewish trade union movement, which by that time was in a state of chaos. Early in 1905 all the Jewish tailoring trade unions in the capital renounced their independence and 'threw in their lot' with the Amalgamated Society of Tailors.[64] At its peak in mid-1906, the AST had sixteen affiliated Jewish branches, which represented in the region of 10,000 members.[65] By 1908 the total membership of the five remaining London branches stood at just 168.[66] This was due to the dissatisfaction, distrust, frustration and anti-alienism manifested by the Manchester Executive of the AST. These factors made it impossible for the AST and the previously independent London Jewish tailoring unions to work together.[67]

The role of Anglo-Jewry in the fate of the Jewish tailoring trade unions of London and Leeds highlights the socio-economic differences that prevailed between the Jewish community of Leeds and that of the capital. Although re-admitted in 1656, the Jews of England did not achieve total emancipation until 1871. By that date members of the long-established Anglo-Jewish community had risen to political, social and financial heights. The sudden influx of alien immigrants after 1881 unsettled an Anglo-Jewish elite that exerted covert controls and restricting pressures on the daily lives of the Eastern European community of the capital through the Jewish educational, religious, charitable and housing organizations.[68]

Accusations that immigrant Jews were stealing the jobs of the host working population led men such as Samuel Montagu to reconsider their attitude towards trade unionism. Previously trade unionism had been thought subversive, restrictive and irreligious, but in the early 1880s Montagu adopted the new Liberal line which accepted the organization of labour as a beneficial and

---

[63] For detailed accounts of the 1889 East End Jewish tailors' strike see Fishman, *East End Jewish Radicals*, pp. 169–79 and L. Gartner, *The Jewish Immigrant in England*, pp. 122–6. For the 1912 tailors' strike see Fishman, *East End Jewish Radicals*, pp. 294–301 and R. Rocker, *The London Years* (London, 1956), pp. 218–26.

[64] *Amalgamated Society of Tailors' Journal* September 1905, Archives of the National Union of Tailors and Garments Workers.

[65] Amalgamated Society of Tailors Annual Report, 1906. Archives of NUTGW.

[66] Ibid., 1908.

[67] Amalgamated Society of Tailors Journal, August 1906, and *JC*, 9 August 1907.

[68] Gartner, *Jewish Immigrants*, chs 7 and 8 and p. 156; and V. D. Lipman, *Social History of the Jews in England, 1850–1950* (London, 1959), ch. 3 and pp. 105–6.

controlling facet of working-class life. He also saw it as a means of accelerating the acculturation and Anglicization of the immigrant work force, thus steering them away from attitudes and actions likely to influence an increasingly xenophobic public. To this end he provided the necessary finance and sponsorship to establish the London Tailors' Machiners' Society in 1886. But while supporting some of the ethics of trade unionism, Montagu insisted that under his patronage the Society adopt a moderate course which excluded the use of strike action.[69] This stipulation led to friction between Montagu and the Society's secretary, Lewis Lyons, and, by 1887, to the departure of Montagu and the collapse of the Society. Two years later the strike of East End Jewish tailors roused further anxieties. Both Montagu and Lord Rothschild intervened to secure a settlement. Montagu personally pledged £100 on behalf of the masters as a sign of their good will. After the passing of the Aliens Act in 1905, which found support amongst some members of Anglo-Jewry, the establishment relaxed their guard and took a less public role in the industrial affairs of the Jewish proletariat.

The absence of an old-established and respected Anglo-Jewish community in Leeds meant that the responses and restrictions operating in London were lacking. The Leeds Jewish Board of Guardians was not founded until 1878; there was no equivalent in Leeds of the Jewish Free Schools of London and other provincial cities, no Reform religious movement and no Jewish 'charitable' housing organizations. The city had no Jewish aristocracy to arbitrate in industrial disputes, or to accelerate a return to work in order to avoid anti-alien attacks. Neither was the Jewish proletariat of Leeds faced with the choice of a multiplicity of Jewish friendly societies, burial societies and a Federation of Synagogues as existed in the East End of London and which created a diversion from the so-called 'benefits' of trade union membership. In fact, by the early twentieth century the Leeds Jewish tailors' union was offering its members kashrus – the preparation of food according to the tenets of the Jewish law – burial and prayer facilities.[70] It is unclear whether this was in order to compensate for the paucity of such facilities within the community or to contradict the view that trade unionism was irreligious.

The final factor, the efficiency, availability and stability of trade union leaders, underlines the importance of leadership in the context of nascent immigrant trade unions. The examples of London and Leeds in the years between 1872 and 1915 prove that full-time salaried general secretaries versed in English trade unionism and the needs of both the host and alien work force were vital to the well-being and success of the tailoring trade unions of the two cities. In Leeds between 1894 and 1915 the tailors were led by just two full-time general secretaries. The first, Sam Freedman, originally a working tailor, was a member of the early tailors' union and involved in the merger between the Leeds gasworkers and the Jewish tailors. It was Freedman who recommended

[69] *JC*, 12 March 1886.
[70] Ibid., 29 May 1908.

his union's affiliation to the General Federation of Trade Unions[71] and the Labour Representation Committee,[72] and initiated the attendance of a representative of the Amalgamated Jewish Tailors', Machiners' and Pressers' Trade Union at the Annual Conference of the TUC. Between 1895 and 1915 only the year 1898 was marked by the absence at the TUC conference of a Leeds Jewish tailoring trade unionist.[73] By comparison 1895 was the only year when a representative from a London Jewish tailoring union, or indeed any London Jewish union, attended the conference.[74] The Leeds Jewish tailoring trade union's leadership clearly manifested a desire to assimilate with, and to be accepted as part of, the English labour movement. Freedman's successor in 1906 was Moses Sclare. In his former position as an officer of the Glasgow branch of the Amalgamated Society of Engineers Sclare had been involved in running one of the country's best-established trade unions. As a result of his association with the ASE and local Glasgow labour and socialist movements Sclare had met members of the Labour Representation Committee and leading trade unionists and socialists from Britain and overseas. He was therefore fully cognizant of the necessity for his union to remain part of the national movement. From 1906 onwards, in his capacity as general secretary, Sclare never lost sight of the need to cooperate and interact with local English trade unions and labour activists. Under Moses Sclare's leadership the years between 1906 and 1915 represent a period of unprecedented branch and membership expansion for the Leeds Jewish Amalgamated Tailors', Machiners' and Pressers' Trade Union.

With the exception of two Leeds graduates, Joseph Finn and John Dyche,[75] general secretaries of the East End mantle makers' union during the 1890s, London lacked comparable leadership. The one individual whose name runs like a thread through the history of London tailoring trade unionism from 1885 until 1912, Lewis Lyons,[76] exhibited flaws of character which denied London the leadership and continuity given by men such as Freedman and Sclare.

[71] *Yorkshire Factory Times*, 16 February 1900.
[72] Ibid., 27 February 1903.
[73] Annual Reports of the Conference of the TUC, 1892–1915. Library of the TUC, London.
[74] Ibid., 1895.
[75] Joseph Finn (1860–1946) was an immigrant from Eastern Europe. After the 1885 Leeds Jewish tailors' strike Finn was forced to leave the city. He spent the following eight years in the United States, returning to London in 1893. He was then appointed secretary of the United Ladies' Tailors' Trade Union, a position he held until 1895. Although by the turn of the century Finn had retired from active trade unionism, he retained his concern and involvement with both the British and Jewish labour movements until his death. Finn was succeeded as secretary of the United Ladies' Tailors by John Dyche, another Leeds Jewish trade union activist. After his retirement from the mantle makers' union in 1900 Dyche went to New York where, in 1904, he was appointed General Secretary and Treasurer of the International Ladies' Garment Workers' Union, a position he held until 1914.
[76] Lewis Lyons was born in England of German parents in 1862. By trade a tailor's machiner, he was involved with the organization of labour from an early age and became a member of the SDF in the early 1880s. Lyons led a number of Jewish unemployed marches and demonstrations in the 1890s. In 1911 he was elected to sit on the Tailoring Trade Board but had to retire from that and his controversial role as secretary of several East End trade unions owing to ill-health. Lewis Lyons died in July 1918.

Lyons' inability to manage financial matters, whether the union's or his own, as well as his talent to create internal disquiet and conflict, were at odds with his obvious charisma which led to his being called back time and again to organize newly founded societies. Between 1885 and 1912 Lyons led, or was involved in running, no fewer than a dozen Jewish tailoring trade unions. He was alternately criticized and driven from trade union ranks and then implored to return. By the outbreak of World War I the surviving London Jewish tailors' unions employed secretaries with the experience and pragmatism necessary to ensure a stable future for their membership. In this way they were in no doubt aided by the long overdue decision to appoint paid officials.

In conclusion, it is clear that the strengths and weaknesses of Jewish tailoring trade unionism in London and Leeds resulted from a combination of factors, though some weighed more heavily than others. The structure of the Leeds clothing industry, with its dimension of separation yet interdependence and its concentration on wholesale consumer markets encouraged the continuing use of medium to large-scale production units, an acknowledged asset in the formation and maintenance of trade unions. The complex infrastructure of London's tailoring trade with its locational, craft and market separations bred small units which weakened attempts at combination. Regional variations in industrial structure were reflected in the organization of the local indigenous work force, an exogenous factor in the success or failure of the Jewish tailoring trade unions of London and Leeds. In the 1850s London was the centre of 'new model' unionism; in the following decade it was deprived of this role. The strength of cotton and coal pushed the centre of gravity to the industrial north where spatial and economic advantages made industrial expansion viable and attractive. Leeds offered a variety of industrial, geographic and demographic advantages to industry and, in addition to wholesale clothing, was a centre for engineering and textile manufacture.[77] It was an industrial environment which facilitated and encouraged the foundation and duration of trade unions. As early as 1860 Edward Baines, Liberal Member of Parliament for Leeds, was quoted as saying that 'scarcely any trade in Leeds is without its union'.[78] By the close of the decade there were a reported twenty-eight trade unions in Leeds,[79] amongst them the local branch of the Amalgamated Society of Tailors.[80] By 1876 the Jewish working tailors had followed suit, founding a union which appears to owe its origins to emulation of local example. But though it has been said that from the mid-1890s Leeds exemplified organizational stagnation,[81] by 1911 9 per cent of the city's tailoring work force was organized.[82] This was

[77] For the background to Leeds industrial, demographic and social history see ed. D. Fraser, *A History of Modern Leeds* (Leeds, 1980).

[78] E. D. Steele, 'Leeds and Victorian Politics', *University of Leeds Review*, 17:2 (1974) pp. 260–1.

[79] Fraser, *History of Modern Leeds*, p. 357.

[80] Amalgamated Society of Tailors Annual Report, 1868. Archives of NUTGW.

[81] E. P. Thompson, 'Homage to Tom Maguire', in Briggs and Saville, *Essays in Labour History*, p. 302.

[82] *Yorkshire Factory Times*, 15 August 1912, and Annual Report of the General Federation of Trade Unions 1912, Archives of the GFTU, London.

almost double the national average for the clothing industry, which was 5 per cent,[83] and almost on a par with the 9.5 per cent of engineering workers affiliated to the Leeds branch of the Amalgamated Society of Engineers.[84] Three years later the proportion of organized local clothing workers had increased to 19 per cent.[85] This impressive increase in support was attributable to a combination of factors. Legislation in the form of the Trade Boards Act of 1909 and the National Insurance Act of 1911 had increased the attraction of trade union affiliation. On a local level, between 1911 and 1913, both Leeds clothing unions, the Amalgamated Jewish Tailors, Machiners and Pressers and the Amalgamated Clothing Operatives, achieved significant advances in pay and hours for their members and thus underlined even more the benefits of organization.[86]

London was, by comparison, a 'trade union desert'.[87] By the start of the 1870s the capital's major industries were concentrated on finished consumer goods.[88] Heavy industry had moved north. The industries that remained – emphasizing commodities and luxury items for the population of a thriving metropolis – were dominated by small-scale units of production and the fickle dictates of fashion and season. This was a structure which did little to advance the cause of trade unionism. Eric Hobsbawm has shown that in London 'the area which curved from Camden Town to Stepney and the river was poorly organised.'[89] With such a weak example from the indigenous working community it is not surprising that trade union organization amongst alien immigrants who had no previous experience of combination in the Pale – in Eastern Europe trade unions were in embryonic form as late as the 1880s and early 1890s[90] – was, until the final years of the period under examination, to say the least fragile. Trade union support was further debilitated by the adverse effects of the 'busy and the slack'. Seasonality was more pronounced and divisive in the capital, which depended far more on the vagaries and idiosyncracies of style and consumer, than did the wholesale-based Leeds tailoring trade.[91]

[83] H. Clegg, *History of British Trade Unionism* (London, 1964), p. 468.

[84] *Decennial Census 1911* and 61st Annual Report of the Amalgamated Society of Engineers, Modern Record Centre, University of Warwick.

[85] *Yorkshire Factory Times*, 30 January 1913; Leeds Jewish Amalgamated Tailors', Machiners' and Pressers' Trade Union Annual Report, 1915, and Amalgamated Society of Tailors Annual Report, 1915. Both: Archives of NUTGW.

[86] The Smith Award which followed the Leeds Jewish tailors' strike of 1911 marked the most significant amelioration in wages and hours in the history of Leeds Jewish tailoring trade unionism. The major advance was the reduction of the working week – in two stages – from 61 hours to 54 hours with no accompanying wage reduction. The Leeds Jewish tailors' union's success resulted in a number of Jewish tailoring workers in other provincial cities requesting the union to open branch offices. For full details of the Smith Award see the *Jewish Chronicle*, 13 March 1911. In 1913 the executive of the Amalgamated Union of Clothing Operatives negotiated increases of between ¾d. (for women) to 3½d. (for men) per hour on the minimum rate laid down by the Tailoring Trade Board.

[87] E. Hobsbawm, *Worlds of Labour* (London, 1984), p. 142.

[88] For details of the capital's industrial structure see G. Stedman Jones, *Outcast London*, ch. 1, and P. G. Hall, *The Industries of London since 1861* (London, 1962).

[89] Hobsbawm, *Worlds of Labour*, p. 142.

[90] See E. Mendelsohn, *Class Struggle In The Pale* (New York, 1970).

[91] Thomas, 'A History of the Leeds Clothing Industry', p. 26.

While events taking place 'beyond the ghetto' were instrumental in determining the direction and success of organization amongst the Jewish tailoring workers of London and Leeds other influences were solely the result of the ethnic nature of the Jewish tailoring work force. In both cities class division and exploitation within the confines of the ghetto stimulated trade union membership. But in the small-scale sweatshops the demands of kinship, religion and the nexus of community frequently deflected aspiring or even active trade unionists. Long-term trade union membership, and therefore enduring trade unions, were further hampered by the transient nature of the Jewish work force. After 1881 the alien population of England, particularly that of London's East End, was of a mobile nature. Many Eastern European immigrants looked upon America – the 'Goldene Medineh' – as their final destination and used England merely as a staging post, it being cheaper to travel to America via England than to travel direct.[92] Of the three-quarters of a million aliens estimated to have passed through England in the years betwen 1881 and 1911 only an estimated 105,000 to 120,000 remained as permanent settlers.[93] Therefore the volume and composition of the alien work force was subject to continual fluctuation.[94] In general terms the Leeds Jewish immigrant community was of a more settled nature. Recent research has revealed that a large proportion of the city's Eastern European population originated from within a seventy-five mile radius of the city of Kovno.[95] These emigrants came with the sole intention of settling in Leeds and becoming a part of its expanding wholesale clothing work force, willing to accept the sweating and exploitation that was an integral part of the sub-divisional tailoring trade. Without knowledge of its people or its language, many aliens arrived in England clasping a piece of paper upon which was written the legend, 'LEEDS'.

The proximity in the capital of a resident Anglo-Jewish elite did not stifle Jewish trade unionism, but it did inhibit its effectiveness. So did the lack of reliable leaders. However, in spite of craft and ethnic differences, neither in London nor Leeds did Jewish trade unionism take place in a vacuum. It reflected local and national patterns of organization and responded to contemporary political and economic conditions. The antagonisms that existed between English and alien workers stemmed from a mutual concern for economic welfare plus, undeniably, that degree of anti-semitism that is to be found beneath the surface of all levels of English society. In spite, or because, of this, members of the English labour movement supported Jewish workers in times of industrial strife and encouraged their combination even within their own societies. Their actions were not altruistic. Organization of the resident alien work force was seen as the only means of ensuring wage rates and conditions

[92] In 1902, after the dissolution of the Atlantic Shipping Ring, tickets from Hamburg to America via England cost £5 15s. while those direct from Germany to the United States cost £7 15s.
[93] Gartner, *Jewish Immigrant*, p.49 and V.D. Lipman, *Social History of the Jews in England*, pp.161–3.
[94] *Board of Trade Report on Volume and Effect of Recent Immigration into the United Kingdom 1894*, Parliamentary Papers 1894, LXVIII, p.573 (London, 1894).
[95] Information from Dr G. Raisman.

acceptable to the English working man. The alien worker had to be made to realize that it was to his advantage to unite with his English counterpart. In Leeds, by 1915, the assimilation of the Jewish tailoring work force had reached the point at which they were able to participate on equal terms with their English counterparts in the formation of the first national clothing workers' trade union, the United Garment Workers' Trade Union. In London, the diverse nature of industry and the reluctance of almost 50 per cent of Jewish tailoring trade unionists to sacrifice their autonomy and 'Jewish identity' resulted in total fusion not being possible until 1938.[96]

---

[96] Until the rise of Fascism and Nazism highlighted their vulnerability the members of the London Ladies' Tailors' Trade Union had fought against fusion with the national clothing workers' union. By 1938 Jacob Fine and Mick Mindel were able to persuade their members of the benefits of amalgamating with the National Union of Tailors and Garment Workers.

PART II
Gender

4

Jewish Women and the Household Economy in Manchester, *c.*1890–1920

Rickie Burman

The history of the Jewish immigrant in England has to a large extent been that of the Jewish male. Little attention has been directed to the experiences of women in either standard works or their critiques,[1] and emphasis has been given to the typically male-associated, public arenas of trade unionism, paid work and political activity. This essay starts with the premise that a consideration of the lives of Jewish women is not merely of peripheral interest, but that it represents an important dimension without which any consideration of immigrant life is incomplete.[2]

Two factors may be adduced to explain the lack of interest in Jewish women. Firstly, a pervasive andro-centric view, which sees women as peripheral to the main thrust of history: women are defined in relation to men and are not perceived as active agents.[3] Secondly, the fact that women's activities are relatively under-represented in the documentary record has made it more difficult to piece together evidence about their lives. The problem of evidence has been at least partly resolved by the development of a new form of historical methodology. Oral history has the capacity to open up new areas of inquiry and to allow evidence from a new direction, shifting the focus of research and bringing recognition to substantial groups of people previously ignored in the

[1] See L. Gartner, *The Jewish Immigrant in England, 1870–1914* (London, 1960) and J. Buckman, *Immigrants and the Class Struggle: The Jewish Immigrant in Leeds, 1880–1914* (Manchester, 1983).

[2] The research for this paper was undertaken while I was working as Research Fellow at the Manchester Studies Unit, Manchester Polytechnic. I should like to thank my former colleagues, Rosalyn Livshin and Bill Williams, for their assistance and support.

[3] This reflects a more general historiographical tendency. See, for example, S. Rowbotham, *Hidden from History: 300 Years of Women's Oppression and the Fight Against It* (London, 1973).

historical record.[4] It has thus been of particular importance in documenting the lives of immigrant communities and women.

This essay draws upon an oral history archive of over 450 tapes recorded with some 300 Jewish interviewees in Manchester, to examine Jewish women's role in one crucial aspect of the immigrant experience: the financing and management of the household economy.[5] The concern here is specifically with the economic role of Jewish women after their marriage. Athough considerable attention has been directed to the economic life of the immigrants, there has been no real attempt to place male breadwinning activities within the context of the household economy. We can calculate how much the immigrants earned, yet know little about how much was needed to keep and reproduce the workers and their families: we know of the seasonal unemployment that characterized the immigrant trades, but not how the immigrants managed to survive the slack periods.[6] Philanthropists expanded on the need for thrift, but what strategies were available to the immigrants themselves?[7] Writers argue about the individualism or entrepreneurial ambitions of Jewish men, working long hours in poor conditions, but rarely is reference made to the way in which their economic contribution related to the household economy as a whole; to the needs or aspirations of the women of the family; and to the role which female members may have played in defining a family's economic position and social status.[8]

These oversights are rooted in a view which sees Jewish women as preeminently homemakers, model exemplars of the ideal of female domesticity. Although some recognition is given to the fact that Jewish women worked prior to marriage, it is assumed that, following their marriage, their economic activities ceased and they became financially dependent upon their husbands, with their concerns narrowly focused upon the home. Such a view takes as given the content of women's domestic role. Female domesticity is seen as unchanging and self-explanatory, existing outside time.

This essay challenges this static view of Jewish women's economic role. It

[4] P. Thompson, *The Voice of the Past: Oral History* (Oxford, 1978), pp. 5–8.

[5] The oral history interviews were recorded by Bill Williams, Rosalyn Livshin and myself, as part of a wider research project on the history of Manchester's Jewish community, based at the Manchester Studies Unit. The archive is now located at the Manchester Jewish Museum. Of the 150 interviews drawn upon for this study, 44% were male and 56% female; 14% were themselves immigrants and 80%, although British-born, had at least one parent of immigrant origin.

[6] See, for example, Gartner, *Jewish Immigrant*, pp. 95–9, for information on wages and Buckman, *Immigrants and the Class Struggle*, on seasonal fluctuations in the wholesale clothing trade.

[7] The need to encourage thrift among the immigrants emerged as a major preoccupation at the Conference of Jewish Women [Voluntary] Workers, held in 1902. In a report in the *Jewish Chronicle*, 30 May 1902, Hannah Hyam urged all philanthropic 'visitors' to 'encourage working men and women to join thrift societies, to save all that is possible during the busy season'.

[8] A useful critique of the stereotype of the immigrant worker as aspiring entrepreneur is provided in Buckman's *Immigrants and the Class Struggle*, pp. 4–20. However, Buckman neglects to comment on the economic contribution of immigrant women, implicit in several of the examples he cites. In one case, a small master argues that he is 'worse exploited' than any worker, unable to make a living 'unless he kept lodgers'. In another, the rise of an immigrant from slipper-maker to factory worker and, by 1900, property owner is traced with only incidental reference to the labour of his wife who 'dealt in property, took in lodgers, and machined slipper-tops in her spare time'. Ibid., pp. 18 and 123.

will seek to look beneath the overlying domestic ideology to discover the actual activities of Jewish women in England around the turn of the century. Feminist historians, such as Davidoff and Hall, have traced the development of the domestic ideology in England to the period between 1780 and 1850, when the roles of men and women and their respective social locations became a matter of considerable debate.[9] Whereas it has been demonstrated that, prior to this period, the household represented the primary unit of production, with men and women each contributing as active economic partners, the late eighteenth century saw the development of the concept of the separation of spheres and the emergence of the domestic ideal. A sharp distinction was drawn between the spheres of home and work, with women being excluded from the latter. Although there has been a tendency for historians to accept at face value the literature of the time, it is becoming increasingly clear that the rigid demarcation between home and work primarily reflected middle-class mores and moralism, and was often more prescriptive than real in a working-class context.

For working-class women, 'home' and 'work' did not represent incompatible or mutually exclusive options. The opposition of these two categories simplified and concealed a reality which was in fact much more complex, with women engaging in many different forms of paid work, conducted either in their own homes, or in the home of others. Although these activities were often overlooked, for example in the Census figures,[10] which severely under-represent the scale of married women's employment, the picture is now being corrected, in particular through the use of oral history. For example, Elizabeth Roberts has indicated the significant economic contribution made by working-class women between 1890 and 1914, even in areas like Lancaster and Barrow, where a low level of formal participation in the workforce is recorded;[11] and Joanna Bornat, writing on women in the Colne Valley of West Yorkshire, has emphasized the important interrelationships which may be concealed by too rigid a demarcation between the spheres of home and work.[12]

In order to do justice to the complexity of women's economic involvement, a dichotomous presentation between women's work or non-work has therefore been avoided here. The model proposed instead is a gradation indicating varying levels of economic involvement, ranging from the role of principal breadwinner, at one end of the spectrum, to supplementary activities, such as

[9] L. Davidoff et al., 'Landscape with Figures: Home and Community in English Society,' in eds A. Oakley and J. Mitchell, *The Rights and Wrongs of Women* (London, 1976) and idem, 'The Separation of Home and Work? Landladies and lodgers in 19th and 20th Century England', in ed. S. Burman, *Fit Work for Women* (London, 1979); C. Hall, 'The Early Formation of the Victorian Domestic Ideology,' in Burman, *Fit Work for Women*.

[10] For a discussion of the difficulties of using Census figures with regard to female employment, see S. Alexander, 'Women's Work in 19th Century London', in Oakley and Mitchell, *The Rights and Wrongs of Women*.

[11] E. Roberts, 'Working Class Women in the North West', *Oral History*, 5:2 (1977), pp. 7–30 and idem, 'Working Class Standards of Living in Barrow and Lancaster, 1890–1914', *Economic History Review*, 1977, pp. 306–21.

[12] J. Bornat, 'Home and Work: A New Context for Trade Union History', *Oral History*, 5:2 (1977), pp. 101–23.

the accommodation of lodgers, at the other. Whilst my focus is primarily on Jewish women of the first generation, the actual immigrants who were themselves born in Eastern Europe, but who settled and brought up their own children in England, it should be noted that the majority of our Manchester interviewees were born between 1890 and 1910 and were, in most cases, the children of immigrants. Most of the evidence cited here is therefore derived from the interviewees' recollections of their parents, rather than directly from the immigrants themselves.

My analysis of 150 of the 300 interviews conducted in Manchester suggested that around two-thirds of the mothers of the interviewees were engaged in some form of economic activity after the birth of their children. Of the seventy-seven instances of women working, five were acting as principal breadwinners, twenty-four had an independent economic role which made a substantial, although secondary, contribution to the household economy; eight were working in joint partnership with their husbands, fifteen assisting their husbands in some way, and the remaining twenty-five supplementing the family income by either taking in home work (buttonholing, cap-making, etc.), accommodating lodgers or opening up small shops in their homes. In several cases, women adopted a number of these individual strategies, either simultaneously or at different points in time.

About 50 per cent of those working independently from their husbands, whether as principal breadwinners or in a secondary or supplementary capacity, were running shops, the majority of them selling different varieties of food. Most commonly, these were grocery or milk shops, but they also included eggs, sweets and, in one case, a chip shop. The remainder sold drapery or clothes, with high-quality gowns at one end of the market and second-hand clothes at the other. There was one example of a newsagent and tobacconist. In addition, five examples were found of women acting as credit drapers, collecting weekly payments for goods sold on credit, and four of market traders. Four women were involved in dressmaking, two in cap-making, and other occupations included a hen dealer, a midwife, an unofficial nurse who also sat with the dead, and the attendant of a ritual bath, or *mikveh*. These figures give some impression of the range and level of intensity of women's work, but they do not convey the dynamism or flexibility of these operations. To illustrate this, a number of case histories will be presented, indicating the varying levels of women's economic participation, according to the gradation outlined earlier.

The clearest examples of women acting as primary breadwinners occur when they are faced by adverse circumstances – the death or illness of a husband, his inadequate earning power or, in a small number of cases, his separation or emigration. A good example here is given by Lily Gerber, born in 1904 to immigrant parents who married in Manchester *c*.1880. Although her father had been a tailor's presser, he suffered from acute pneumonia and, by the time that Lily was born, was no longer working, his wife having assumed the role of principal breadwinner. She rented premises from a former off-licence and opened separate grocery and dairy shops. Lily describes her routine:

My mother used to get up at five o'clock, and at half-past five she used to go to the bakehouse ... to get her bread and cakes. And she used to take it round to all her customers ... she used to have a basket and she used to put everybody's order in the basket, so many *baigels* and *kichels* for this one and this, and she used to take it round. Now our shop was open from half-past six in the morning till 12 o'clock at night, for a ha'penny candle and a bunch of firewood for a penny. We sold everything from a pin to – goodness knows what. We sold everything in that shop.[13]

More dramatic was the case of Mrs Mannheim, who came to Manchester from Holland *c.*1900, when her eldest daughter married there. The mother of fourteen children, she had carried on the family business in Holland, making ladies' coats, when her husband died at the age of forty-one. In Manchester she set up a tailoring factory, which operated on two storeys of the four-storey house, where she lived with her younger children. The factory had twelve machines, and produced costumes and mantles for sale to shops and market traders. Mrs Mannheim also opened up a gown shop in Cross Lane, Gorton. Her granddaughter remembered her as 'very regal-looking': 'She was like Queen Victoria. She ruled us over. We were all dead frightened of her.'[14]

Not in all cases were women's efforts crowned with such success, however. Two examples highlight the difficulties which a woman might encounter when left to act as sole support for a young family, with little business experience and no skilled trade to draw upon. Here, an interviewee recalls the difficult situation faced by his mother when his father, a cabinet-maker, died *c.*1910, leaving her with seven children to support: 'The problem was how were we to exist, because the oldest one was twelve, the youngest was one month.'[15] A Jewish charitable organization provided her with some money to start a small shop, but 'It wasn't a success in the sense that she made any surplus of it, it simply was a means of keeping us alive until some of us got work and others, you know, managed to fend for themselves in one way or another.' His mother was hampered by two basic problems: 'She hardly spoke English at the time and certainly she didn't understand anything about the economics of small shop-keeping or anything of that kind.' Nevertheless, she 'somehow or other managed to acquire this knowledge, and kept this shop till she died'.

Another woman's husband, a former tailor, died *c.*1911, leaving four children between the ages of one and nine. This woman was unusual in that she provides the single example of a Jewish woman working as a charwoman, an occupation commonly assumed by Gentile women of the area. Her son notes that she lacked any experience in a skilled trade. He recalls: 'She did *any* jobs. She did washing for people. She'd go to people's houses as a home help ... She'd go

---

[13] Interview J91. See R. Burman, 'The Jewish Woman as Breadwinner: The Changing Value of Women's Work in a Manchester Immigrant Community', *Oral History*, 10:2 (1982), pp. 27–39, for similar examples of women opening up shops in the home. A more detailed account of the work involved is provided in R. Burman, 'Growing Up in Manchester Jewry – the story of Clara Weingard', *Oral History*, 12:1 (1984), pp. 56–63.

[14] Interview J222.

[15] Interview J63.

and help someone in a shop as an assistant for a day, anything. Where there was a few shillings to be made, she went.'[16]

These last two women were forced into the position of breadwinners, whilst having no skills or resources to draw upon. More numerous, however, were cases where women, whose husbands were still economically active, pursued an independent career. Mrs Bloom emigrated from 'a small place in Kovno Geberne, Lithuania' in the 1880s and soon after met her husband, who, partly at her instigation, set up a tailoring workshop in Manchester. Although the workshop did reasonably well, and they had ten children to care for, Mrs Bloom earned an independent livelihood, not in the family workshop, but out on the markets over 'the length and breadth of Lancashire'. Her daughter recalls: 'My mother had never been in the workshop ... She was always on the markets. From the time that I recollect my mother, she'd always been going on the markets. She always told us, "Don't depend upon your husband's wage. Go out and earn your own."'[17]

In several instances, women started small businesses to supplement their husband's income, and these proved so successful that they came to make a substantial (and sometimes the major) contribution to the household economy. Mrs Menackerman started up a 'hen business' from her home in Townley Street, Cheetham, around 1920, to help out her husband, who was a market draper.[18] Things were 'very, very hard' at that time, and the Menackermans had nine children to support. The business soon developed into a major enterprise, involving all the family members. Hens were purchased from a dealer, taken to be slaughtered, then plucked, cleaned and finally delivered to the customers' homes. Mrs Menackerman had customers over a wide area of North Manchester, and her son estimates that she delivered fifty to one hundred hens a week. Although her profit margins were low, Mrs Menackerman still played a prominent breadwinning role. A neighbour from Townley Street remarked: 'From the time I knew them, Mrs Menackerman was, sort of, the one who seemed to be the highlight of the family ... She sold the chickens and Mr Menackerman would go to the slaughter-house with her and, you know, help her.'[19]

Following the gradation characterizing differing levels of economic involvement, the next level relates to those women engaged in a joint enterprise with their husbands, or those described as 'assisting' in their husband's business. In practice, it is often difficult to distinguish between these two categories, since the manner in which the woman's involvement is described closely reflects the perception of the person speaking. Thus, one interviewee related how her father came to England from Cracow as the agent of an incandescent mantle company, and later established his own business importing and wholesaling incandescent mantles in Manchester. She continues: 'My mother used to go

[16] Interview J88.
[17] Interview J186.
[18] Interview J177.
[19] Interview J84.

and help. She was a better businessman than my father. My father was really, really no businessman to speak of at all ... But mother really was a sharp businesswoman. She did all the business advising at that time, as far as I remember.'[20] In this more middle-class family, the interviewee's mother is described as 'helping out', despite the evident prominence of her role.

The same problem of definition applies as we approach the end of the spectrum, where women engage in subsidiary economic activities, supplementing the family income in small but significant ways. Popular strategies here were those which could be carried out in the home, for example dressmaking, home work (buttonholing or machining for a tailoring firm), or the accommodation of lodgers.[21] Some women also carried out miscellaneous activities, acting as unofficial midwife, tending the sick or sitting with the dead. In several cases, respondents denied that their mothers worked, but subsequent questioning revealed that they had been economically active. Thus, one interviewee says of his parents. 'My father was a cabinet-maker, and my mother was only a housewife.' However, he later mentions, incidentally, that his sister learnt dress-making from his mother. This gives rise to the following exchange:

Q: Your mother didn't work?
A: Not as work, she was a dressmaker, she used to do a little bit at home as well, yes, to implement, I suppose, the wages, yes...
Q: But she only did it sort of occasionally? On the side?
A: Oh yes, it was a sideline.[22]

This interchange suggests that, by this interviewee's generation at least, perceptions of women's work had been influenced by the prevalent domestic ideology to the extent that paid work performed by women within the home on an intermittent basis was not classified as 'real work'. For the majority of the immigrant generation, however, as we have seen, the sharp demarcation between home and work did not apply, and it was not necessarily seen as a matter of shame for a woman to engage in paid work after marriage.

Several examples may be cited of women who took an evident pride in their resourcefulness and who, like Mrs Menackerman, continued their economic activities long after it was financially necessary for them to do so. Mrs Glantz had worked as a cap-maker prior to her marriage and, even before she was widowed, had taken in work to do at home. When her husband died, she withdrew one of the older children from school to look after the younger ones, and went out to work in a cap factory; she also brought work home at night. Even when, many years later, two of her sons became successful manufacturers, she refused to move house or stop working. In the words of her daughter, 'She was working when she was eleven, and she worked till she was seventy-five,

---

[20] Interview J15.
[21] Davidoff, 'Landscape with Figures', highlights the importance of lodging as a form of subsistence employment, which supplemented the family income without requiring the women of the household to work in the public domain.
[22] Interview J239.

when she died. She couldn't do without work, and she was happy working. And she didn't need to as she grew older, but she worked.'[23] Another woman whose shop had served as the mainstay of the family found it difficult to accommodate to the loss of her shop, when she eventually moved during World War II: 'Mother was so used to handling money and meeting people. If a neighbour came in for a change of a shilling, she'd be happy. She missed the shop very much.'[24]

These extracts suggest that, contrary to the middle-class view held at the time, immigrant women seem not only to have engaged in paid work, but also to have derived considerable satisfaction from it. While, to some extent, their economic initiatives were related to sheer financial necessity or adverse family circumstances, despite the hard work, some women also enjoyed the sense of autonomy and independence which paid work brought them. An active economic involvement often gave women a greater degree of power and influence within the home. Mrs Mannheim, with her own factory, was compared to Queen Victoria, and Mrs Menackerman was described as 'the boss': 'She was the boss – in everything ... Well, we looked to her as the figurehead. She was the boss – she was the worker sort of thing.'[25] Mrs Paulcovitch, who ran a chip shop, took all the major decisions,[26] and it was said of another woman, who set up a successful dairy shop: 'We looked up to her like – she was like a queen. We daren't make a move without we asked her, you know.'[27] In contrast, another interviewee, asked who controlled the household, replied 'My father – father, yes', and added, by way of explanation: 'My mother never worked from being – worked very little until she married, quite young ... and er [after marriage] never worked.' [28]

It is possible that the particular configurations of life in Eastern Europe gave these immigrant women an extra confidence in developing their own initiatives. Members of the established Anglo-Jewish community, like their Gentile middle-class peers, drew a sharp distinction between the spheres of home and work, which corresponded neatly with a demarcation of sexual spheres. The immigrants from Eastern Europe drew upon a different tradition: whilst they also perceived the woman's domestic role as of primary importance, this did not necessarily entail exclusion from the economic sphere. Rather, it was opposed to the male sphere of religious study and scholarship, and assigned to her the more general responsibility to provide for her family and contribute to the household economy in whatever way she could. This reflects a pattern of female responsibility commonly found in pre-industrial societies and evident also among working-class families even following industrialization.[29] In a comparative study, 'Women's Work and the Family in Nineteenth-Century Europe', Scott

[23] Interview J279.
[24] Interview J280.
[25] Interview J177.
[26] Interview J191.
[27] Interview J97.
[28] Interview J61.
[29] See R. Pahl, *Divisions of Labour* (Oxford, 1984).

and Tilly suggest that, 'Whether in the cities and towns of Europe and in America, the patterns of work of married women resembled older, pre-industrial practices ... Whether they worked outside the home or not, married women defined their role within the framework of the family economy.'[30]

There are indications that traditional values and assumptions continued to influence the way in which the immigrants from Eastern Europe adapted to life in England. The fathers of several interviewees were said to have been *yeshiva bochers*, students at religious seminaries, prior to their emigration; and interviewees sometimes refer to their fathers as dreamy and remote, lacking in practicality, while their mothers appear as resourceful, businesslike and, often, assertive. The grandmother of one interviewee (in fact Mrs Menackerman's mother) developed a successful career as a market trader, and rented a house specifically as a warehouse for her stock. Her husband is described as 'an extremely Orthodox, religious, well-learned man, very highly respected'. Asked, 'Did he play any part in the business?' the interviewee replied, 'No, he was learning and learning and learning all the time.'[31]

Although, as a result of the economic demands and opportunities of their new environment, such dedication to religious scholarship was relatively rare among the immigrant men, many of the women maintained an active interest in the economic development of the family. As has been shown, they frequently took economic initiatives on their own account. They were also often the driving force behind their husbands, for example, encouraging them to set up on their own or applying for work on their husbands' behalf.

One impressive woman raised the capital for her husband to establish a large furniture and upholstery business by herself opening up a 'gents' outfitting shop', while her husband continued to work as a cabinet-maker. Her daughter, the second of eight children, assisted her in the shop. She relates: 'My mother was a very ambitious woman, and she was very strong, and we opened a business. It was to allow my father to proceed with his business, you see, he needed money. And my mother and I worked in that shop until I was twenty-three or four, and then I got married and they sold ... and my father opened a large manufacturing business.'[32] The menswear shop was based in the front of their home in Chorlton-on-Medlock, and the interviewee's parents subsequently managed to buy the three small shops adjacent to their own. In this case, the interviewee's mother employed a maid, washerwoman and ironing woman. This freed her to look after the shop and thus make an independent contribution to the economic progress of the family. It is interesting to note that this woman came from a relatively affluent background in Eastern Europe: her father had been a hotel-owner and, according to her daughter, 'she had never had to wash a cup in Russia'. For this woman, then, it was perhaps preferable to engage in business and employ domestic servants than to carry out menial work.

[30] J. Scott and L. Tilly, 'Women's Work and the Family in Early 19th Century Europe', *Comparative Studies in Society and History*, 17 (1975), p. 59.
[31] Interview J177.
[32] Interview J153.

Even where women did not engage in paid work, they still played a central role in the management of the household economy, and this aspect of their work will be discussed in the second section of this essay. Before concluding this section, however, a further case study will be cited to illustrate the dynamism inherent in women's economic activities. For, while a gradation for women's work has been suggested, to indicate their varying levels of economic involvement both within and outside the home, it is important to stress that this gradation was by no means static. Women adopted different strategies at different points in time, responding to the opportunities available to them, the pressures to which they were subject, and the constraints which placed limitations on their actions.

Amelia Jenkins came to England as an immigrant from Kovno in Lithuania at the age of fifteen in 1905. She married here, but subsequently returned to Russia, where she set up a dressmaking workshop with ten machines. Returning to Manchester with two young children, she worked at home sewing buttons on khaki uniforms, before setting up a shop, also in the home, selling drapery and children's clothes, which she made up for herself from remnants bought cheap at a mill. Later, from about 1914 through to the 1920s, she worked with her husband, a cap-maker, selling caps on the markets of Lancashire and Yorkshire. Her daughter relates: 'My mother was a very adventurous woman. Nothing daunted her. She wasn't afraid of anything.' When she discovered a new market, 'it was sort of sacred'.[33]

This market experience stood her in good stead when the family moved to Ireland in 1925, following a scarlet fever epidemic in which one of the children died. Here, Mrs Jenkins became a 'traveller' (agent), obtaining orders for caps which her husband and children then made up. According to her daughter, she caused quite a stir: 'Me mother went round as a traveller. Now in Dublin at that time it was unheard of for a lady to go around in business like that. They'd never heard or seen it before. And she was only young, she was very nice-looking, spoke very nicely, ginger hair. And she made her own style.' After a few years, the family returned to Manchester. The Jenkins wanted the children to have the company of other Jewish children and more job opportunities, as they grew older. Now Mrs Jenkins took over a grocery shop in the family's home in Julia Street, Strangeways. By this time she had eight children.

This career history indicates Mrs Jenkins's versatility and her centrality to the household economy. But it also highlights the often discontinuous nature of women's work. Mrs Jenkins's daughter explains that, 'Every time she built a business up, she stopped and had a baby, and by the time she got back again somebody had taken her place, or somebody had started off with her line, and she'd have to start from rock-bottom again. But she was never discouraged, she always, you know, started again.'[34] Despite her evident capability and determination, Amelia Jenkins's economic activities had to be fitted around her demanding domestic commitments.

[33] Interview J219.
[34] Ibid.

II

The evidence from Manchester suggests that, with very few exceptions in the immigrant generation, even those women who were not engaged in paid work played a central role in managing the household economy. This accords with the general evidence for working-class families at that time.[35] In almost all cases where the information was available, interviewees gave their wages to their mother, and it seems likely that their fathers did the same, although less evidence is available. The majority of the interviewees, both male and female, 'tipped in' their entire wage and received back what their mothers felt they could afford for spending money. In several cases, interviewees mention that they continued 'tipping in' their wages until they left home to marry or became engaged. As one woman, born in 1900, related, 'I gave my money to my mother right to the day I got married. Every bit. I never kept any.'[36] She would receive back only 2s. or 3s. spending money, 'enough to go to the pictures'. When her brother started work, he also handed in his pay packet.

Another interviewee described how, on a Friday evening, the family would tip all their wages in and their mother would give them spending money: 'The first time ever she said, "Well, don't give me your wages, just give me so much", was when I got engaged'.[37] Prior to this, he had to hand her all his wages and rely on her generosity; if he ran short towards the weekend, he would hope to wheedle some more money from her. One woman, born 1907, was encouraged to budget for herself. Although she at first 'tipped in' all her wages, her mother then asked her to keep money back to pay for her own expenses, but to give her a certain amount for food. She explained: 'You just gave so much a week in. If you earned £3, the average was about 25s. to give your parents. You gave your parents about 25s., and you had to buy your own clothes ... your own shoes, your own holidays.'[38]

The evidence from Manchester suggests the persistence of the household as a single economic unit well into the 1920s. Just as children of school age were expected to assist in family businesses, delivering milk or bread before school or in lunch-breaks, or taking on jobs as errand-boys or lather-boys, so, when they started work, they were expected to pool their resources in the family economy. Most interviewees were eager to start earning and making their contribution, although some resented the constraining influence which their mothers continued to exercise over their movements. One interviewee complained that,

If you went for a job, and you got the job, you couldn't leave it, unless your mother said so. If my mother said, 'Leave it, you're not being paid enough. Don't worry, we'll

[35] See for example, Bornat, 'Home and Work', Roberts, 'Working Class Women in the North West', and E. Ross, 'Women's Neighbourhood Sharing in London before World War One', *History Workshop*, 15 (1983), pp. 4–27.
[36] Interview J186.
[37] Interview J272.
[38] Interview J279.

manage', then you left the job. If my mother said, 'No, you're learning the trade, you're not leaving', and you saw all your pals were earning more than you were, you got rather annoyed, but you couldn't leave, because of that right hand.[39]

To the mother fell the difficult task of juggling often slender resources to meet diverse, competing needs. Although, as indicated by Rowntree's 'poverty cycle',[40] the pressures often eased as the older children reached breadwinning age, and some families were able to improve their standard of living by 'moving up' to a better district or superior accommodation, a new pressure descended on Jewish women at this time. This was the problem of providing a dowry and wedding expenses for their daughters. The strict control exercised by one interviewee's mother over the household finances enabled her to save enough to provide dowries for her nine daughters. Her daughter recalls that the earnings of 'each one helped to get the other married'. In addition, with nine daughters to be married, it was regarded as important to keep a presentable home:

We were reckoned in the bigger houses, but what was in our pockets, nobody knew... But my mother always kept a lovely house and always brought nice plants home and was very house-proud. She used to say, 'I've nine girls and a person wants to see what they're coming into. First impression is the best.' Nice curtains, nice home, nice furniture.[41]

It is interesting that this interviewee's mother chose to embark on a market career in order to increase the family income, rather than seeking to enhance the family's status by refraining from work, as occurred in some aspiring families.

Two exceptions were found to the pattern of household management outlined. In one case, to which reference has already been made, both parents, although immigrants, came from relatively affluent backgrounds and settled into the middle-class community of English-born Jews already established in the suburb of Higher Broughton. The father, who had come to Manchester as a representative of a Cracow firm, established his own business in the city, importing goods from the Leipzig trade fair. Although his wife 'assisted in his business', and is described by their daughter as 'a better businessman than my father', it was the latter who had control of the household finances and allocated to his wife a housekeeping allowance. Their daughter, born in 1902, remembers, 'Two pounds was the sum total of my mother's housekeeping allowance.'[42]

In the second case, a woman who had been widowed for nine years and had established a successful credit drapery business, remarried a Romanian immigrant (*c.*1913), who attempted to extend his control over the household economy. After her years of independence, it must have been difficult for her 'to write down everything she bought in Yiddish, grocery, hen, fish', so that in the evening, when he came in from synagogue, he could inspect the list and give

[39] Interview J94.
[40] B. Seebohm Rowntree, *Poverty; A Study of Town Life* (London, 1941).
[41] Interview J186.
[42] Interview J15.

her the money. This shift from female to male control of the household resources increased in the succeeding generation.[43]

Jewish women in Manchester round the turn of the century, like the Londoners who featured in Maud Pember Reeves's study, sometimes had to manage on 'round about a pound a week'.[44] In order to make ends meet, they adopted a range of economizing strategies. A shoe with a hole could be blocked up with cardboard,[45] coke cinders discarded from the nearby boiler works could be picked over and recycled,[46] and clothes made at home from remnants. Here, the daughter of Amelia Jenkins describes how her mother managed to provide her children with new clothes, as customary at the Festival of Passover (Pesach), despite very difficult financial circumstances:

I can remember one year, it was Pesach, and the children had nothing new, and we didn't know what to do. My mother had a piece of material, and we sat down the night before, and sewed all through the night, and the next morning there was little dresses, and it was white stockinette material, and she'd even made them little socks to match, out of the same material. And everybody had a little new dress. There was five younger than me, four girls and a boy, and she'd made every single one of them something new. She tried her best, you see, to make it as bright as she could.[47]

Mrs Jenkins adopted a similar strategy, when almost destitute, earlier in her married life:

My mother had a great big navy blue serge skirt, very full, pleats all round. Things were very bad, and she sat one day and thought, 'What can I do?' And she was in her room and she picked up this skirt and looked at it. She got hold of it, cut it, unpicked it, pressed it and washed it, and she made school caps out of it, and it made two dozen school caps. And she sold them in a shop, and that gave them something to buy food with and carry on with.

Similar economies could be made with food. Many of the traditional Ashkenazi Jewish recipes, such as chopped herring or *belzel* (stuffed chicken neck), provided ways of using cheap ingredients in an appetizing way or making a small quantity of meat or fish go a long way. Here, the son of a widow describes with some relish a 'special soup' which his mother made, using bones but no meat:

We had a special soup my mother made: it was a beautiful soup, and, as I'm talking to you now, the taste is in my mouth. I used to love that soup. But, in later years, we called it 'the poor soup'. We knew the way it was made: my mother would get some bones, onion, a potato. She'd fry the onions, then put water and bones in with them, and then when

---

[43] Interview J104.

[44] Maud Pember Reeves, *Round About a Pound a Week* (London, 1977) was a detailed account of working-class women's daily lives in Lambeth first published in 1913. Based on a four-year survey of daily budgets and other information, it sought to answer the question, 'How does a working man's wife bring up a family on 20s. a week?'

[45] Interview J279.

[46] Interview J254.

[47] Interview J219.

that was well boiled up, put cornflour and flour in, thicken it, then put boiled potatoes in. That was the meal. I think it cost 'flumpence', that. Again, we've all lived to a good age on it.[48]

A common strategy was to go to the fish and fruit market at the end of the day, when the vendors were ready to throw their remains away, and to get them 'either for nothing or for a very nominal sum'.[49] For those who could not afford to buy a chicken, even for the festival of Passover, a solution was to 'buy a very little chicken for peanuts'. To keep it in the cellar and feed it until it was ready for slaughtering at Passover time.[50]

In terms of accommodation, many families were forced to live for years in houses infested with bugs or mice. Housewives struggled valiantly to maintain a high standard of cleanliness and to keep the bugs at bay, with little effect. Here, an interviewee recalls how his father, a tailor's presser, would take out a loan to have part of the house painted and papered, again before Passover: 'We never kept 'em away. You used to get it decorated, and managed to get a few pound, and they just come out again ... [We] used to get it papered and er the walls were sometimes red with the blood of them, if you hit one. It was all over like that, you know.'[51] Some families hoped to afford better accommodation by sharing with relatives or friends or taking in lodgers. But often, even with lodgers, only the rent of poor-quality housing in Red Bank or Strangeways could be met. Conditions were cramped and beds were shared, between two or three children, and, in at least one case, three adults.[52]

Even with all these economies, survival was not assured, particularly in the tailoring trades with their seasonal fluctuation in labour demand. The most common strategy employed at such times was to buy goods 'on tick', although few shops would extend credit for more than two or three weeks.[53] One way to avoid debts and rent arrears was to do a 'moonlight flit', disappearing from accommodation overnight. Although it has been suggested that Jewish families used the pawnbroker less commonly than non-Jews of a similar class, some examples of pawning were found. When one interviewee's father, a cabinet-maker, was out of work, his wife, who was an invalid, could do little to help. The family therefore had to resort quite frequently to pawning to make ends meet or to purchase the food for their Sabbath meal:

When me father was working and we could afford it, we had a tablecloth – they brought piles of linen from Russia. But when he wasn't working, which was frequently in those days ... we had newspaper then on the table and the brass candlesticks that they brought from Russia, I used to take to the pawn-shop for 9d ... that week we'd have meat ... And we used to put the candles, Friday night, in pop bottles, because the candlesticks were pawned for 9d.[54]

[48] Interview J94.
[49] Interview J273.
[50] Interview J94.
[51] Interview J214. These visitors were sometimes known as 'the red army'.
[52] Interview J279.
[53] Interview J273.
[54] Interview J107.

The pawning of the tablecloths or candlesticks made it possible to celebrate Sabbath in the appropriate spirit, even if 'a bottle of pop' was substituted for wine and 'pop bottles' for candlesticks. This interviewee related that she would go to the pawnbroker 'whenever Father wasn't working, and whenever we couldn't borrow from anybody else'.

Before resorting to the pawnbroker, help would be sought through the various support mechanisms which existed within the immigrant community, most commonly through family networks. Financial assistance might be given, or, often, help in kind, and in a time of crisis a family might move in to the home of a sibling or parent. Interviewees quite often mention extended family members resident in their homes. Members of a particular family often clustered in particular streets or areas. For example, Mrs Menackerman lived in the same street as her mother and sister, with a third sister living round the corner.[55]

Landsleit, or immigrants coming from the same area in Eastern Europe, offered a secondary source of assistance, as did neighbourhood networks in Manchester.[56] Although few interviewees mentioned actual financial assistance from neighbours, there are numerous examples of mutual aid from both Jewish and non-Jewish neighbours. Assistance was given at times of sickness, death and childbirth; clothes might be passed on between neighbours and food borrowed.[57] On Yom Kippur, the Jewish fast day, a non-Jewish neighbour might offer to feed the children of a Jewish family while their parents were in synagogue. In one case, when a young woman was widowed, the neighbours helped her to obtain stock for a shop, and a woman renting the end house of the terrace offered to exchange houses with her, so that she could have a window display; all the neighbours also made a point of buying from her shop.[58]

In an example of neighbourhood assistance probably deriving from Eastern European traditions, a woman who ran a grocery shop jointly with her husband would place a washing-basket in the middle of the shop and say to her customers in Yiddish, 'Give a *ndove*', that is, a gift for charity. People would put in a quarter-pound of tea, half a pound of lentils, butter, sugar, flour, bread or herring, and the shopkeeper's children would take the basket round the back-streets by night, leaving it at the house of a family known to be in need.[59]

Although instances of individual acts of charity abound, application was only made to formal institutions, such as the Jewish Board of Guardians, as a final resort. This was one of a number of survival strategies which might be employed in times of extremity, when a woman's efforts at scrimping and saving and the safety net of mutual aid proved insufficient to meet the extent of a family's crisis. When a widow with six young children fell ill before her attempt

---

[55] Interview J117.
[56] Cf. Ross, 'Women's Neighbourhood Sharing'.
[57] One interviewee (J155) described how, when she had her tonsils removed, 'a neighbour who sold hens' (Mrs Menackerman) brought her a warm new-laid egg to drink raw every day.
[58] Interview J241.
[59] Interview J273.

at setting up a small business could reach fruition, and she became bedridden, her sister and neighbours helped out with food and cooking, recourse was made to the pawnbroker, and free food and clothing obtained from the Jewish Soup Kitchen and other charitable agencies. Finally, the youngest child was sent to the Norwood Jewish Orphanage.[60] In another case, a child was adopted by a relative in Liverpool.[61]

For some women, the tensions of making ends meet were too great and the task too hopeless. Mental breakdown and depression occurred, and the 'yellow cab' might appear to remove a person to the 'lunatic asylum', 'a place to be shunned and never to be talked about'. In one tragic case, the wife of a chronic gambler, in despair, committed suicide: 'She couldn't stand it any more, you see, she couldn't feed the family, and she owed bills ... So she went and threw herself into the claypit pond at the back of the Jewish hospital.'[62]

It may be suggested that, in the absence of the Welfare State, the pressures on women of the immigrant generation were such as to necessitate their active involvement in economic endeavours, despite the prevalence of the domestic ideology at that time. Certainly, writers such as Elizabeth Roberts and Sally Alexander have indicated the active contribution of working-class women more generally to the household economy, even when they did not, in a formal sense, 'go out to work'.[63] At the same time, it is also possible that the considerable degree of initiative and resourcefulness exhibited by the immigrant women may be related in part to the experience and role expectations that they brought with them from Eastern Europe. Even if few women in England supported husbands who were religious scholars, they still assumed a wide-ranging responsibility for the domestic economy, which in their eyes did not exclude a breadwinning component.[64] In their paper on women's work in nineteenth-century Europe, Scott and Tilly advocate a model of social change which posits 'a continuity of traditional values and behaviour in changing circumstances. Old values coexist with and are used by people to adapt to extensive structural changes ... Behaviour is less the product of new ideas than of the effects of old ideas operating in new or changing contexts.'[65]

Although the context had changed, women continued to combine their domestic commitments with economic endeavours, to manage the household economy and to operate the family as a collective economic unit. Although there were immigrants who conformed to the division of labour enshrined in the domestic ideology, many women preferred to improve their family's status in a

[60] Interview J43.

[61] Interview J5.

[62] Interview J273.

[63] See Alexander, 'Women's Work in 19th Century London' and Roberts, 'Working class Women in the North West'.

[64] Burman, 'The Jewish Woman as Breadwinner'. For an examination of the changing significance of women's domestic activities to Jewish religious life, see R. Burman, '"She looketh well to the ways of her household": the changing role of Jewish women in religious life, *c.*1880–1930', in ed. G. Malmgreen, *Religion in the Lives of English Women, 1760–1930* (London, 1986), pp. 234–59.

[65] Scott and Tilly, 'Women's Work and the Family in Early 19th century Europe', p. 42.

more direct way, by themselves working to increase the family income, improve their standard of living, or to save up sufficient to provide attractive dowries for their daughters. At the same time, the immigrant women were adaptable and open to new ideas and opportunities, which they sometimes used to further traditional ends. Thus an insurance agent working in one of the immigrant areas of Manchester found a ready market for endowment policies, which were used as a strategy to save for dowries.[66]

It is in the next generation, that of the interviewees for this study, who were born mainly between 1890 and 1910, that a major change in women's economic role becomes apparent. Interviewees emphasize that, for their generation: 'In those days, not the rule but the custom was ... a Jewish girl got married – it was her duty to stay at home and look after her home and husband ... Those days, a man was king in his castle ... It was a very rare thing for a Jewish girl to get married and go out to work.'[67]

As Catherine Hall found for married women in Birmingham in the 1920s and 1930s,[68] in this generation the domestic idyll is not simply accepted as an ideal; it is enacted in practice: Thus an analysis of the Manchester oral history interviews suggests that only around 38 per cent of married women of the interviewee generation, as against 66 per cent of their mothers, worked at some time after marriage. Where women did engage in paid work, they often demonstrate a certain ambivalence. One interviewee speaks with great pride of her mother's competence as a businesswoman, but elsewhere she notes that she herself 'wouldn't have dreamt' of working after marriage. She comments: 'None of my friends went to work. We thought we were having a good time staying at home, but I thought it was easier going to work actually.'[69] When her husband became seriously ill with tuberculosis, she tried to help at his business, and later sold bags for a relative, telling him, 'Well, I've never done it in my life, but I'll have a go. I was very good at jumble sales and selling flags.' Despite this experience, she defines clearly what she perceives as her role: 'My husband was ill for forty years on and off, and I think I was sent into this world to do a job, which was to look after him.'

At this period, it becomes more common for men to manage the household economy while their wives' concerns become more narrowly focused upon the physical and emotional needs of their husband and children and the creation of comfort in the home.[70] Here, the wife of a civil servant, who worked as a machinist when she was single, describes her daily routine after marriage:

He used to come home on the dot of twenty past five, and I used to have his cup of tea ready. He used to say, 'I'd like to unwind, I'll have a cup of tea.' ... So on the dot of

[66] Interview J20.
[67] Interview J66.
[68] C. Hall, 'Married Women at Home in Birmingham in the 1920s and 1930s', *Oral History*, 5:2 (1977), pp. 62–83.
[69] Interview J280.
[70] Cf. Hall, 'Married Women at Home' and P. Stearns, 'Working Class Women in Britain, 1890–1914' in ed. M. Vicinus, *Suffer and Be Still: Women in the Victorian Age* (Chicago, 1973).

twenty past five I had the front door open, and he used to come in and have his drink and read the papers. While he was reading the papers, I used to take the children upstairs, bath them and get them ready for bed. And ... then he'd go upstairs to say goodnight to them and I used to put the dinner out. And this used to go on regularly, for years and years and years.[71]

This quotation contrasts sharply with those cited earlier to illustrate the prominent economic role played by many of the immigrant women. The man of the house has now become the sole breadwinner and the pivot of the household, whose routine structures precisely the activities of his wife and children. For many women of this generation, the separation of home and work, and the demarcation of sexual spheres, had now become a reality.

III

In a paper published in 1982, I documented the change which took place in the ideal or conception of the Jewish woman's role, following migration from Eastern Europe.[72] Here I have focused, rather, on what actually happened in practice, in particular in the immigrant generation. The evidence drawn from 150 oral history interviews suggests that such a transition did not take place as a sudden transformation following migration. Despite the hopeful comments of middle-class Jewish observers, as early as 1901, that 'Jewish women are seldom allowed by their husbands to go out to work.'[73] the majority of immigrant women in fact continued to play an active economic role, although this was rarely recognized, as a result of the artificial distinction drawn between home and work.

By the 1920s, however, this generalization about Jewish women was becoming increasingly accurate. Increased prosperity and a striking decline in family size meant that the once crucial economic contribution of women was often no longer required. By refraining from paid work, women increased the level of domestic comforts of their husband and children, and also furthered the status of the family, by demonstrating that the husband earned sufficient to keep his wife at home.

It should be noted that this transition, in values and in practice, paralleled closely more general developments among the English lower-middle and aspiring working classes. Such a parallel was by no means coincidental, for the children of Jewish immigrants were subject to similar pressures, which were reinforced by the influence of the established Anglo-Jewish community; and, for them, Anglicization, the process of becoming English, almost by definition entailed conforming to the values and behavioural norms of the English middle classes.

---

[71] Interview J66.
[72] Burman, 'The Jewish Woman as Breadwinner'.
[73] C. Russell and H. Lewis, *The Jew in London* (London, 1901), pp. 186–7.

Interviews Cited

J5   Male, born 1901, Ancoats, Manchester, to Lithuanian father and Latvian mother. Father an umbrella-maker, mother ran a newspaper and tobacconist's shop. Interviewee started work as a jeweller, later became a teacher; married a sales assistant.

J15   Female, born 1902, Higher Broughton, Manchester. Father from Cracow, mother from Romania. Parents engaged in importation and wholesaling of incandescent mantles and later electrical fittings. Interviewee married a fuel consultant and did not undertake paid work.

J20   Male, born 1905, Higher Broughton, Manchester. Both parents English-born. Father an insurance agent. Interviewee started work as a tailor's cutter, later became an insurance agent.

J43   Male, born 1911, Hightown, Manchester to Austrian father and Lithuanian mother. Father an artist and later a picture-faker, mother a cigarette-maker prior to marriage; after she was widowed, she tried to establish herself as a credit draper. Interviewee a waterproofer.

J61   Female, born 1911, Strangeways, Manchester, to Russian father and Polish mother. Father a tailor's presser, mother not engaged in paid work after marriage. Interviewee a clothing machinist when single.

J63   Male, born 1905, Cheetham, Manchester, to Russian parents. Father a cabinet-maker, mother opened a small grocery shop in the home when she was widowed. Interviewee started work as an office boy, became a political party worker.

J66   Female, born 1902, Lower Broughton, Manchester, to Romanian father and Austrian mother. Father a tailor, mother a buttonhole hand when single. Following her marriage she took in home work and opened a shop in her home. After she was widowed she opened a boarding-house. Interviewee a tailoress when single, married a clothing machinist who later became a civil servant. She ceased to engage in paid work after marriage.

J84   Female, born 1920, Cheetham, Manchester, to English-born father and Russian mother. Father ran a trouser-making workshop; mother, a former tailoress, assisted him. Interviewee became a secretary.

J88   Male, born 1907, Strangeways, Manchester, to Russian parents. Father a tailor, mother worked as a charwoman after marriage. Interviewee became a raincoat machinist.

J91   Female, born 1904, Strangeways, Manchester, to Lithuanian father and Polish mother. Father a tailor's presser. Mother worked as a cap-maker when single, and ran dairy and grocery shops after marriage. Interviewee worked as supervisor in a raincoat manufacturing firm when single, and for a period as a waterproofing 'passer' after marriage.

J94   Male, born 1915, Strangeways, Manchester, to Austrian father and Polish mother. Father a tailor's cutter, mother a cap-maker. Interviewee started work as a clothing machinist and became a raincoat manufacturer. His wife also worked in the tailoring trade prior to marriage.

J97   Male, born 1900, Hightown, Manchester, to Romanian parents. Father a tailor's presser, mother ran a dairy shop after marriage.

J104   Female, born 1901 in Austrian Galicia and came to England in 1904 with parents. Father had been an estate valuer in Galicia, but died soon after migration. Mother became a credit draper. Interviewee worked as a clothing machinist when single, but did not undertake paid work after marriage. Her husband was a credit draper.

J107   Female, born 1892, Salford, to Lithuanian parents, Father, who had worked as a mechanic at a flour mill in Lithuania, became a cabinet-maker; mother did not go out to work after marriage. Interviewee worked as a picture-faking canvasser before her marriage to a clothing machinist in 1913, and continued this work during World War I.

J153   Female, born 1895, Strangeways, Manchester, to Russian parents. Father a cabinet-maker and later a furniture manufacturer; mother ran a gents' outfitting shop. Interviewee assisted her, prior to her marriage to a sewing machine salesman.

J155   Female, born 1918, Cheetham, Manchester, to parents from Warsaw. Father a tailor, mother ran a grocery shop. Interviewee worked as a shop assistant when single.

J177   Male, born 1911, Cheetham, Manchester, to Austrian parents. Father a cap-maker, and later a market draper, mother a hen dealer. Interviewee became a textile dealer.

J186   Female, born 1900, Salford, to Lithuanian parents. Father a tailor, mother a market draper. Interviewee worked in tailoring, waterproofing and market trades when single, ran a shop after marriage.

J191   Male, born 1898, Red Bank, Manchester, to Lithuanian parents. Father a tailor's presser, mother for a time worked as a market trader, and later ran a chip shop. Interviewee began work in a cotton mill, and later became an auctioneer.

J214 Male, born 1902, Strangeways, Manchester, to Galician father and Romanian mother. Father a tailor's presser, mother did not go out to work after marriage. Interviewee became a raincoat machinist, and later a union organizer. His wife was also a raincoat machinist.

J219 Female, born 1910, to Russian father and Lithuanian mother. Father a cap-maker, mother at different times ran a dressmaking workshop and a drapery shop, and worked as a market trader. Interviewee worked as a clothing machinist when single.

J222 Female, born 1907, Lower Broughton, Manchester, to Russian father and Dutch mother. Father a tailor. Interviewee worked as a shop assistant when single, and did not go out to work after marriage.

J239 Male, born 1909, Kiev, Ukraine, to Russian parents. Emigrated to England with family in 1914. Father a cabinet-maker, mother did some dressmaking at home. Interviewee became an upholsterer.

J241 Female, born 1916, Hightown, Manchester, to Lithuanian father and Latvian mother. Father a tailor, and later a raincoat manufacturer, mother a buttonhole hand prior to marriage. Interviewee a clerical worker when single.

J254 Female, born 1918, Strangeways, Manchester, to Austrian father and Romanian mother. Father a cap-presser, mother ran a sweet and grocery shop. Interviewee a raincoat machinist prior to her marriage.

J272 Male, born 1912, Lower Broughton, Manchester, to Latvian parents. Father a decorator, mother a housekeeper when single in Riga, but did not undertake paid work after marriage. Interviewee became a raincoat cutter, and later a dealer in raincoats and handbags. He married a comptometer operator, who gave up her work on marriage.

J273 Male, born 1909, Strangeways, Manchester, to immigrants from Austrian Galicia. Parents ran a grocery shop. Interviewee became a doctor, and married a secretary, who gave up work on marriage.

J279 Female, born 1907, London, to Austrian father and Polish mother. Father a tailor's cutter, mother a cap-maker when single. She continued to do home work after marriage, and when widowed returned to work in a cap factory. Interviewee a raincoat machinist both before and after her marriage to an engineer.

J280 Female, born 1901, Cheetham, Manchester, to Polish father and Russian mother. Father a waterproofer, mother worked as a 'buttonholer' when single and kept a grocery shop after marriage. Interviewee worked as a raincoat machinist prior to her marriage to a raincoat manufacturer.

PART III
Culture

5

The Acculturation of the Children of Immigrant Jews in Manchester, 1890–1930

Rosalyn Livshin

This essay focuses upon the children of Jews who emigrated from Eastern Europe to Manchester around the turn of this century. In particular it examines the way in which these children were introduced to English culture and an English way of life and what effect this had upon them in terms of their culture, religion and sense of identity. The information is drawn from research that was carried out at the Manchester Studies Unit of Manchester Polytechnic using both documentary and oral evidence. The author was involved in collecting the oral evidence of hundreds of older members of the Manchester Jewish community and this oral archive adds another very important dimension to the source material available to the historian of modern Anglo-Jewish history.[1] It was indispensable to this study because it provided material through which the effects of Anglicization could be examined.

Although this essay focuses upon the children of immigrants who settled in Manchester, it must be realized that the pressures and influences they experienced were in many ways common to the children of immigrant Jews throughout the country. What differed between communities was not the pressures and influences but how they were brought to bear and with what intensity. This study illustrates how pressures and influences which were nationwide were responded to and dealt with in the sizeable provincial Jewish community of Manchester.

The children of immigrants were exposed to Anglicizing influences from many directions. They were introduced to them from an early age from the wider society in which they lived. Through mixing with non-Jewish children on the streets they learned English songs and street games such as 'bobbe and

---

[1] This archive is now available at the Manchester Jewish Museum. Each interviewee has been given a number, preceded by 'J', and this will be cited below.

kibbs', 'piggy and stick', and 'weak horse'.[2] They were also introduced to the popular reading matter of the time – comics and magazines such as the *Wizard* and the *Rover*, the *Magnet* and the *Gem*.[3] Many of the children would go to their local cinemas, often the Saturday matinees, where they eagerly imbibed the films of that era.[4] As they got older they were attracted to other forms of English entertainment such as the theatre, dance halls, music halls or cafés, according to their tastes and the social environment in which they were brought up.[5]

They were exposed to the Anglicizing influences of the wider society not only informally through leisure and entertainment, but also formally through its institutions. Many of the children of immigrants attended the Board Schools in their areas, particularly Southall Street School in Strangeways[6] and Waterloo Road School in Hightown.[7] These schools played an important role in introducing the children to English culture and an English way of life.

However, not only were Jewish children exposed to Anglicizing influences from without, so to speak, from the wider society, but they were also exposed to them from within, through the very institutions of the Jewish community itself, including the Jews' School, the Jewish Lads' Brigade and the Jewish Girls' Club. Specifically Jewish organizations promoted the values and culture of the wider society among Jewish youth. Why were the institutions of the Jewish community concerned to promote Anglicization? To answer this question it is necessary to look briefly at the make-up of the Manchester Jewish community.

The immigrants from Eastern Europe came to a Jewish community in which there already existed an established, Anglicized Anglo-Jewish community, which had grown up during the course of the nineteenth century, through immigration from Germany or from other parts of England. These earlier settlers were for the most part people with capital who had been attracted to Manchester retailing, the professions or the manufacture and export of textiles.[8] This community was one whose image and reputation stood high in the non-Jewish world. It was seen as respectable, honourable in its dealings and well known for its benevolence. Such remarks could frequently be found in the *Manchester Guardian* from 1840 onwards.[9] This emphasis on credit and respectability put pressure on the Manchester Jewish community to ensure that the reality corresponded to the ideal. The established community feared that

[2] Described by J91, J266, J94 and J102.
[3] Described by J94 and J43.
[4] Described by J75, J55, J151, J7, J40 etc.
[5] Described by J254, J24, J21, J40, J214 and J242.
[6] Southall Street School Girls Log Book, 17 June 1892 and Manchester School Board Managers, Minutes, 15 October 1894, 25 January 1897, 21 February and 29 August 1898.
[7] Waterloo Road School Mixed Log Book, 10 June 1899, 23 September 1901, 24 January 1903, 31 May 1904 and 13 June 1907.
[8] B. Williams, *The Making of Manchester Jewry, 1740–1875* (Manchester, 1976), pp. 12, 15 and 34; A Briggs, *Victorian Cities* (London, 1963), p. 85.
[9] *Manchester Guardian*, 22 January 1848, 10 and 21 February 1949, quoted in Williams, *Manchester Jewry*, p. 165. Manchester Hebrew Association (MHA) *30th Annual Report, 1868*, pp. 11–12.

any deviation from this ideal would bring anti-Jewish feeling against the whole community including themselves. It was therefore their task to ensure the maintenance of the respectability and high standards of all Jews.[10]

With the growth of immigration from Eastern Europe, the established community was faced with a new social element which threatened to distort the accepted image of local Jewry. The immigrants created a new pattern of Jewish settlement, evolved a new occupational structure and brought with them a more Orthodox religious outlook. As Bill Williams has pointed out, they formed a distinctive working-class community, with its own culture and subject to seasonal trades and poverty.[11] It was this which posed a threat to the image of the Anglo-Jewish community, not only in Manchester. As the editor of the *Jewish Chronicle* put it in a leader on the foreign poor in 1881:

they form a community within the community. They come mostly from Poland; they as it were, bring Poland with them, and they retain Poland while they stop here. This is most undesirable: it is more than a misfortune, it is a calamity. We cannot afford to 'let them slide'. Our outside world is not capable of making minute discrimination between Jew and Jew and forms its opinion of Jews in general as much, if not more, from them than from the Anglicised portion of the community. We are then responsible for them.[12]

The Anglo-Jewish community feared that as long as the foreign Jews remained apart, they would attract hostility and abuse and would never be fully accepted as British citizens by the general population. As the editor of the *Jewish Chronicle* put it: 'The constant influx of foreign coreligionists so different in speech and habits as they are, from the general population, must tend to keep alive the lingering feeling that Jews are not and cannot be Englishmen, which still holds possession of so many minds.'[13]

In the eyes of the established community the answer to this problem lay in the transformation of foreign into English Jews. Anglo-Jewry believed that the immigrants, in accepting the hospitality of England, owed a reciprocal duty of becoming Englishmen.[14] Consequently, the great drive within the Anglo-Jewish community in the face of this problem was to Anglicize the immigrant by all means in their power. In particular it looked to the Jewish schools as one of the best means of achieving this. It was believed that the English education of a Jewish school would assure that the young foreigner would be turned out a young Englishman. In this way hostility would be disarmed.[15]

The Manchester Jews' School aimed to do this by adopting the methods of the schools in the wider society. Learning the English language was an important first step towards Anglicization. It was the key to English life and

[10] Williams, *Manchester Jewry*, pp. 57, 77 and 79.
[11] Ibid., pp. 173, 176 and 180.
[12] *JC*, 12 August 1881.
[13] Ibid., 4 May 1883.
[14] Ibid., 12 August 1881.
[15] Ibid., 12 August 1881 and 4 May 1883.

culture.[16] Great emphasis was placed on speaking English, whilst anything to do with Yiddish was frowned upon. An aspect of this was described by a daughter of immigrants who attended the Jews' School from 1905 under the headship of Miss Raphael.

... it was Miss Raphael and she said, 'Tauba's not a name. You can't go through life with a name like Tauba, so ask your mother what she would like.' I went home and my mother said 'You were named Tauba, I would like it to stay that way.' Well she wouldn't accept it ... so I not liking to argue with the headmistress said, 'Well shall I say Tina.' So I went back and I said 'Mother said Tina.' She said 'That isn't a name either, would you like Matilida?' I said 'Indeed not!' I thought it was a dreadful name, I don't know why. Anyway we came to the conclusion that Tilly would be best, so Tilly it was.[17]

In this way names were changed to make them more acceptable to an English-speaking country, even though, as in this case, the parents of the child were opposed to such a change – Tilly having been named after her grandfather. Not only were Yiddish names disliked but there was a certain disdain for Yiddish as a language, as described by a teacher of that period:

I think there was a kind of ... prejudice against Yiddish, you know, I think so a bit ... I just think there was a prejudice against Yiddish somehow, it was kind of degrading to speak Yiddish in a certain, to a certain degree. I think it was rather, that's why Yiddish has never taken on in Manchester, you know much, they've never had, been able to sustain a Yiddish play, you know here, the Yiddish theatre was never encouraged in Manchester.[18]

The establishment's great dislike of Yiddish partly stemmed from the fear that it kept immigrants isolated and apart from the English community and partly from the belief that Yiddish was an 'uncivilised, uneducated jargon.'[19] The teaching of English to immigrant children was hoped to have 'a distinctly civilising influence upon them',[20] and was believed to be a step towards introducing them to 'the higher stage of culture offered by English life'.[21] These beliefs indicate a certain judgement about the language and culture which the immigrants had brought with them.

Not only did the teaching of English help to Anglicize the children but so did many aspects of the school curriculum. The children learned English literature, history, geography, songs and games, and they celebrated Empire Day, Armistice Day and May Day festivities.[22] As well as this, at Waterloo Road

---

[16] L. P. Gartner, *The Jewish Immigrant in England, 1870–1914* (London, 1960), p. 240.
[17] Interview J53.
[18] Interview J98.
[19] *JC*, 23 May 1917 and 8 June 1923.
[20] *Jewish Ladies' Visiting Association 10th Annual Report, 1893–4* (Manchester, 1894), p. 7.
[21] *JC*, 12 August 1981.
[22] Southall Street Girls Log Book, Recitation for 1891–2 and 1892–3, and 22 May 1914. *Suggestions for the Considerations of Teachers and Others concerned in the Work of the Public Elementary Schools* (Manchester, 1905), pp. 36, 58, 61, 131–4; *MHA 55th Annual Report* (Manchester, 1894), p. 6; Waterloo Road Mixed Log Book, 28 May 1913 and 11 November 1918; A. H. Garlick, quoted by J. S. Hurt in ed. P. McCann, *Popular Education and Socialization in the Nineteenth Century* (London, 1977), p. 182; Southall Street Infants Log Book, 1 May 1911.

School, nearly every class decorated their room in a Christmas fashion, even though four-fifths, that is 1,000 of the children in 1907, were Jewish.[23]

School also had another role to play in introducing immigrant children to the English way of life. Not only what was taught, but also the atmosphere and setting within which children were taught, and the social behaviour expected of them were important in introducing them to an English middle-class code of behaviour. The type of behaviour expected is perhaps nowhere better illustrated than in the Manchester Jews' Girls' School under the headship of Miss Raphael. As one pupil recalled,

We were all well trained, she was terribly keen on good manners, she was continually comparing us to the royal family, so of course we had to have good manners. They wouldn't do this at the palace or so on or so forth ... I suppose she thought she was raising our views and our ideals by doing this but it was a bit much for children that were brought up in an ordinary Jewish home, you know.[24]

The Head's preoccupation with the royal family was further illustrated by her insistence that the girls wore white pinafores over their dresses as Princess Mary did in the royal household schoolroom. Manners were continually being mentioned in the Annual Reports, as for example in 1893, when an advance in manners and deportment, as well as learning, was noted.[25]

The inculcation of good habits by the Headmistress was constantly recalled by former pupils of the school. Sheila, who attended the school from 1917 to 1923 related how 'she made a fetish of neatness and tidiness, it didn't matter what you wrote but whether you wrote, whether you had good handwriting and no blots, you see.'[26] Neatness and tidiness were very important in the school. This girl was in fact very clever and would do all her sums correctly, but she was always making blots and because of this Miss Raphael saw her as inferior. She was never praised for her good work because she didn't fall in with the standards and values of the school. There were those at the school, including teachers, who believed that Miss Raphael was more concerned with etiquette and the girls being ladies, walking and eating at table properly, than with cleverness. She would give out framed mottos to girls, such as 'Be good sweet maid, let who will be clever', and she would often lecture the girls on behaviour.[27]

The work of school in introducing the children of immigrants to English life and culture was continued and furthered by the clubs, namely the Jewish Lads' Brigade, Jewish Girls' Club and Saturday evening social gatherings at the Jews' School. These clubs, modelled on non-Jewish clubs and organizations, were yet another way in which the established Anglo-Jewish community attempted to deal with the problem of producing respectable English citizens who would be a credit to the Jewish community.

[23] Waterloo Road Mixed Log Book, 20 December 1907 and 21 December 1911.
[24] Interview J53.
[25] Ibid.
[26] Interview J268.
[27] Interview J93.

In examining the Manchester Jewish Lads' Brigade (JLB) and the associated Grove House Lads' Club, it becomes evident that the desire to keep boys off the streets, and out of trouble, and to provide them with discipline and character-forming activities, were important stimuli behind its creation.[28] The avowed object was 'to instil into the rising generation from its earliest youth, habits of orderliness, cleanliness and honour so that in learning to respect themselves they will do credit to their community'.[29] The Brigade sought to produce a strong and manly Jewry by improving the physical fitness of the children. Whilst physical fitness was an aim of all Brigades, it was particularly important to the JLB, since it was the means by which the community could put an end to the reproach that Jews lowered the physical standards of the country. From its foundation the Brigade aimed to 'iron out the ghetto bend',[30] and to convert 'the narrow shouldered, round shouldered, slouching son of the Ghetto ... into an erect and self respecting man, a living negation of the physical stigma which has long disfigured our race'.[31]

The production of a strong and manly Jewry, it was felt, would enable it to take its part in the defence of its adopted country.[32] At the same time the Brigade aimed to produce loyal and worthy citizens, as described by this son of Russian parents: 'It built up character and it taught a boy how to be a good citizen and ... to be loyal to his country because we were Jewish boys don't forget, no country in the world, let's be fair, offered a Jew the hospitality that was offered in England'.[33] The Brigade boys were often reminded that they were Jewish and that their conduct must be exemplary, especially at camp, when the eyes of the non-Jewish world were upon them. The Brigade saw camp as an opportunity for instilling good will between Jew and Gentile since there the good conduct of Jewish boys under discipline could be illustrated.[34]

Also, by attracting Jewish boys to its club, the Brigade hoped to remould them in the image of its offices. The ghetto image was to be replaced by another, as described by this son of Lithuanian parents:

> If it wasn't for the officers, I don't know, we'd have been, we'd probably have been a load, lot of ruffians, because they taught us more or less manners and how to behave and discipline so this is what we needed. We had, we had to get all the rough edges of this *shtetl* business you know, eh fiddler on the roof, eh atmosphere away from yer and this is where the discipline came in.[35]

Anything that was reminiscent of foreign habits or behaviour was to be replaced by what was called the best of English characteristics. The boys were to learn such English ideals as good comradeship, healthy sport, and playing the game.[36] By

---

[28] *Jewish Lad's Brigade (JLB) Annual Report, 1910* (London, 1911), p. 7. Reprint from *JC c.* 1897, p. 1.
[29] *JLB Annual Report, 1907* (London, 1907), p. 4.
[30] *JC*, 28 January 1910.
[31] Reprint from *JC* (as n. 28), p. 2.
[32] *JC*, 13 May 1899.
[33] Interview J51.
[34] *JC*, 9 April 1909 and 2 August 1907, and interview J55.
[35] Interview J142.
[36] *JC*, 18 February 1921 and *JLB Annual Report 1929* (London, 1929), p. 9.

Anglicizing the children and encouraging them to be patriotic, well behaved and to take a pride in upholding the Jewish good name, the Brigade hoped to maintain a good image of the Jewish community and to dispel any anti-semitic feeling that existed in the wider society.[37] Just as with the Jews' School, these aims were particularly important to those who founded and supported the JLB. These were the people who represented the established Anglo-Jewish elite in the town and who were particularly sensitive to the views of the non-Jewish community by virtue of their greater contact with it.

It is thus evident that the children of immigrants were being introduced to English culture and an English way of life from within the Jewish community as well as from without. Through its institutions the Jewish community sought to bring home the message of the wider society that Jews were welcome in England so long as they became loyal and worthy English citizens. In Anglicizing the children, teaching them English subjects, culture and an English code of behaviour the establishment was encouraging the substitution of new values for the old. The pressure being put on the children was not one of adding to the old culture, letting it slowly evolve and change, but rather one of telling the children that they should adopt a new culture – an English, middle-class, public-school culture – at the expense of the old. This was said and done in no uncertain terms – the culture and language the immigrants brought over being seen as uncivilised and backward, whilst English culture was seen as modern and enlightened.

Whilst the main aim of the established Jewish community was to Anglicize the children through school and club, it was hoped that this would be done without weakening their Jewish sympathies – the child was to be an Englishman but an Israelite as well.[38] And so the Jews' School taught Hebrew as well as secular subjects,[39] and provision was made for Hebrew instruction at the Board Schools.[40] This Hebrew instruction was, however, to be enlightened and Jewish beliefs and duty were to be inculcated in a modern way.[41] This type of religious education conformed to the established Anglo-Jewish community's view of Judaism, which was highly Anglicized. The religion of the immigrants and the foreign methods they used in their *chevras* were believed to be medieval and uncultured and the *cheder* was thoroughly despised.[42] The *cheder* was believed to hinder the Anglicization of the children by perpetuating the old native habits of the immigrants and their Yiddish language.[43] The *chedarim* were seen as 'curious survivals of a bygone age' and the *Melammed* taught what was believed to be an antiquated form of Judaism.[44]

---

[37] *JC*, 9 August 1907 and 2 March 1906.
[38] *JC*, 4 May 1883.
[39] *MHA 5th Annual Report* (Manchester, 1843), pp. 5–6 and *JC* 27 November 1908.
[40] Manchester School Board Managers Minutes 12 October 1891, 26 June 1893 and 3 September 1900; Waterloo Road School Mixed Log Book, 10 June 1899.
[41] *JC*, 4 May 1883.
[42] Ibid., 14 April 1899. Letter from M. H. Valentine, Manchester.
[43] Ibid., 22 July 1898.
[44] Ibid., 1 and 22 July 1898.

Despite the attempts of the established Anglo-Jewish community to provide for the Hebrew instruction of Jewish pupils at school, this was believed to be completely inadequate by the parents. They distrusted the English method of teaching Hebrew knowledge and the standards reached, and they saw Western teaching as shallow, superficial and not inspired by the spirit of true piety.[45] Many parents therefore sent their boys to private *chedarim* of which there were forty-six in Manchester in 1921,[46] or to the Talmud Torah, founded by East European immigrants in 1879.[47] These institutions and the influence of the children's homes provided some of the counter-pressures to the great forces of Anglicization and assimilation. The effects of these will now be examined.

It is evident from the interviews that the children very quickly picked up the English language, even though for the first few years of their lives many of them heard mainly Yiddish spoken at home. Yet, whilst they spoke English well, their ability to speak in Yiddish was not so good. From the interviews there is definitely evidence of a decline in spoken Yiddish. Many would reply in English to parents speaking in Yiddish, as for example this son of Russian parents, born in Manchester in 1910, 'Me father couldn't speak English at all and I couldn't speak, eh Yid—; he spoke yiddish and I couldn't the Yiddish, I understood it but I couldn't speak it ... I understood it but I couldn't speak it, only the odd words now, but I couldn't have a conversation with me father at all.'[48] Whilst he could not speak Yiddish he obviously could understand it. On the other hand there were a minority of children who did reply to their parents in Yiddish. These were often the oldest children in a family,[49] or those who had been born abroad and brought over as youngsters – as in the case of the boy in the next extract, who was born in Galicia in 1907. His father, who was a very strict Orthodox *Hassid*, compelled him to speak only Yiddish at home.

Father was different from other people, you see. First of all he was a great *Hassid*, he spoke no English and if we spoke English in the house and he overheard us, we were liable to be slapped, you see. And if he caught me reading an English book and was able to get hold of the book, he would throw it on the fire. So when I saw him coming I'd throw the book under the sofa ... if I was too late and he grabbed hold of it first it went into the fire, you see. In a way I'm grateful to him because he did that, it's delayed ... gratitude, you see. It meant that we spoke Yiddish and if he hadn't been so strict we probably wouldn't have been able to speak Yiddish.[50]

Whilst this parent made a concerted effort to preserve Yiddish, there were other homes in which the parents rarely spoke in Yiddish themselves. Such parents had often emigrated to this country as youngsters or had been in

[45] C. Russell and H. S. Lewis, *The Jew in London*, (London, 1901) p. 24; *JC*, 6 November 1903 and 15 May 1908; Letter from I. Wassilevsky, Cheetham.
[46] I. W. Slotki, *Jewish Education in Manchester and Salford*, (Manchester, 1928) p. 11.
[47] I. W. Slotki, *Seventy Years of Hebrew Education* (Manchester, 1950), pp. 9–10.
[48] Interview J100.
[49] Interview J49.
[50] Interview J99.

England for some years. Other parents, on coming to Manchester as adults, had picked up English gradually at work, in the street or through their children, or they had made a conscious effort to learn it by attending Derby Street Night School.[51] Those children who were brought up in homes where Yiddish was no longer spoken obviously could barely understand the language, let alone speak it.

That Yiddish was rarely used for conversation by the children of immigrants in Manchester was indicated by the following son of Russian immigrants. He was amazed by the contrast he saw in America. 'I know in America, oh thirty years ago I remember eh seeing girls in America, dressed up girls, teenage girls, eh, speaking Yiddish in the buses and so on ... but these Jewish girls I remember seeing used to speak in Yiddish in the bus, I was amazed, you know, oh I can understand two elderly people but young girls!'[52] This was obviously not a usual sight in Manchester. There a strong English culture passed on to the children of immigrants through the established Jewish, as well as through the surrounding non-Jewish community, had led to a decline in use of the language. This contrasts with the situation in a city like New York, where a vibrant Yiddish culture existed by the twentieth century.[53] Unlike the older-established American communities where Yiddish did not thrive, in the newer cities the smaller and less powerfully established communities were often unable to exert any great influence, at least at first, upon the vast waves of immigrants who contributed to their growth. As a result the forces of assimilation, while present, were not powerful enough to prevent the myriad cultures the immigrants brought with them from taking root. The more cosmopolitan nature of these cities was hospitable to the transplantation of different cultures, although in time assimilatory pressures did take their toll.

The degree to which Yiddish, as a language, culture and art, never really got off the ground in Manchester illustrates the strength of acculturation pressures upon the immigrants and their children. The number who consciously tried to perpetuate Yiddish was very small and their efforts on behalf of the language met with general indifference. Most parents accepted that learning English was an inevitable and necessary step, at least for their children. However, this step led to more than the adoption of a new language at the expense of the old.

There is evidence that the absence of a common spoken language between parents and children led in some homes to a lack of communication. As one interviewee put it, 'I couldn't have a conversation with me father at all.'[54] The lack of conversation between immigrant children and their parents is highlighted by the gaps of knowledge many children had about their families. At its most extreme, for example, one interviewee did not know where her mother was born, whether her parents were married when they emigrated, when they came

[51] Interviews J90, J50 and J180.
[52] Interview J55.
[53] I. Howe. *World of Our Fathers*, (New York, 1976), pp. 417–555.
[54] Interview J100.

and why, nor many details about her mother's occupation.[55] This ignorance about the family's past was by no means uncommon. The lack of knowledge was perhaps more due to the children's lack of interest in such things, as this daughter of immigrant parents explained: 'We had not, we hadn't got that eh liking for the past that seems to be so common nowadays. We, eh, we wanted to emancipate ourselves and to become more modern, and ... but in those days you, your whole idea was to get rid of all these old things.'[56]

This lack of interest in their own past, their desire to be modern and part of modern society, a desire encouraged by school, led children to undervalue their own culture and heritage and caused some to be ashamed of the Yiddish of their elders. The feeling is described by this son of Russian immigrants, who is relating how his uncle used to speak Yiddish in his barber's shop in Strangeways.

he was one of those fellows, that eh, wanted the Yiddish language to stay on as a language, you know, even in the shop, many times he'd be speaking Yiddish with his Yiddish customers because a lot of them were the older type, you know, old friends of his. And I used to say like, you know, have a bit of sense, ther's goyim in the shop, you know, it's not nice. He said, 'I've got them *in drerd*' he used to say. He said, 'Does anyone complain when you hear French people speaking on a bus or something like that?' He said, 'Why should I be ashamed of eh?' Yes he used to ... he didn't care a damn.[57]

Embarrassment at one's parents' broken English and foreign ways was particularly sharp at moments when these were contrasted with English cultural norms. One girl vividly related how she had returned to the Jews' School early, without her mother's permission, after being discharged from the fever hospital. She was made to stand on a form with two other late girls holding slates over their heads.

My mother was a heavily built woman ... I could hear somebody with a heavy tread. I thought that sounds like my mother, oh please G—d don't let her come in. Anyhow it was. The door bursts open and me mother comes in. She takes one look and sees me there with a slate over my head and the other two girls. So she comes up to me and she says, in Yiddish 'pherd' that means horse, 'beheme' that means cattle, 'meshugene' that means barmpot. 'If the *meshugene* teacher will tell you to climb on the roof and jump down will you do it?' Now the teacher stood there. There are 52 kids in the class killing themselves laughing. There's me stood there with the two other girls. Don't know what to do. If I don't obey my mother I'm a naughty girl, but my teacher hasn't told me to get down, I'm in trouble, great trouble ... My mother goes across to the teacher ... 'Tell me Mrs, are you a teacher or are you a wardress' – ha, ha she saw the chain you see. The teacher was trembling and as it happens she was a Christian teacher, her name was Miss Collins. She said '... come down, you too'. She said 'Did you ask her did she sleep ...', I have to laugh myself. There's 52 kids in the class. 'Did you ask her if she slept last night? Do you know she's not long out of the fever hospital? Did you ask her if..?' ..ha, ha, ...

[55] Interview J75.
[56] Inteview J268.
[57] Interview J7.

I'm dithering, all the kids are tittering with laughter and I'm standing there. Well you can imagine it for yourself, can't you? That isn't enough humiliation. From under the shawl my mother takes out a *baigel* 'Do you know what a *baigel* is? Round, with an egg, ha, ha, and salt in a paper. And Miss Collins said 'Eat your breakfast.' How can you stand in front of a crowd of tittering children. If I lived through that morning of humilation and shame, I can't tell you.[58]

This incident, in which the child felt humiliation and shame, shows the obvious dilemma of a child caught not only between two voices of authority but between two cultures. Her immigrant mother was very different from the English ladies the pupils were expected to admire and imitate. She was a heavy woman with a heavy step, forceful, assertive and not easily intimidated. Her manner and broken English were a source of great embarrassment and ridicule in the confines of the Jews' School, whose values and ideals the children were imbibing.

Whilst many would not go so far as to say they were ashamed of their parents' Yiddish language and foreign ways, many children were keen for their parents to become more modern and more Anglicized. Often, the more foreign families in the neighbourhood were spoken of rather disparagingly, as by this daughter of immigrants, whose parents had been in England for about thirty years:

A: They were, she was very, a real greener like you used to say. A very greener type of woman.
Q: What does that mean?
A: Well, very foreign, you know, she still thought she lived in the *heim* as they called it ... The girls were twins. She always denied they were twins, she probably thought she'd get an *einhorre*, that's what I mean, that type of thing, she was very foreign in her ways ... And very natural, you know what I mean. One of the boys was named Myer and he, he was a bit off his food and she'd sit on the front doorstep with him, shoving teaspoons of egg down his throat, '*Esse*, Michele, *esse, esse, esse*,' you know. Well my mother would never do that outside, you know what I mean, a bit more refined, sort of thing. I mean very greenified we used to say. But my mother had already learnt to be more of the English, you know, with us going to school.[59]

Thus we see how the foreigners, the greeners, were associated with rather uncivilized behaviour, whilst the English were believed to be more refined.

In this way the children picked up certain attitudes towards their own culture and past which began to have an effect on their religious observances. One of the most obvious practices affected by the desire to become modern and Anglicized was the wearing of a *sheitel* (a wig). The *Jewish Chronicle* regarded this practice as a filthy, horrible and disgusting tradition, backward and long outdated.[60] These attitudes filtered down to the children, so that while a number of their immigrant mothers wore *sheitels*, very few of the daughters ever put one on. For many of the children of immigrants the wearing of a *sheitel* was

[58] Interview J107.
[59] Interview J151.
[60] *JC*, 22 February and 7 March 1924.

something which they found ridiculous and repulsive, and something which they tried to persuade their immigrant mothers to stop doing.

We hated it, we used to say 'Take if off! We don't like you in it!' We were, we were religious at home, but we were more modernized, you know. We didn't like to see my mother with a *sheitel* because my mother had lovely hair, nice wavy hair, you know, and to cover it over, they used to say 'It looks like a *parach*, like a scabby head.' She had a *sheitel* with a fringe here and ... eh no we didn't like it but she used to put it on for the *Yomtovim* to go to *shul*, you know.[61]

This girl's mother had obviously arrived at the compromise, under pressure, of not wearing her *sheitel* all the time, but just on festivals. Her children just did not like it. They thought of it as old-fashioned and they wanted her to be more modern. Modern in their minds meant being more English. To wear a *sheitel* was foreign and un-English; not to wear one was described as progressive.[62]
   It is evident that the attitude the childen absorbed was one more pressure upon their observance of Judaism. This was something that the established community had not particularly realized. They had intended to make English Jews – and they had emphasized the English side of things to help this along, but what they found themselves faced with, and what they began to realize in the 1920s, was that the whole thing had gone too far. The *Jewish Chronicle* began to report a lack of religious spirit, religious apathy and disintegration amongst Jewish youth.[63] The realization dawned that what was needed was to Judaize the children, not to Anglicize, so that as one person put it 'they shall enthuse about their Isaiah, their Judas Maccabaeus, their Jehuda Halevi and their Maimonides as they do about their Nelson, their Shakespeare and their Cromwell.'[64]
   In the 1920s therefore, there is growing concern amongst the Anglo-Jewish community about the pace of assimilation and initial attempts to revive an interest in Jewish history and religion. Jewish clubs like the Jewish Lad's Brigade (JLB) began to come under attack for their lack of religious atmosphere and religious content and for their part in the decline of religious observance.[65] In Manchester football, cricket and basketball matches with non-Jewish clubs were played on Saturday afternoons, home and away, involving the desecration of the Sabbath. Despite criticism, this did not change until after World War II.[66]
   The revival in interest in Jewish history and religion by the Anglo-Jewish establishment was reflected in the Jews' School, where, from 1920, more time began to be spent on Hebrew and religious instruction and the religious

[61] Interview J151.
[62] Interview J94.
[63] *JC*, 20 March 1908, 23 August 1907 and 11 March 1910.
[64] *JC*, 20 March 1908.
[65] *JC*, 9 July 1920, 2 March and 26 January 1923.
[66] *JC*, 9 January 1931; Grove House Lads' Club Managers, Minutes, 7 October 1918, 6 October 1931 and JLB, Annual Report 1919, p. 46.

syllabus was overhauled. More attention began to be paid to Jewish festivals and a more Jewish atmosphere was aimed for.[67]

The decline in religious observance amongst Jewish youth recognized by the Anglo-Jewish community is illustrated in the tapes, although the whole subject is very complex. It is undoubtedly true that the life of the wider society to which the children were introduced through school, club and leisure activities opened them to a whole series of external influences and temptations current in a modern industrial society. These influences and pressures forced each child to make a whole series of choices between participation in the activities of the wider society and the observance of Judaism. However, the degree to which each child was affected by these influences differed and was affected by the choices and compromises that had already been made by his or her immigrant parents.

There were, for example, children of religious families, who nevertheless were so attracted by the sports played at school and club that they desecrated the Sabbath, as in the case of this boy who played football for the JLB:

A: I remember the time that eh I used to play football for the team, you see one time and eh my father was very religious at the time and he wouldn't let me play. He wanted, all he wanted me to do was to go to the synagogue on Saturdays, you know what I mean. And eh I was playing football and eh I had to get my football boots out on a Saturday afternoon and eh I had to throw them through the cellar window to somebody who was waiting and then walk out. He says to me eh 'Wo gehst du?', that means were are you going? and I says eh 'I'm only going to the park', he says 'okay then, be back in time', and I used to go and play football.

Q: And he didn't know?

A: He didn't know. He didn't know at the time, no.

A: [Wife] None of the boys' parents knew that they were playing football, they used to wash their jerseys themselves.

A: Yes we used to wash our jerseys ourselves. Did I tell you . . . I used to send mine to the laundry as a matter of fact. It used to cost me about 3d, 3 pence in those days, anyway.[68]

For some the temptation of informal leisure activities, such as Saturday matinées, or the cafés in town, led them to ignore the Sabbath observances.[69] Other children, brought up in Orthodox homes, continued to observe the religious practices of their parents until they left school and started to work, as in the case of this son of Romanian parents. When he left school his mother did not want him to go into the normal Jewish trades. She wanted him to learn a 'proper' trade and found him a job in the laboratory of a manufacturing chemist's shop. That job entailed him working half day Saturday. 'It broke my father's heart. I couldn't help it, ha. My father used to bring me to *shul*, to the *Roumanishe shul*, every *Shabbos*. But mother. It was mother, mother was the boss

---

[67] *MHA Annual Reports:* 81st (1920), p. 6; 82nd (1921), p. 6; 83rd (1922), p. 7; 86th (1925), pp. 6 and 13.

[68] Interview J100.

[69] E.g. interviews J75, J55 and J142.

... I had to work on the Sabbath, oh yes it was 6, eh 6½ days, yes 6½ days a week, till 12 o clock.'[70] This example only goes to illustrate how complex a matter the whole question of religious observance was – this boy working on the Sabbath at the behest of his mother. For other children who worked on the Sabbath, they were merely following the example of their father, who had already made this choice.[71]

For a few children religion seemed to be altogether meaningless and irrelevant to the conditions in which they found themselves, as described by this son of a widowed Russian immigrant, whose family lived in poverty.

No it was hard to get used to it. Because there was nothing to offer as youngsters, there was, what could they offer us? To go in a room with a lot of old men, speaking a language that we didn't understand, praying to something and saying what the hell are we praying to? What's he doing for us? He's giving us nothing. So it made a lot of us eh agnostics in those days or more, I would say, more or less atheists. We couldn't believe in it because there was ... we saw what was going on, even though we don't understand it properly but we did know there was something, there had to be something better than that ... In your own little tin pot way, being ignorant and everything, you could say well there must be something better. Now there's nobody up there doing it for us, so what are we going to *shul* for? And in fact all the boys of round about our area were like me, felt the same way. I don't know who was the leader of this movement but as much as possible we kept away from it.[72]

To this boy and those like him religion did not provide any answers to their problems and their poverty. For some children the answers instead seemed to lie in the philosophy of the left – a philosophy which filled the void created by doubts about religion. For others the philosophy of the left gradually drew them away from religion towards the atheism of communism.[73] Then there were other children who despite the influences to the contrary continued to maintain a high degree of religious observance. 'Business was closed on *Shabbos*, yes, eh but Sunday working till 4 o'clock, from 9 o'clock till 4 ... we always closed, always closed on the festivals, yes, *Sukkos* and eh *Shavuous*, that's right, *Shavuous* we closed ... I was brought up in, on *Jewishkeit*, that I daren't tear paper, you see tear paper on *Shabbos*, I daren't open an envelope on *Shabbos*.'[74]

Whilst each individual made his or her own choices and each maintained observance to differing degrees, a definite trend is none the less evident amongst the children of immigrants, suggesting a growing laxity in observance for the majority. Even those who continued to maintain a relatively high degree of observance did not do so in exactly the same way as their parents. The strength of Anglicization pressures was leading to a subtle change in the way the children conceived of and looked at religion. Religion was slowly becoming relegated to one aspect of the children's lives: it was not something which was

[70] Interview J40.
[71] Interviews J142 and J251.
[72] Interview J94.
[73] Interviews J24 and J28.
[74] Interview J266.

all-encompassing as it had been for Orthodox Jews in Eastern Europe.[75] The effect of this relegation meant that children no longer looked to the Rabbi or Jewish learning for guidance but sought it from other, often non-Jewish sources. As a result, the higher Jewish learning which had been revered and respected in eastern Europe suffered neglect in England as its place was taken by secular education and knowledge.[76] The religion-orientated value system operating in eastern Europe was being replaced by one in which religion played little part.

Nevertheless, although such a change was taking place, no matter how much a child compromised with religious observance, very few were willing to give everything up and marry out of their faith. The majority were willing to drift about between two poles, opting sometimes to maintain an aspect of the religion and sometimes not – but this drifting took place within defined boundaries, beyond which few were willing to venture. The boy earlier quoted who found religion irrelevant and who called himself an atheist was yet quick to point out that both he and his friends in the street all married Jewish girls.[77] Jewish boys may have taken out non-Jewish girls but when it came to marriage, the majority married a Jewish girl. Some explained that they would have missed the Jewish atmosphere and food on a Friday night,[78] others that they could not have done such a thing to their parents, as in the case of this Jewish girl who courted non-Jewish boys, although she would not have married one.

Oh, I couldn't possibly. My, my parents would be so upset. In fact in some religious houses they'd go into mourning for a week, you know, and they wouldn't even talk to you ... And especially the mother, if they went to *shul*, they'd think what would the other people say about them ... But um, I felt as though I wouldn't do it, not while they were alive.[79]

In conclusion, the evidence shows how within one generation foreigners were turned into English Jews. The pressures towards acculturation accumulated from all directions were too strong not to have their effect. For a few children the pressures were so great that they identified almost totally with the English people amongst whom they lived. They had grown up and gone to school amongst non-Jews, and the similar nature of the conditions of life which they and their non-Jewish neighbours faced seemed to make their religious differences insignificant.[80]

There were others for whom the pressures towards acculturation were mitigated and whose Jewish identity was reinforced by the influence of their home environment, their religious education or the activities of religious youth groups such as the Sinai League or the Talmud Torah Study Circle.[81] The

[75] R. O'Brien, 'The Establishment of the Jewish Minority in Leeds' p. 439.
[76] Howe, *World of Our Fathers*, p. 8; *JC*, 23 August 1907 and *JC* Supplement for June 1921.
[77] Interview J94.
[78] Interview J71.
[79] Interview J295.
[80] Interview J54.
[81] Manchester Sinai Association Pamphlet; *JC*, 9 October, 27 March and 7 August 1925 and 13 January 1928.

activities of the early Zionist youth groups and Hebrew Schools, such as Junior Mizrachi and the Ha'ivri Schools in the 1920s, also played a role in fighting assimilation by fostering Hebrew language and literature and aiming to give a sense of Jewish identity and purpose.[82]

Yet no matter how much the children's Jewish identity was encouraged, all had been influenced to some degree by the pressures of Anglicization. The great majority felt themselves to be English Jews. Some were more English than Jewish, others more Jewish than English, but almost all had combined identities. The Yiddish language and culture of the immigrants was not their inheritance. Judaism was, but not quite in the same way, since the pressures which had eroded the one were also eroding the other. It was for a later generation to realize the need once again to stress Jewish values, religion and history, although unfortunately a lot of the damage had already been done.

Yet, while the children of immigrants were succumbing in varying degrees to the pressures of acculturation and were becoming English in habits and outlook, they found that they still had to face those elements in the wider society which reminded them of their birthright and which had been the spur for their integration in the first place – namely anti-semitic feeling. For a boy to be told he was an alien, after growing up in England and almost giving his life as a soldier in World War I, illustrates the naivity of the belief that if you became English, if you assimilated then anti-semitism would cease. Here is the reaction of a soldier to such anti-semitic statements.

Oh yes I remember, no not so much before the First World War but during it. The cry was Britain for the British, and there was a man, Fred Brocklehurst, he was a barrister. He used to go about spouting 'Britain for the British, send all the foreigners back.' And I remember, I remember it well, when I was wounded and I came back to Manchester. I was on crutches and I remember Webber – you've heard of Pifco haven't you? He was the man that started it and he was an Austrian, and he came to me one day and he said 'Listen,' he says, 'what are you Yiddisher boys doing?' He said 'This Fred Brocklehurst, Britain for the British, you're letting him get away with it. He's got a meeting at Houldsworth Hall tomorrow afternoon at 3 o'clock.' And I was in hospital blues at the time and on crutches. I was in hospital in Manchester. So I got a few Yiddisher boys, also in blues, and when Fred Brocklehurst started his speech – so he went 'Britain for the British and the aliens there and they're taking away, oh yes, they're taking our homes and they're taking our jobs.' That was not before the First World War but during it. So I shouted out, I said, 'Mr Brocklehurst, will you answer me a question? He said 'Yes what is it?' I said 'You say Britain for the British. What is the position of a man who came over here from Russia long before the war, brought up a family here. He's got half a dozen sons all fighting in the British army, several of them wounded – would he have to go back to Russia?' He said, 'It's a hard case, but we couldn't make any exceptions.' I said 'Well I can make an exception.' And I went on my crutches towards the platform and I threw my crutch at him. So there was an uproar. In those days a wounded soldier could commit murder and get away with it. You see, somebody gave me my crutch and the meeting ended up in uproar.[83]

[82] *JC*, 30 December 1921, 24 February and 6 October 1922, 5 October 1923 and 26 October 1928.
[83] Interview J208.

Interviews Quoted

J7   Born 1916, Strangeways. Parents emigrated from Poland in *c.*1910. Father a tailor. Barber.

J21   Born 1902, Lithuania. Emigrated with parents in *c.*1905. Father a baker and then greengrocer. Machinist.

J34   Born 1910, London. Settled in Manchester 1917. Parents emigrated from Latvia in 1897. Father a cabinet maker and part-time Rebbe. Waterproof machinist.

J24   (Husband to above). Born 1899, Strangeways. Parents emigrated from Lithuania and Russia. Father a tailor. Waterproofer.

J28   Born 1904, Staffordshire. Parents from Russia and England. Father a tailor. Settled in Manchester *c.*1914. Office Worker.

J40   Born 1904, Lower Broughton. Parents emigrated from Romania in 1903. Father a tailor, mother a midwife. Laboratory assistant.

J43   Born 1911, Rydal Mount. Parents emigrated from Austria and Russia in 1880s. Father an artist and then shopkeeper, mother ran a weekly payment business after father died. Waterproofer.

J49   Born 1907, Lower Broughton. Parents emigrated from Lithuania in 1904. Father a rag merchant. Did a secretarial course but stayed at home.

J50   Born 1902, Redbank. Parents emigrated from Poland in 1902. Father a baker and confectioner. Office worker.

J51   Born 1907, Broughton. Parents emigrated from Romania. Father a traveller. Waterproof cutter.

J53   Born 1900, Cheetham. Parents emigrated from Russia and Germany in 1880s. Father a tailor. Machinist.

J54   Born 1910, Manchester. Parents from England and Russia. Father ran a vegetable and fruit business. Attended a London University.

J55   Born 1903, Hightown. Parents emigrated from Russia in *c.*1900. Father ran a phonograph shop and then opened a wholesale embroidery business. Shirting Manufacturer.

J71   Born 1893, Strangeways. Parents from Lithuania. Father a slipper maker. Fent business and weekly payments.

J75   Born 1902, Redbank. Parents from Russia. Father a shoemender, mother a ritual bath attendant. Worked in tailoring/raincoat workshops.

J90   Born 1891, London. Parents emigrated from Austria *c.*1886. Settled in Manchester 1893. Father a draper and auctioneer. Draper, auctioneer and Gents outfitter.

J91   Born 1904, Strangeways. Parents emigrated from Russia 1880s. Father a tailor's presser, mother kept a dairy/grocery shop. Machinist.

J93   Born 1887, Cheetham. Parents from Lithuania. Father a watch-seller. Teacher.

J94   Born 1917, Strangeways. Parents from Russia and Austria. Father a tailor, mother a capmaker. Machinist.

J98   Born 1897, Cheetham. Parents from Russia. Father had a grocery shop. Teacher.

J99   Born 1907, Galicia. Emigrated with parents in 1914 to London and to Manchester in 1917. Father a Chassidic Rabbi. Rabbi.

J100   Born 1910, Strangeways. Parents emigrated from Russia in 1905/6. Father a master cabinet maker, mother a dressmaker. Traveller.

J102   Born 1912, Hightown. Parents born in Manchester. Father a machinist. Machinist and klapper.

J107   Born 1895, Salford. Parents emigrated from Lithuania *c.*1884. Father a cabinet maker. Picture canvasser.

J142   Born 1905, Hightown. Parents emigrated from Lithuania 1891/2. Father a tailor. Tailor and professional musician.

J142   (Brother to above). Born 1893, Cheetham. Tailor.

J151   Born 1900, Glasgow. Parents emigrated from Russia and Lithuania in early 1880s. Father a traveller, waterproofer and part-time Rebbe. Settled in Manchester 1902. Machinist.

J180   Born 1909, London. Immigrant parents settled in Manchester 1914. Father an agent for a film company. Teacher.

J208   Born 1893, Warrington. Parents from Russia. Settled in Manchester 1900. Father the manager of a furniture shop. Manager of a money-lending business.

J214   Born 1900, Strangeways. Parents from Austria and Romania. Father a presser. Raincoat machinist.

J242   Born 1902, Strangeways. Parents from Austria. Father a presser, 'picture faker' and a beadle. Waterproofer.

J251   Born 1913, Hightown. Parents from Russia and England. Father a second hand furniture dealer. Librarian.

J254   Born 1918, Cheetham. Parents from Austria and Romania. Father a capmaker, mother ran a grocery/sweet shop. Machinist.

J266   Born 1894, Old Town, Manchester. Parents emigrated from Poland in 1880s. Father a slipper maker. Waterproof/raincoat cutter.

J268   Born 1912, Hightown. Parents emigrated from Russia and Roumania in 1890s. Father a wholesale cotton merchant. Teacher at a Training College.

6

The Other Self: Anglo-Jewish Fiction and the Representation of Jews in England, 1875–1905

Bryan Cheyette

In a recent study of minorities in an 'open society', Geoff Dench has argued that:

Members of national minorities in modern states are subject to powerful contradictions. On the one hand they are regaled with promises of free and equal participation in society for all individuals – if not perhaps at once, then in a little while. On the other they are faced with a continuing reality of communalism, among themselves as well as in national minorities, whereby groups identifying themselves in terms of common origin, race or culture tend to stick together. This discrepancy creates tremendous dilemmas for them, and throws up moral and political issues for society as a whole.[1]

Whilst this basic contradiction between a particularist 'communalism' and a universalist promise of 'equal participation in society' is apparent in all aspects of British-Jewish life, it is nowhere more apparent than in the evolution of the Victorian Jewish novel.

Jewish novelists, like Jews in general, had to negotiate between the national culture of their host society and their own cultural heritage. By straying too far along the particularist road, Jews were always open to charges of 'clannishness'.[2] Writing in English, for a predominantly non-Jewish audience, the Jewish writer was especially sensitive to the mediating role in which he or she attempted to reconcile the universalist values of British liberal culture with particularist Jewish experience. This mediating position arose historically with the publication of the earliest Anglo-Jewish novels in the first half of the nineteenth century, all of which represented virtuous Jewish characters in their fiction during the campaign lasting three decades for Jewish political and civil

---

[1] Geoff Dench, *Minorities in the Open Society: Prisoners of Ambivalence* (London, 1985), p. 1.
[2] Ibid., p. 10.

rights.[3] This campaign centred around the debate over whether England was to remain a particularist 'Christian nation' or adopt the universalist liberal principle of 'liberty of conscience'.[4] The best-known early Anglo-Jewish novelist, Grace Aguilar, in her *History of the Jews in England* (1847), mediated between these two positions by arguing that:

In externals and in all secular thoughts and actions, the English naturalised Jew is an Englishman, and his family is reared with the education and accomplishments of other members of the [English middle class] community. Only in some private and personal characteristics and in religious belief, does the Jew differ from his neighbour.[5]

In this account, Aguilar emphasizes the liberal construction in which Jews were turned into 'Englishmen of the mosaic persuasion' by relocating Judaism in the private sphere and making it merely a matter of personal 'conscience'. But Aguilar could also highlight the Christological defence of Judaism, especially in *The Spirit of Judaism* (1842) and 'The Perez Family' (1850), a short story set in Liverpool. In these works, Aguilar developed a form of 'Jewish Protestantism' or 'Christianized Judaism' and stressed the toleration of Jews and Judaism not for its own sake but as an extension of Christian values.[6]

Yet even such an Anglicized Judaism, which accorded with English culture, could not eschew its communal function and operate purely as a non-conformist, privatized religion. By the same token, English liberal values were also 'communalist' and were not entirely emptied of their particularist 'Christian' content. The still dominant Christian discourse of 'transcending' Judaism was reflected in the liberal *quid pro quo* of Jewish 'emancipation' – the idea that Jews would eventually adopt the dominant values of society after they had become citizens – which was made with some urgency in Victorian Britain.[7] Thus, when William Hazlitt typically identified Jewish emancipation with a Whiggish 'progress of civilization', this universalist position could just as easily be read in particularist terms by linking the 'progress of civilization' with a specific Jewish messianic purpose within Christendom.[8] Homi Bhabha has labelled this ambivalence as the '*double* vision' of racial discourse which constructs 'a subject of difference that is almost the same, but not quite . . . in

[3] For these novelists see Linda Zatlin, *The Nineteenth-Century Anglo-Jewish Novel* (Boston, 1981), p. 30 and *passim*.

[4] Richard Davis, *The English Rothschilds* (London, 1983), pp. 81–4. See also M. C. N. Salbstein, *The Emancipation of the Jews in Britain* (London, 1982).

[5] Cited in Israel Finestein, 'Some Modern Themes in the Emancipation Debate in Early Victorian England', in ed. Jonathan Sacks, *Tradition and Transition: Essays Presented to Chief Rabbi Sir Immanuel Jakobovits* (London, 1986), p. 144.

[6] Beth-Zion Lask Abrahams, 'Grace Aguilar: A Centenary Tribute', *Transactions of the Jewish Historical Society of England*, 16 (1945–51), p. 142 and Zatlin, *Nineteenth-Century Anglo-Jewish Novel*, p. 39.

[7] For a recent discussion of this point see Andrew Benjamin, 'Kitaj and the Question of Jewish Identity', *Art and Design*, Winter 1988, p. 61.

[8] *Tatler*, March 1831. For the prevalence of these beliefs in early nineteenth-century Britain see W. H. Oliver, *Prophets and Millennialists: The Uses of Biblical Prophecy in England from the 1790s to the 1840s* (Oxford and Auckland, 1978), *passim*. See also Finestein, 'Some Modern Themes', pp. 131–46.

which to be Anglicized, is *emphatically* not to be English'.[9] That is, behind an idealized Jewish Self – which represented the potentialities for liberal progress – is a particularist Other which, by its very presence, contradicts the promise of 'emancipation'.

Sander Gilman, from a social psychological perspective, has illustrated the mechanisms by which this discourse of difference is internalized by Jews. He argues that a minority community tends to accept the 'mirage of themselves' generated by the majority culture which necessarily results in a form of 'self-hatred'. That is, in Gilman's terms, an 'illusionary definition of the self' is caused by minorities accepting the dominant image of the Other. This ambiguity, according to Gilman, results in two common definitions of racial difference which are internalized by Jews. The first definition of racial difference he has called the 'liberal fantasy', where 'anyone is welcome to share the power of the [majority culture] *if* he abides by the rules that define that [culture]'. The second, contradictory definition of racial difference, however, excludes participation in the dominant culture. This Gilman has called the 'conservative curse':

On the other hand is the hidden qualification of the internalized reference group, the conservative curse: The more you are like me, the more I know the true value of my power, which you wish to share, and the more I am aware that you are but a shoddy counterfeit, an outsider. All of this plays itself out within the fantasy of the outsider.[10]

It is this 'double vision' that 'plays itself out' in the Anglo-Jewish novelist. This was especially apparent by the 1870s since mass Jewish immigration – with an identifiable Yiddish sub-culture – had by this time begun to establish large Jewish populations which were seriously to challenge the 'liberal fantasy' of a Jew 'differing from his neighbour' purely in terms of his private religious beliefs.[11] It is in this context that I will now turn to three novelists – Benjamin Farjeon, Julia Frankau and Israel Zangwill – who, from differing perspectives, all attempted to transcend the Jewish Other in their fiction and replace it with an idealized image of selfhood. This resulted, inevitably, in a radically ambivalent construction of Jewishness.[12]

To some extent, Benjamin Farjeon can be said to be the first novelist to have brought the apologetic tradition of early Anglo-Jewish fiction into the twentieth century.[13] In a letter to the *Jewish Chronicle* he quotes, with some satisfaction, a

[9] Homi Bhabha, 'Of Mimicry and Man: The Ambivalence of Colonial Discourse', *October*, 28 (1984), pp. 126–8.

[10] Sander Gilman, *Jewish Self-Hatred: Anti-Semitism and the Hidden Language of the Jews* (Baltimore, 1986), p. 2.

[11] For a detailed account of this racial discourse, see my forthcoming *Jewish Representations in English Literature and Society, 1875–1925: A Study in Semitism.*

[12] For a recent theoretical discussion of ambivalence, see Homi Bhabha, 'The Other Question...', *Screen*, 24 (November–December 1983).

[13] B. Cheyette, 'From Apology to Revolt: Benjamin Farjeon, Amy Levy and the Post-Emancipation Anglo-Jewish Novel, 1880–1900', *Transactions of the Jewish Historical Society of England*, 29 (1982–6) makes out this case, pp. 257–60.

reader's response to the *The Pride of Race* (1900): 'This work of yours is more than any novel; it is the lifting of a great people in the eyes of those who depreciate them; it is teaching them how good and kind and unselfish poor Jews are and can be.'[14] Significantly, *Solomon Isaacs* (1877), Farjeon's first novel concerning Anglo-Jewry, was read in periodical form to 'Jewish working people' as part of the Association for Free Lectures to Jewish Working Men and their Families. Most of Farjeon's forty novels, not just the four dealing with Jewish themes, were part of the 'massive flood of printed matter poured out upon [the lower classes]' which was designed 'to improve their minds and souls'.[15] Like Aguilar, who constructed Jews in liberal terms in the context of the campaign for Jewish emancipation, Farjeon 'moralized' the working-class Jewish immigrant in a bid to lessen the 'fear' caused by mass Jewish immigration into England.[16]

Where Farjeon differs from his mid-Victorian counterparts, however, is in the Disraelian construction of Jewish identity based on a belief in Jewish racial superiority. Aaron Cohen, the idealized central character of *Aaron the Jew* (1894) is, like his author, 'deeply interested' in 'the Jewish Working Men's Clubs in the East End'.[17] During one of his lectures to them Cohen argues that:

there is no historic family in England or elsewhere the record of whose deeds can vie in splendour with the record of the Jew. His history is at once a triumph of brain power and spiritual vitality, and the proudest boast a Jew can make is that he is a Jew. (vol. III, p. 6)

Farjeon reflected this form of chauvinism throughout *Aaron the Jew*, stating at one point that 'nations that oppress the Jew' will necessarily 'fall into decay' (vol. III, p. 190) and making out a case for a special Jewish racial ability with regard to music (vol. I, pp. 57–8). Just as 'all is race' for Disraeli,[18] Farjeon notes that: 'as a rule, vices, virtues and all classes of the affections are hereditary, and the religious sentiments are not an exception. Aaron had studied the subject, and was conscious of the solemn issues dependent upon it' (vol. III, p. 15). This position is diametrically opposed to Aguilar's liberal construction of Jews as being 'Jews only in their religion – Englishmen in everything else'.[19] In fact, unlike the 'Jewish Protestantism' of a Grace Aguilar or Benjamin Disraeli, Farjeon is at pains in *Aaron the Jew* to differentiate between 'Christian' and 'Jew' in primarily racial terms.[20] Aaron adopts a

[14] *JC*, 8 February 1901, p. 8.
[15] Louis James, *Fiction for the Working Man, 1830–1850* (Oxford, 1963), p. 135. See also *Jewish Chronicle*, 7 May 1875, p. 95 and 23 November 1877, p. 12.
[16] Gareth Stedman Jones, *Outcast London: A Study in the Relationship between Classes in Victorian Society* (Oxford, 1971), ch. 15 is the best account of this 'moralizing'.
[17] Benjamin Farjeon, *Aaron the Jew* (3 vols; London, 1894), volume III, p. 4. Page numbers of this novel and subsequent fiction will be cited in the body of the text. Unless indicated otherwise, quotations will be from first editions.
[18] Benjamin Disraeli, *Tancred* (London, 1927 edn), p. 153.
[19] Cited in Abrahams, 'Grace Aguilar', p. 145.
[20] Ibid., for Aguilar's 'Jewish Protestantism' and for Disraeli see Todd Endelman, 'Disraeli's Jewishness Reconsidered', *Modern Judaism*, 5 (1985), pp. 109–23.

'Christian' daughter and her refusal to accept Judaism and marry a Jew is said to provide incontrovertible 'proof' of Jewish difference:

Once a Jew, always a Jew, whether he follows the Mosaic laws or disregards them. So powerful is the seed of Judaism that it can never be entirely destroyed in the heart of one born in the ancient faith. We who are Jews know this to be incontrovertible; you who are Christians may not be able to understand it. (vol. II, pp. 194–5)

The construction of Jews as a separate 'historic family' was seen by Farjeon as a positive act, a means of representing cultural difference in Disraelian terms as a mirror image of 'religion, property and natural aristocracy'.[21] By the 1870s, in fact, with the universalist mid-Victorian liberal consensus under threat, particularist racial explanations of social questions were increasingly widespread. 'Englishness', in particular, was constructed as a 'completed' identity which was rigidly fixed in the past.[22] The rhetorical equivalent of this increasingly powerful representation was an emphasis on the deeds of 'historic Judaism' which similarly highlighted Jewishness as a 'completed' identity rooted in past glory and the 'pride of race'.

As Martin Weiner has shown, the construction of 'Englishness' in terms of the 'aristocratic' values of stability, tranquillity and spirituality countered the bourgeois ideals of economic and technical innovation. After the 1850s, the 'emotions laden onto the cultural symbol of England as a garden' made many Victorians uneasy about an increasingly 'modern' – urban, industrial and democratic – Britain. For this reason, the new dominant bourgeois culture in England adopted many of the values of the old aristocracy.[23] This general cultural ambivalence towards the modernization of England meant that the emancipation and acculturation of the Jewish upper and middle classes was perceived as peculiarly double-edged. The progressive liberal, on the one hand, might well have viewed the shedding of a particularist Jewishness as a symbol of the 'modernity' of a future England. However, an exclusivist conservative could just as easily understand Jewish assimilation as a denial of the cultural values and past history which was said to constitute 'Englishness'. This doubleness was reflected in both Disraeli and Farjeon – and many members of Anglo-Jewry's elite – who represented their own material progress as the natural ascent of a racial aristocracy.[24]

In fact, in his speech to the East End 'Jewish working men and their families', Farjeon articulates the beliefs and values of rural England:

In the country men were brought into closer contact with nature, while in the town one

---

[21] Benjamin Disraeli, *Lord George Bentinck: A Political Biography* (London, 1905 edn), p. 323 and ch. 24 *passim*.

[22] For this construction of 'Englishness' in the late 1870s, see eds Robert Colls and Philip Dodd, *Englishness: Politics and Culture 1880–1920* (London, 1986), p. 22 and ch. 1 *passim*.

[23] Martin Weiner, *English Culture and the Decline of the Industrial Spirit 1850–1980* (Cambridge, 1981), p. 10 and ch. 1 *passim*.

[24] For examples of this see Robert Huttenback, 'The Patrician Jew and the British Ethos in the Nineteenth and Early Twentieth Centuries', *Jewish Social Studies*, 40 (Winter 1978), pp. 49–62.

moved in an atmosphere of mammon, of deceit, of fashion, false feeling and conventional ties and one is compelled to bring into play the meanest portion of oneself. In the country there is more simplicity, less humbug.[25]

Farjeon defines 'humbug' in his talk as 'assuming a superiority to which we are not entitled' and echoes the common unease, in late Victorian England, at the rise of a new elite based not on 'blood' and land but on money alone.[26] Continuing this theme of 'prosperous knavery', Farjeon argues that 'in receiving more than our due, we commit a kind of moral larceny' which re-emphasizes the fixed place of his working-class audience within an already 'completed' social hierarchy.[27] The distinction between 'good' and 'bad' ways of making money is especially important in these terms as it associates 'good' money with the rural values of the English upper classes.

Farjeon's *The Pride of Race* is an extended illustration of this theme as the novel distinguishes between the unacculturated first-generation Jewish immigrant and the second-generation English-born 'Jewish gentleman'. The alliance between Jews and the English upper classes is complete in this novel and is confirmed by the sympathetic gentlemanly narrator who tells us that 'a man may be both a Jew and a gentleman; I have met with many such and have learned from them much that is worth learning' (p. 3). To be sure, the reader soon 'learns' that it is now 'common' for 'a member of [the] English aristocracy and of the Church of England [to] marry a Jew' as 'the Jews, who have the reputation of being an exclusive race, are broadening out and becoming assimilative' (p. 89). Raphael Mendoza, the son of the self-made millionaire Moses Mendoza, is the prime example of this 'assimilative' spirit as he marries into an impoverished English aristocratic family and becomes a Member of Parliament. Once again, a Disraelian construction of Jewishness prevails in Farjeon's novel. In the words of a fictional British Cabinet Minister, the ancestry of 'indigent Jews living in the poorest quarters of the city ... outvies the noblest of ours' (p. 62). Moreover, even though Moses Mendoza makes his wealth the 'wrong' way on the Stock Exchange, he diverts it all, by the end of the novel, into the impoverished English aristocracy. In this way, Farjeon legitimizes both new wealth and the moral worth of the Jewish immigrant who, instead of disrupting the established social hierarchies, even donates a battleship to the nation (p. 71).

It is interesting to see the extent to which a Disraelian construction of Jewishness pervaded late Victorian English culture. This was, however, only one way of rewriting the mid-Victorian liberal consensus concerning Jews. Other less paternalistic forms of rewriting this consensus were especially apparent in the Anglo-Jewish novel of the 1880s. Julia Frankau, writing under the pseudonym 'Frank Danby', published four novels on Jewish themes, beginning with *Dr Phillips: A Maida Vale Idyll* (1887), which departed radically

---

[25] 'Mr B. L. Farjeon on "Humbug"' *JC*, 7 May 1875, p. 95.
[26] Ibid. For examples of this unease see Ruth apRoberts, *Trollope: Artist and Moralist* (London, 1971), pp. 166–7.
[27] 'Mr B. L. Farjeon on "Humbug"', p. 95.

from the Victorian apologetic tradition. Frankau was particularly influenced by French naturalism. In her view, 'the realistic representation of life was the only desideratum of novel writing, the only consideration that would make it worth while'.[28] As P. J. Keating has demonstrated, a naturalistic focus on 'the realistic representation of life' helped introduce greater freedom in both subject matter and style in depicting the working classes in fiction at the turn of the century. And, just as this freedom was to eventually spill over into the English novel as a whole, it also broadened the concerns of the Victorian Anglo-Jewish novel.[29] Julia Frankau was especially friendly with George Moore who, in the 1880s, was one of the main proponents of French naturalism in England.[30] Significantly, Moore dedicated his first novel, *A Mummer's Wife* to James Davis, Julia Frankau's brother. Like George Moore, Frankau published her novel with Henry Vizetelly, who had been jailed for three months for publishing Zola's *L'Assommoir* and *Nana* in English translation in 1885. *Nana*, in particular, had a direct impact on both Moore's *Esther Waters* (1894) and Frankau's *Dr Phillips*. As with Moore's novels, *Dr Phillips* was suppressed in England and the United States on 'account of its realistic treatment', as it was part of a wider attack on the conventions and sexual mores of Victorian fiction.[31] It is in the context of this new freedom that Frankau's early fiction, along with Amy Levy's *Reuben Sachs* (1888), can be said to have rewritten the apologist Anglo-Jewish novel.[32]

   Dr Phillips concerns the degeneracy of a talented Jewish doctor who gives up the 'pure' world of science for the world of Mammon. As part of his decline, Benjamin Phillips marries for money and has a Gentile mistress, Mary Cameron, around whom the novel largely revolves. It is the view of Anglo-Jewry through Mary Cameron's eyes that indicates the novel's main debt to *Nana*. In Zola's Rougon-Macquart saga, Nana, the prostitute, is the symbolic centre of the corrupt French Second Empire. In particular, she 'devours' Steiner, a 'terrible' Jewish plutocrat who is 'noted for his sudden passions' and whose 'furious appetite for women' ruins him.[33] Phillips is similarly characterized by 'an Eastern virility that brooked no denial' (p. 94) and, like Steiner, Phillips squanders his fortune because of his uncontrollable appetite for Mrs Cameron. However, the sexual explicitness of Frankau's novel resulted in a general outcry against *Dr Phillips*. *Punch*, for instance, commented that Frankau's 'advanced' book 'should never have been written. Having been written, it should never have been published. Having been published, it should not be read.'[34] The

---

[28] 'Death of "Frank Danby"', *JC*, 24 March 1916, p. 22.

[29] P. J. Keating, *The Working Classes in Victorian Fiction* (London, 1971), pp. 125–38.

[30] W. C. Frierson, 'The English Controversy over Realism in Fiction, 1885–1895', *PMLA* (June 1928).

[31] R. Schneider, *Bibliography of Jewish Life in the Fiction of England* (New York, 1916), p. 6. For the Vizetelly trials see ed. George Becker, *Documents of Modern Literary Realism* (NJ, New Jersey, 1963), pp. 350–5 and 369–82.

[32] For a discussion of Amy Levy's *Reuben Sachs* in this context, see Cheyette, 'From Apology to Revolt', pp. 260–3.

[33] G. Holden (ed.), *Nana* (1972, Penguin translation), p. 116.

[34] Cited in Gilbert Frankau, *Self-Portrait* (London, 1944), p. 22.

moral looseness of *Dr Phillips* undoubtedly contributed to the 'storm of indignation' which it caused within Anglo-Jewry.[35]

Nevertheless, it was Frankau's claim, in the novel, that large sections of the Jewish middle classes in Britain are 'entirely unemancipated' (p. 192) which was specifically noted by the established Jewish community. In her Preface to the second edition of *Dr Phillips*, Frankau directly addressed the question of 'unemancipated' Anglo-Jewry and argued that her novel was not an attack on all Jews but on a 'small and little known section of [Jewish] society before it yields to the influences of advanced civilization and education'.[36] In a bid to show the consequences of a particularist Anglo-Jewry which has not 'progressed' since its emancipation, Frankau focuses on a section of London Jewry whose 'Deity is Gain' (p. 15). Here is Frankau's equivalent of Zola's corrupt Second Empire – a 'decaying' society whose only value is the 'acquisition of wealth':

It is a fact little understood that here, in the heart of a great cosmopolitan city ... there is a whole nation dwelling apart in an inviolable seclusion, which they at once cultivate, boast of, and are ashamed at. There are houses upon houses in the West Central districts in Maida Vale, in the City, which are barred to Christians, to which the very name of Jew is an open sesame.

All the burning questions of the hour are to them a dead letter; art, literature and politics exist not for them. They have but one aim, the acquisition of wealth. Playing cards at each other's houses is their sole experience of the charms of social intercourse; their interests are bounded by their homes and those of their neighbouring brethren. (p. 168)

And, just as Nana becomes the moral yardstick in Zola's novel, Mary Cameron becomes 'splendid' (p. 114) besides the degeneracy that surrounds her: 'It was strange to see this beautiful woman of loose morals accepted and moving among these heavy, coarse-featured narrow-minded Jewesses' (p. 168). Clearly, Frankau internalized a racial discourse about Jews. This is particularly apparent with reference to the influence of Zola's fiction in which semitic motifs appeared frequently.[37]

Frankau, however, differs from her non-Jewish counterparts in her recognition of the complexities of Jewish self-hatred in *Dr Phillips*. Thus, she notes that 'socially ambitious' Jews belong to a class of people who 'see in every Christian a probable "swell", in every Jew a direct descendant of an old clothesman or a hawker' (p. 9). By the end of the novel, after causing the death of his wife, Phillips leaves a Jewish milieu and 'became in time the Jew-hater ... It irritated him to see [Jews] walking about the neighbourhood, that new Jerusalem which they have appropriated with their slow and characteristic walk' (p. 337). Moreover, one need only compare *Dr Phillips* with H. G. Well's *Marriage* (1912) – which also centred around the common theme of the corruption of

---

[35] Montague Frank Modder, *The Jew in the Literature of England* (Philadelphia, 1944 edn), p. 325.
[36] Cited in Zatlin, *Nineteenth-Century Anglo-Jewish Novel*, p. 98.
[37] For a useful discussion of this subject see E. F. Randell, 'The Jewish Character in the French Novel, 1870–1914', unpublished Ph.D. thesis, (Harvard University, 1940), pp. 20–51.

'pure' science by 'Jewish materialism' – to see the relative ambivalence of Frankau's treatment of this subject matter compared to Wells's outright hostility.[38] For Wells, that is, 'Jewish materialism' symbolized the degeneration of England as a whole, whereas, for Frankau, it applied only to one 'bad' section of Anglo-Jewry. This section would disappear in time, according to Frankau, and, presumably, assimilate into a relatively healthy English culture.

The naivety of Frankau's radical assimilationism becomes apparent when we learn of the use that Arnold White made of *Dr Phillips* in his anti-semitic *The Modern Jew* (1889). This work examines the 'fatal' domination of the 'English nation' by 'cosmopolitan and materialist influences'. In this context, White describes *Dr Phillips* as a 'brilliant but sinister' novel which demonstrates the 'aloofness of Israel' and the inability of Jews in general to lose their racial particularity.[39] Frankau herself, after writing *Dr Phillips*, was the victim of a number of anti-semitic attacks and, by 1900, distanced herself – through her sister, Eliza Aria – from any misinterpretation of her early novel:

Dr Phillips was written in extreme youth; it is crude and harsh with immature judgement, but ['Frank Danby'] was bitterly hurt at the use Arnold White made of his boyish generalisations... One day I think Frank Danby will write another Jewish story, but he will write now in a different spirit – in one that will be worthy of the race that he loves.[40]

Aria's article in the *Jewish Chronicle* signalled the publication of *Pigs in Clover* (1903), which resisted exploitation by British anti-semites by reverting back to the Disraelian Jewish stereotype in Farjeon's *The Pride of Race*. Unlike the unremitting 'naturalism' of *Dr Phillips*, *Pigs in Clover* explicitly identifies elements of the 'Jewish plutocracy' with the good of the nation as a whole.[41]

Written in the wake of the anti-semitic outbursts which accompanied the Boer War (1899–1902), *Pigs in Clover*, Frankau's second major novel on a Jewish theme, is at pains to differentiate between the moral and immoral aspects of 'Jewish Finance' in England. To this end, Frankau rather crudely identifies two half-brothers, Karl and Louis Althaus, who symbolize the 'good' and 'bad' aspects of Jewish financial involvement in South Africa during the Boer War. Karl Althaus is, in fact, a thinly disguised amalgam of Alfred Beit and Barney Barnato, who both became millionaires in South Africa. Like Barnato, Karl was born in the Whitechapel slums of London and, like Beit, he wished to use the diamond mines in South Africa for the good of the British Empire.[42] By the end of the novel Karl learns of 'patriotism' under the

---

[38] For an analysis of H. G. Wells's *Marriage* in these terms, see Bryan Cheyette, 'H. G. Wells and the Jews; Antisemitism, Socialism and English Culture', *Patterns of Prejudice*, 3 (Winter 1988), pp. 22–35.

[39] Arnold White, *The Modern Jew* (London, 1899), pp. xi–xii and 145–7.

[40] *JC*, 4 May 1900, p. 22. For an example of an anti-semitic attack on Julia Frankau see ed. D. H. Laurence, *George Bernard Shaw: Collected Letters, 1898–1910* (London, 1972), pp. 609–11.

[41] Zatlin, *Nineteenth-Century Anglo-Jewish Novel*, p. 113 is wrong to argue that 'all Jews receive Frankau's hostility' in *Pigs in Clover*.

[42] For biographical details of Barney Barnato and Alfred Beit, see Jamie Camplin, *The Rise of the Plutocrats* (London, 1978), ch. 3.

acculturating influences of a woman novelist, an English aristocrat and the imperialist Cecil Rhodes (who appears as himself in the book). Karl's racial financial 'instinct' (p. 71) is reined in by these benign figures and he eventually refuses to 'love money, money only, but to his surprise, now, at the root of his heart, pulling at it, he found England' (p. 181). Rather like Farjeon's Moses Mendoza, Karl grows 'beyond money' (p. 253) and, confirming this, the aristocratic Stephen Hayward argues that Karl is 'a thorough good fellow, a gentleman too, for all his want of a coat of arms' (p. 327). By contrast, Louis Althaus, Karl's Polish half-brother, remains 'the descendant of that wheedling ringleted son of a weak race that is no longer a nation' (p. 131) who is without 'a drop of good blood in his veins' (p. 210). Instead of growing 'beyond money', Louis uses his power traitorously and thereby threatens British interests in South Africa. What finally differentiates Karl from Louis, however, is Karl's longing 'for Christianity and its early lessons, for himself and for his people' (p. 97). The logic of Frankau's radical assimilationism was such that only Christianity was able to ensure the necessary transcendence of a 'Maida Vale' Jewish particularity. Clearly, there is a thin line, in these terms, between mediating the dominant culture and being absorbed by it.[43]

By the 1890s, a spate of Anglo-Jewish novels emulated *Dr Phillips* and *Reuben Sachs* by portraying a particularist Anglo-Jewry which either was encouraged to improve itself by marrying into the English upper classes or which was rigidly demarcated into those Jews who were 'coarse and loud' compared to the 'gentle people of their persuasion'.[44] The *Jewish Chronicle* in May 1892 reacted to this shift away from the Victorian apologetic tradition by editorializing that:

In England, Jewish writers have usually felt themselves called upon to portray the seamy side of Jewish life ... It is hard that the Jewish novelist in England should have a keener vision for defects than for beauties, should show on the whole less sympathy with Jews than do those who accept an absurd convention and can at least plead ignorance in justification. Perhaps Mr Zangwill's forthcoming novel, 'Children of the Ghetto', will prove the long-awaited antidote to the literary poison that has been poured in the public ear by several clever and unsympathetic writers.[45]

The *Jewish Chronicle*'s focus on Zangwill was significant since, by the 1890s, he had a national reputation as the editor of *Ariel* – a journal of New Humour – and as the author of *The Bachelor's Club* (1891). In 1889, Zangwill had also published an article in the first volume of *The Jewish Quarterly Review* entitled 'English Judaism: A Criticism and a Classification', which brought him to the attention of Judge Mayer Sulzberger, the head of the recently formed Jewish Publication Society of America (JPSA). Judge Sulzberger, on the basis of this article and two published short stories on Jewish themes, commissioned Zangwill to write a major Jewish novel for the JPSA. After protracted

---

[43] For a recent account of the radical assimilation of the Frankaus see Aryeh Newman, 'From Exile to Exit: The Frankau Jewish Connection', *Jewish Quarterly*, 34:4 (1987), pp. 49–52.

[44] Leonard Merrick, *Violet Moses* (3 vols; London, 1891), vol. II, pp. 79 and 235. For an implicitly conversionist novel see Cecilly Sidgwick's *Isaac Eller's Money* (London, 1889).

[45] 'The Jew of Fiction, and the Jewess', *JC*, 20 May 1892, p. 9.

negotiation, Zangwill was given '*carte blanche* to write exactly what I pleased' and in 1891 began what was subsequently to be known as *Children of the Ghetto: A Story of a Peculiar People* (1892).[46] It was in this context that the *Jewish Chronicle* projected Zangwill as a 'sympathetic' novelist who would act as an 'antidote' to the 'literary poison' of his 'unsympathetic' predecessors. This communal representation of Zangwill as a Jewish novelist who, in the words of a later critic, had 'advanced the cause of the Jew throughout the world', remains to this day.[47] Thus, in a recent edition of *Children of the Ghetto*, it is argued that:

In 1891 a young Anglo-Jewish writer commissioned to write about the London ghetto would wish to demonstrate to the non-Jewish world the problems and virtues of the immigrants, their relationship to the previously established Jews in London, and their aspirations to become accepted into English society.[48]

To be sure, Zangwill was the first writer in England to represent the Jewish immigrants in fiction. His was a unique task, yet it would be wrong to separate Zangwill completely from the Anglo-Jewish novels that preceded him. Zangwill, in particular, fitted uneasily into the apologist tradition of Anglo-Jewish fiction. Whilst negotiating with Judge Sulzberger, he made it clear that he 'could not undertake for any amount of dollars to write a novel that would appeal exclusively to a section' and, a year after publishing *Children of the Ghetto*, he wrote to Clement Shorter, editor of the *Illustrated London News*, saying: 'I must resist the solicitations of editors to shut myself up in the Ghetto.'[49] This ambivalence towards becoming a particularist Jewish writer stems from similar premises to those which underpinned the 'unsympathetic' novelists identified by the *Jewish Chronicle* for its opprobrium. This can be seen, especially, in Zangwill's regular column (1888–91) in the short-lived *Jewish Standard* edited by Harry S. Lewis, where he often benignly referred to the fiction of Amy Levy and Julia Frankau. Using the pen-name 'Marshallik', Zangwill, for instance, devoted a large part of one of his columns 'Morour and Charouseth' (Bitter and Sweet) to a satirical ballad entitled '"Dr Reuben Green: A Study of the Maida Vale Jewish Colony" by Amy Danby', an obvious reference to *Reuben Sachs* and *Dr Phillips*.[50] This ballad resulted in what the *Jewish Standard*, in its subsequent editorial, called 'some little sensation'. Whilst condemning the anti-semites' use of Frankau's and Levy's fiction, the *Jewish Standard* differed from the *Jewish Chronicle* in arguing that 'we are not of those who think that a Jewish writer dealing with his own people is bound to paint everything in a glowing rose colour and to give us a picture suffused with light and no shade.'[51] Six months

---

[46] Bernard Winehouse, 'Israel Zangwill's *Children of the Ghetto*: A Literary History of the First Anglo-Jewish Best-Seller', *English Literature in Transition*, 16 (1973), p. 95 and pp. 93–117 *passim*.
[47] Modder, *The Jew in the Literature of England*, p. 341.
[48] V. D. Lipman (ed.), Introduction to I. Zangwill, *Children of the Ghetto* (Leicester, 1977) p. 13. References to this edition will be cited in the body of the text.
[49] Cited in Winehouse, 'Israel Zangwill's *Children of the Ghetto*', p. 94 and Harold Fisch, 'Israel Zangwill: Prophet of the Ghetto', *Judaism*, 13:4 (1964), p. 414.
[50] *Jewish Standard*, 1 March 1889, pp. 9–10. See also 9 October 1889, p. 14.
[51] Ibid., 'A Misunderstood Marshallik', 8 March 1889, Editorial.

after this editorial, the *Jewish Standard* argued that *Reuben Sachs* was 'an acute diagnosis of the spiritual blight that has come over well-fed Judaism' and Zangwill, in his column, similarly noted with reference to *Dr Phillips* that 'it's no use blackguarding the mirror because it reflects such evil features'.[52] Zangwill's column, moreover, also satirized Mrs Mark Herbert's *Mrs Danby Kaufman of Bayswater* (1890), an apologist riposte to *Dr Phillips*.[53]

In general, the *Jewish Standard*, known as 'the organ of English Orthodoxy', represented the views of a group of Anglo-Jewish intellectuals who, influenced by the impact of modern German-Jewish philosophy on traditional thought, were in self-proclaimed 'rebellion' against an 'official Judaism' which they dubbed 'flunkey Judaism' because of 'its deference to a wealthy oligarchy'.[54] It is not surprising, therefore, that their newspaper should show some 'sympathy' for novels that criticized the materialism of the Jewish middle classes. Zangwill, in particular, in his article in the *Jewish Quarterly Review*, had argued that 'all over the world the old Judaism is breaking down' and, in 1888, he was forced to resign his post as a student-teacher at the Jewish Free School because of the publication of a satirical ballad on Anglo-Jewry.[55] Furthermore, Zangwill's earliest stories, 'Motsa Kleis' (1880) and 'Under Sentence of Marriage' (1888), had specifically poked fun at what he called 'Anglo-Jewish bourgeois life'. Such satire characterized 'Morour and Charouseth' and this column has been accurately described as 'the very breath which gives life to *Children of the Ghetto*'.[56] To be sure, many of the central concerns of Zangwill's fiction can be found in his column. This includes the opening scene in the novel where poor and hungry East Enders are forced to wait in a soup kitchen before they can eat, while their West End brethren make pompous speeches. Generally speaking, the attack on Anglo-Jewry's wealthy elite in 'Grandchildren of the Ghetto', the second half of the novel, is anticipated in much of 'Morour and Charouseth'. In 'Grandchildren', the satiric poem 'Reuben Green', for instance, reappears as the fictive 'Mordecai Josephs' by the heroine, Esther Ansell, exemplifying the generic novel of 'revolt'.

Children of the Ghetto can be especially linked to the fiction of Julia Frankau and Amy Levy because, like them, it centres around the conflict between Jewish particularity and what Esther Ansell, at the end of Book I, calls 'the larger life' (p. 237). This conflict is usually played out in Zangwill's novel in generational terms and is reflected, at its most extreme, in the antipathy of the Anglicized Louis James towards his Orthodox father, whom he publicly rejects as 'an old

[52] Ibid., 25 September 1889, p. 9 and 13 December 1889, p. 10.

[53] Ibid., 28 February 1890, p. 9.

[54] Norman Bentwich, 'The Wanderers and Other Jewish Scholars of My Youth', *Transactions of the Jewish Historical Society of England*, 20, (1959–61), p. 54.

[55] Israel Zangwill, 'English Judaism: A Criticism and a Classification', *Jewish Quarterly Review*, 1 (1889), p. 398 and idem, 'My First Book', *The Idler*, 2 (1893), p. 632.

[56] Bernard Winehouse, 'The Literary Career of Israel Zangwill from its Beginnings until 1898', unpublished Ph.D. Thesis (University of London, 1970), p. 55 and *Jewish Standard*, 30 November 1888, p. 9, for 'Marshallik's' comment on 'Under Sentence of Marriage'. This story is collected in *The Jewish Calendar* (1888–9), pp. 54–79.

Jew who supplies me with cash' (p. 324). A more optimistic, but short-lived, encounter between an Anglicized son and his Orthodox father can be seen in the death-bed reconciliation of Benjamin and Moses Ansell. As Harold Fisch has noted, Zangwill's Anglicized 'children' are desperately in need of self-improvement and, unlike the 'emancipated' second generation in Farjeon's novels, do not yet represent the 'progress of civilization'. The main thrust of *Children of the Ghetto* is, therefore, towards the transfiguration of its central characters who try and resolve the 'double lives' which they lead.[58]

Whilst Zangwill is clearly emulating the Anglo-Jewish novel of the 1880s, he was not simply a 'naturalist' writer.[59] In particular, Zangwill's explicit universalizing in *Children of the Ghetto* distinguishes his work from the Anglo-Jewish novel of the 1880s. By the end of the novel, for instance, Esther Ansell is openly described as 'an allegory of Judaism' (p. 398) which would not have been possible in the naturalist novel of the 1880s. The book's documentary realism – covering the widest range of subject matter and living individuals – can, like its central characters, be said to have been transcended by Zangwill's universalizing vision. This vision is implied in Esther's rejection of the 'ghetto' for a life in America, and it is also reflected in her reading of the New Testament and her wish that she had 'lived in the past, when Religion was happening' (p. 135). As the Proem to the novel makes clear, Zangwill locates Jewish spirituality in a historic 'ghetto' which has long since disappeared. Zangwill's characters, in these terms, are but 'vestiges of the old gaiety and brotherhood ... the full *al-fresco* flavour [has] evaporated' (p. 7). This view, at its most extreme, results in a Christological construction of contemporary Judaism as an outmoded religion, an 'endless coil of laws' (p. 230). Because of this view of Judaism, the main thrust of Zangwill's art and politics after *Children of the Ghetto* was an attempt to transcend Jewish particularity.

In his article on 'English Judaism' Zangwill not only anticipated the 'break down' of the 'old Judaism' but also hinted at a grand synthesis of 'the scientific morality of Moses and the emotional morality of Christ'.[60] By the time of *Dreamers of the Ghetto* (1898), this synthesis is brought to fruition in a poem at the beginning of the book entitled 'Moses and Jesus'. Ten years later, Zangwill's play *The Melting Pot* (1908) articulated a view of America as the universalist ideal which was implicit in the end of *Children of the Ghetto*. In these terms, America is 'God's Crucible, the great Melting Pot, where all the races of Europe are melting and reforming'.[61] In particular, the intermarriage between David Quixano, a Jewish immigrant who came to the United States after his family was slaughtered in a Russian pogrom, and Vera Revendal, a Russian

[57] *Jewish Standard*, 'Opening of the Soup Kitchen – Wednesday Evening', 21 December 1888, p. 10. See also ibid., 22 June 1888, p. 10.
[58] Fisch, 'Israel Zangwill: Prophet of the Ghetto', pp. 415–16 to which I am indebted for my analysis of Zangwill.
[59] Ibid., pp. 407–8 for Zangwill's rejection of naturalism.
[60] Israel Zangwill, 'English Judaism', p. 403.
[61] Israel Zangwill, *The Melting Pot* (London, 1925 ed), p. 33.

Christian aristocrat, illustrates the transcending powers of the 'melting pot'.[62] Zangwill's view of the 'melting pot' in fact complemented his political Zionism, which has recently been described by David Vital as a means of creating a non-particularist 'Jewish' nation.[63] It was according to these notions that Zangwill justified to Theodore Herzl, leader of the Zionist movement, his own inter-marriage:

Jews must become a people like any other. It is a positive duty to 'marry out'. Much as I value my Zionist activity, I cannot allow it to dwarf my larger sense of what the world needs, and what perhaps I exist to help to teach ... I do not care to help [Zionism] except as a political movement ... I am not sure, however, that the movement did not make a mistake in allowing itself almost to be captured by the religious party – you lose thousands of the most intelligent men in Judea, who are frightened away by the idea that Zionism is a movement of fanatics.[64]

Zangwill had also written to Herzl, regarding the possibility of his wife's conversion to Judaism, that 'the gates of Judaism are kept by clericism and she could no more become a Jewess than I could become a Jew.'[65] For Zangwill, Zionism would radically eliminate Jewish difference and would construct a nation state that would be 'Jewish only through the preponderance of its Jewish population'.[66] The mirror image of Zangwill's politics was his view of the 'melting pot', which can be similarly interpreted as a belief in a universalized Judaism as 'the future religion of all Americans'.[67] *Dreamers of the Ghetto*, Zangwill's collection of fictional portraits of the most famous Jewish apostates – including Christ, Spinoza, Heine and Disraeli – is a paradoxical expression of this universalized particularism. Zangwill intended his collection of stories to be a grand Arnoldian synthesis of 'Hebraism and Hellenism' where the 'most intelligent' non-particularist Jews can, finally, resolve the ambivalence of their own 'double lives'.[68]

Geoff Dench has rightly argued that the modern state has a 'dual character'. Formally, 'it is committed to progressive "universalist" values' but it still operates 'through traditional "national" vehicles tied to the destiny of particular communities'. Whereas the dominant national majority can interpret 'universalist prescriptions in partisan ways', this is not possible for weaker minority communities who lack 'the power to turn [these] contradictions in their favour'.[69] This results, according to Dench, in minority behaviour which, he states, 'can best be understood as attempts to minimize punishment for the

[62] For a useful analysis of Zangwill's play see Neil Larry Shumsky, 'Zangwill's *The Melting Pot*: Ethnic Tensions on Stage', *American Quarterly*, 27:1 (March 1975), pp. 29–41.
[63] David Vital, *Zionism: The Formative Years* (Oxford, 1982), pp. 356 and 438.
[64] Ibid., p. 354, citing letter to Herzl, 21 December 1903.
[65] Ibid.: 5 November 1903.
[66] *Jewish Territorial Organization*, ITO Pamphlet Number One (London, 1905), cited in Vital, *Zionism*, p. 438.
[67] Shumsky, 'Zangwill's *The Melting Pot*', p. 31.
[68] For this argument see Maurice Wohlgelernter, *Israel Zangwill: A Study* (New York, 1964), ch. 7.
[69] Dench, *Minorities in the Open Society*, p. 8.

majority. They need to act in ways which satisfy both communalist demands from the masses as well as the integrationist expectations of the national *elite*.'[70]

This describes well the project of the novelists that have been discussed in this essay. The fiction of all three writers 'minimizes punishment from the majority' by taking prevalent Jewish representations – such as the Jewish financier or, in Zangwill's case, the Jewish alien – which are then re-written in terms which make them 'acceptable' to the majority values of English culture. At the same time, Frankau and Zangwill, to some extent, resist the apologetic imperative of the Jewish community and, instead, radically conform to the 'integrationist expectations of the national elite'. And yet, the very construction of a 'Jewish novel' in Britain which differs in style and subject matter from its 'non-Jewish' counterparts signifies the very otherness which the 'universalist' writer would wish to transcend. Caught in this 'double bind', many Anglo-Jewish novelists before 1945 constructed a particularist novel with a universalist message, whether it be the plea to 'intermarry', as in the novels by Louis Golding, or, in the case of Samuel Gordon's *Sons of the Covenant* (1900), the need to 'decentralize' the Jewish East End so that it would, supposedly, no longer be a source of anti-semitism.[71] These contradictions were most clearly articulated by Israel Zangwill, who attempted to reconcile his Zionism, radical assimilationism and international reputation as a 'ghetto' novelist. To varying degrees, such contradictions were inevitable in a society which both promoted and denied racial difference as a means of constructing a particularist national identity which could not, by definition, be synonymous with its 'Anglicized' Other.

---

[70] Ibid.
[71] *JC*, 4 January 1901, p. 8, and 26 July 1901, p. 6, for this interpretation of the novel.

PART IV
Politics

7

The Transformation of Communal Authority in Anglo-Jewry, 1914–1940

David Cesarani

Before World War I, communal authority in Anglo-Jewry was located in a few highly centralized institutions dominated by London Jewry. The Board of Deputies represented Jews nationally, the Anglo-Jewish Association (AJA) handled its international affairs, while the London-based Jewish Board of Guardians, United Synagogue and Federation of Synagogues supplied welfare and spiritual needs, with parallel organizations in non-London centres. These institutions existed on a voluntaristic basis, but had acquired a high degree of potency within the Jewish population. Over the years, they had arrogated to themselves a mediatory function between the Jewish population and the British state which became enshrined in custom and, in certain cases, embodied in statute. Their authority rested also on the dispensation of patronage and philanthropy. Since they relied on private funding and acted as intercessors, high office in them was dependent upon wealth and standing in the majority population. Their power structure was, consequently, characterized by oligarchy and plutocracy: they were dominated by a small number of men, scions of an interlocking network of illustrious families which had been present in the British Isles for over one and a half centuries.[1] The reigning ideology of this elite can be typified as 'assimilationism', expressing their commitment to British citizenship and culture combined with a proud adherence to Judaism and compatible elements of Jewish tradition.[2]

[1] See V. D. Lipman, *A Social History of the Jews in England, 1850–1950* (London, 1954), chs. 3–4; I. Finestein, 'The New Community, 1880–1914', in ed. V. D. Lipman, *Three Centuries of Anglo-Jewish History* (London, 1961), pp. 107–23; Eugene Black, *The Social Politics of Anglo-Jewry, 1880–1920* (Oxford, 1989), pp. 1–3, 8–70.

[2] See I. Finestein, *Post-Emancipation Jewry: The Anglo-Jewish Experience* (Oxford, 1980); S. Cohen, *English Zionists and British Jews: The Communal Politics of Anglo-Jewry, 1895–1920* (Princeton, 1982), pp. 163–83; B. Cheyette, 'From Apology to Revolt; Benjamin Farojen, Amy Levy and the Post-Emancipation Anglo-Jewish Novel, 1880–1900', *Transactions of the Jewish Historical Society of England* 29, (1982–6), pp. 253–65.

On occasions, sections of the Jewish population had rejected the authority of the officially constituted leadership and challenged its power. Most, however, accepted its exclusive right to represent British Jewry: the pattern of authority and subordination was maintained intact until 1914. World War I ruptured this continuity, inaugurating twenty years of prolonged intra-communal strife as a result of which the structure of politics within Anglo-Jewry was transformed. By 1940 its official leader, the President of the Board of Deputies, was the foreign-born son of poor immigrants and a Zionist actively engaged in the struggle for a Jewish State in Palestine. The Board of Deputies had been reformed and democratized and was dominated by the immigrants of the period 1870–1914 and their descendants. A similar revolution had occurred in the Federation of Synagogues fourteen years earlier. Although the old leadership still dominated the United Synagogue, it was forced to cope with a truculent, strongly Zionist Chief Rabbi, J. H. Hertz, and a more assertive, self-confident rabbinate. There was also an efflorescence of political activity outside the ambit of the traditional structures. The Zionist Federation of Great Britain and Ireland (ZF) had become a major national organization and a power base in British Jewry. Significant prestige attached to those associated with the Zionist funds, in contradistinction to older-fashioned philanthropic causes such as the Board of Guardians. New bodies had sprung up during the 1930s composed of delegates from synagogues, Jewish friendly societies, Jewish trade unions, left-wing organizations and youth groups which had either been denied representation on the Board of Deputies until recently – or which were still excluded.

These developments have become familiar landmarks in Anglo-Jewish historiography.[3] Equally widely accepted is the connection between change in communal leadership and the advance of Zionism institutionally and ideologically within Anglo-Jewry.[4] In this version of events a conjunction is made between the 'rise' of the immigrants and their children and the ascent of Zionism to ideological hegemony over British Jewry. The immigrant and first generation of British-born Jews are perceived as the vehicles for Zionism: their assumption of power within Jewish communal organizations is ascribed largely to a desire to see Zionism triumphant.[5]

There are a number of weaknesses in this analysis which suggest the need for a re-evaluation. Despite the 'triumph' of Zionism, there was no mass migration

[3] See, for example, Lipman, *Social History*, p. 183; I. Finestein, *A Short History of Anglo-Jewry* (London, 1957), pp. 163–8; N. Bentwich, 'The Social Transformation of Anglo-Jewry, 1883–1960', *Jewish Journal of Sociology*, 2: 1 (1960), pp. 16–24.

[4] H. M. Brotz, 'The Position of the Jews in English Society', *Jewish Journal of Sociology*, 1: 1 (1959), p. 106; L. Stein, *The Balfour Declaration* (London, 1961), pp. 445–9, 458–9; G. Shimoni, 'Selig Brodetsky and the Ascendancy of Zionism in Anglo-Jewry (1939–1945)', *Jewish Journal of Sociology*, 22: 2 (1980), pp. 125–32 and idem, 'The Non-Zionists in Anglo-Jewry, 1937–1948', *Jewish Journal of Sociology*, 28: 2 (1986), pp. 106–10. A more critical view of the role of Zionism, 1917–20, is presented by Cohen, *English Zionists and British Jews*, pp. 215–18.

[5] Cf. I. Finestein, 'Profile of a Community: Anglo-Jewry since 1933', *Jewish Quarterly*, 30: 4 (1983), pp. 19–20 and idem, 'Changes in Authority in Anglo-Jewry since the 1930s: A Critical View', *Jewish Quarterly*, 30:2 (1985), p. 34, arguing that conditions were ripe for change regardless of the impact of Zionism.

to Israel, even after 1948, indicating that the rhetoric and objectives of the movement require a critical elucidation. Nor is there an unequivocal linkage between the Jewish immigrant 'masses' and the Zionist movement. The Zionist Federation was dominated by middle-class Jews, many of whom were well established in Britain. By contrast, large sections of the immigrant Jewish working class were socialist or communist and, therefore, anti-Zionist or indifferent to Jewish nationalism.[6] While Zionism was the focus of many of the struggles that tore apart communal bodies in the 1920s and 1930s, it was only one among many controversies. Through its opposition to political Zionism the old communal leadership aroused the enmity of the nationalist section of the population, but it alienated a wider span of Jewish opinion on a range of other issues.

This essay will argue that the traditional leadership of British Jews suffered a diminution of authority during and immediately after World War I and that the erosion of established forms of communal authority continued throughout the 1920s, accelerating dramatically in the decade before World War II. While Zionism and the Zionist movement played a key role in the delegitimization of the pre-1914 communal hierarchy, it was only one element in a broader process of political and ideological change. The fractiousness of the inter-war years was symptomatic of a protracted dialogue between sections of the Jewish population around the identity of Jews in Britain and the best means for ensuring their survival *in situ*. In this debate, the Jewish left had as much to say as the Zionists, yet the role of the Jewish left has been consistently minimized and marginalized in the historiography of the period.[7] It will be suggested here that Zionism has been wrongly isolated as the motor force for change in Jewish society in Britain, that the Jewish left played a major role in the politics of Anglo-Jewry – in the 1930s in particular – even if its impact was indirect and outside of traditional institutions, and that the behaviour of the Zionists cannot be fully comprehended without an awareness of the strength and enterprise of Jewish socialism.

Most studies of the intra-communal politics of Anglo-Jewry have concentrated on institutional developments, with asides on the social and economic 'background'. Yet social and economic changes in British Jewry, regardless of political movements or ideological shifts, contributed to the deracination of the pre-1914 Jewish elite. An attempt will be made here to elaborate the essential conjunction between the social reconfiguration of the Jewish population, the

---

[6] D. Cesarani, 'The East London of Simon Blumenfeld's "Jew Boy"', *The London Journal*, 13: 1 (1987–8) pp. 46–53.

[7] The strength of the left in the Jewish population was a problem for the official Jewish community then and remains a cause of embarrassment. This may account for its absence from the historical-cultural agenda of British Jews until recently. For innovative attempts to confront the subject, see H. Srebrnik, '"Salud di Heldn!" Jewish Communist Activity in London on Behalf of the Spanish Republic', *Michigan Academician*, 16: 3 (1984), pp. 371–81 and 'Communism and pro-Soviet Feeling Among the Jews of East London, 1935–45', *Immigrants and Minorities*, 5: 3 (1986), pp. 285–304; J. Bush, *Behind the Lines: East London Labour 1914–19* (London, 1984), pp. 185–90; E. Smith, 'East London Tailors, 1918–1939: An Aspect of the Jewish Workers' Struggle', *Jewish Quarterly*, 34:2 (1987), pp. 26–9; S. Kadish, 'Jewish Bolshevism and the 'Red Scare' in Britain,' *Jewish Quarterly*, 34: 4, (1987), pp. 13–19.

restructuring of the collective identity of Jewish communities and the related patterns of communal authority.

Since the political and religious institutions of Anglo-Jewry were highly centralized, any study of authority naturally tends towards a concentration on London. This is reinforced by its predominance in the distribution of Jewish settlement in Britain: while approximately 35,000 Jews lived in Manchester, 25,000 in Leeds and 15,000 in Glasgow between the wars, around 235,000 resided in London, over 100,000 in the East End alone. Hence, developments in London were crucial for determining the overall structure of power and authority. However, parallel developments to those in London occurred in non-London Jewish centres, and an attempt will be made to incorporate these developments, particularly where they had an impact upon the stature and decision making of the central leadership.

I

As was the case for British society as a whole, World War I engendered a social revolution in Anglo-Jewry. Sections of the population that had been powerless and silent acquired authority and articulated their own aspirations. New institutions were created to meet the demands of wartime, while a spirit of popular participation contributed to the democratization of communal affairs. The existing establishment faced challenges to its authority and, by its policies, provoked a crisis of confidence in its leadership that was of permanent significance.[8]

The vast majority of British-born Jews threw themselves into the war effort, but amongst the Russian-born immigrants there was little enthusiasm for the conflict.[9] British-born Jews were deeply embarrassed by the behaviour of their co-religionists. They sympathized broadly with the various experiments which the government undertook in an effort to induct immigrant Jews into military service in 1916–17 and became increasingly intolerant of the opposition aroused by these schemes. In the spring of 1917, the government concluded an agreement with the Russian authorities under which Russian-born Jews would be either conscripted into the British forces or returned to Russia to serve there. The process of negotiations which led to the Anglo-Russian 'Convention' were set in motion by Herbert Samuel, the Home Secretary, who came from the Jewish social elite. Other leading Anglo-Jewish personalities lent their weight to attempts to recruit Russian-born Jews into military units. These efforts were regarded by the immigrants as a gross betrayal: Jews opposed to the imposition of military service on Russian-born immigrants disrupted recruit-

---

[8] A. Marwick, *The Deluge: British Society and the First World War* (New York, 1970), pp. 289–310; J. Williams, *The Home Fronts: Britain, France and Germany, 1914–1918* (London, 1972), p. 1.

[9] See C. Holmes, *Anti-Semitism in British Society, 1876–1939* (London, 1979), pp. 126–36; Bush, *Behind the Lines*, pp. 181–6. Russian Jews had little desire to fight on the same side as Tsarist Russia, from which they had emigrated in search of a freer, better life. Many had left specifically to avoid conscription and had an ingrained hatred of military service.

ment meetings and condemned the Jewish leadership which was acting in complicity with the government.[10] Several thousand finally opted to return, hundreds leaving behind wives and children who eked out a living on the basis of an allowance provided by the Russian Embassy and local government boards. Despite appeals for aid to the official Jewish charities, the Jewish Board of Guardians in London ostentatiously refused to give financial succour to the dependants of returnees, while the Board of Deputies declined to intervene on their behalf.[11] The entire question of military service for Russian-born Jews drove a wedge between native and immigrant Jews, leaving a legacy of bitterness and mistrust.

Soon after the outbreak of war, the government enacted measures to register all enemy aliens and intern those of military age. Thousands of Jews from Galicia, the Austrian-controlled area of Poland, found themselves rounded up and torn from their families and livelihoods. Despite pleas from Jewish friendly societies and the Jewish press, the Board of Deputies refused to intercede in favour of these 'enemy aliens'.[12] The Board's leadership stuck by this policy in the wake of the anti-alienism which followed the sinking of the *Lusitania* in May 1915. It refused to apply for official aid for the victims of anti-German rioting – many of them innocent Russian and Romanian Jewish shopkeepers. After the promulgation of new, stringent measures against enemy aliens, the Board declined to appoint representatives to the tribunals to hear appeals against internment or repatriation. Jewish friendly societies and the B'nai B'rith, a secular national organization of the Jewish middle class, protested against the Board's aloofness and themselves represented Jews at the tribunals. In Manchester, Glasgow and Leeds, local bodies sprang up to undertake this work. These were the germ of the permanent Jewish representative councils which became a feature of Jewish settlements outside London.[13]

The assertiveness of local leadership cadres was reinforced by their experience of war-time responsibilities. As the regulation of civilian life spread ever wider, committees, councils and tribunals were set up to facilitate the participation of experts and representatives of concerned groups. Jews in Manchester, Glasgow and Leeds were appointed to local recruitment committees, relief agencies, conscription tribunals, aliens advisory tribunals and food control committees. The war thus gave office and experience to increasing numbers of Jews, mainly from the middle classes, but also artisans and working-class

[10] Cohen, *English Zionists and British Jews*, pp. 217–18, 252–4.

[11] *JC*, 12 October 1917, p. 5. See also *JC*, 21 September 1917, p. 5.

[12] Marwick, *The Deluge*, pp. 37–8; Board of Deputies of British Jews, Minutes, (hereafter BOD), Board of Deputies Archive, vol. 16, 15 November 1914; *JC*, 30 October 1914, p. 7, 20 November 1914, p. 5.

[13] Marwick, *The Deluge*, p. 131; *JC*, 21 May 1915, p. 5, 28 May 1915, p. 16; B. Williams, *Manchester Jewry: A Pictorial Portrait* (Manchester, 1988), p. 75; K. Collins, 'Growth and Development of Scottish Jewry, 1880–1940', in ed. K. Collins, *Aspects of Scottish Jewry* (Glasgow, 1987), pp. 22–3. JRCs had existed in Manchester and Leeds before the war and the council in Glasgow owed its origins to events in 1913. However, earlier efforts to maintain autonomous communal governing bodies in non-London centres had always foundered and it is arguable that the war forged these new institutions.

representatives from Jewish friendly societies and trade unions. They became more confident of their abilities, aware of the local or regional interests that they knew best and contrasted this with the divergent opinions and actions of the centralized leadership in London.[14]

In May 1917, the representatives of non-London Jewry were enraged by the high-handed behaviour of the London leadership over the matter of Zionism. Since 1915, Chaim Weizmann and a small circle of Zionist activists had been lobbying the government to issue a declaration in favour of a Jewish State in Palestine. Most of the Anglo-Jewish social elite was appalled by such an idea. To them it connoted the existence of a separate Jewish nationality that seemed incompatible with citizenship of another country and, therefore, undermined Jewish claims to civil equality. By early 1917 it appeared that Weizmann and his group were close to achieving their goal. In an attempt to forestall such a departure, David Alexander, the President of the Board of Deputies, and Claude Montefiore, the President of the Anglo-Jewish Association, published a letter in *The Times* invoking their representative offices and denouncing the activity of the Zionists along with the idea of a Jewish State.[15]

Their action, taken without consulting the Board of Deputies, caused outrage even amongst those who were indifferent to Zionism. The letter in *The Times* crystallized the ire of middle-class Jews in the B'nai B'rith. Members of this organization, founded in 1909, had long resented their exclusion from the higher reaches of communal authority, despite their sterling work in communal affairs. The friendly societies, which formed the largest associations of Jews in Britain but had no formal representation on the Board of Deputies, saw in this action a perfect example of oligarchy at work. The non-London Jewish centres were, likewise, insulted by the absence of consultation by those presuming to act in the name of British Jewry. As a result, there was a crowded and stormy meeting of the Board in June 1917 at which Alexander and Montefiore were censured; Alexander was obliged to resign the presidency, while the AJA saw its links with the Board of Deputies temporarily severed.[16]

Zionism split British Jews into warring camps and it was feared this would led to 'schism', with a section of Anglo-Jewry leaving the organized community completely.[17] The anti-Zionist faction formed a League of British Jews, dedicated to the principle that the Jews constituted a denominational group and to the defence of their civil rights (including the right of any Jews to settle in

---

[14] See Collins, *Aspects of Scottish Jewry*, and Williams, *Manchester Jewry: Portrait*, p. 75. For local activities, see, e.g., Manchester appointment of 3 representatives to the advisory committee on interned Galicians, *JC*, 24 August 1917, p. 16. S. Cohen, 'The Conquest of a Community? The Zionists and the Board of Deputies in 1917', *Jewish Journal of Sociology*, 29: 2 (1977), p. 174, notes the phenomenal wartime expansion of these councils, but does not entirely explain it.

[15] Cohen, *English Zionists and British Jews*, pp. 237–9. On the content and significance of anti-Zionism amongst the Anglo-Jewish elite, see chs 5 and 6.

[16] Cohen, *English Zionists and British Jews*, p. 239, W. M. Schwab, *B'nai B'rith: The First Lodge of England, A Record of Fifty Years* (London, 1960), pp. 43–5.

[17] On the threat of schism, see M. J. Landa, *Hibbert Journal*, 61: 2 (1918), pp. 223–33 and Mentor, *JC*, 18 January 1918, p. 12.

Palestine if they so wished!). The League's membership embraced a substantial part of the social, economic and political elite of pre-1914 British Jewry, including several of the Jewish MPs, the paymasters of a clutch of the most important Jewish communal organizations and the heads of almost all of them.[18] Their claim to represent Jews in Britain was, however, weakened by the League's statutory exclusion of non-naturalized foreign-born Jews. This was doubtless a patriotic gesture and in full keeping with the hysterical anti-alienism of the times, but it was of disastrous consequence for their standing in Jewish eyes. By excluding Jewish aliens (and many of the immigrants before 1914 had not bothered to naturalize owing to the expense or lack of urgency), they set themselves apart from a large portion of the Jewish population. Moreover, they tacitly identified themselves with the ultra-patriotic right-wingers who were busily hunting down 'aliens' wherever they could find them, frequently with more than a tinge of Jew-hatred.[19]

The League compounded its apparent abandonment of immigrant Jewry when ten of its leading members published a letter in the *Morning Post* in May 1919, dissociating themselves from two pieces by Mentor (Leopold Greenberg) in the *Jewish Chronicle* which expressed a measure of support for the ideals of Bolshevism. The letter linked these articles to claims, made particularly in the *Morning Post* itself, that foreign-born Jews in Britain were acting as carriers for subversive ideas. The Leaguers protested that 'the publication of these articles can have no other effect than to encourage the adoption of the theoretic principles of Russian Bolsheviks among foreign Jews who have sought and found a refuge in England.'[20] The object of the letter may have been only to distance the sort of Jews whom the League represented from Greenberg's erratic journalism, but its effect was quite different. It was widely interpreted as an expression of concurrence with the anti-Bolshevism of the *Morning Post* and kindred papers which referred explicitly and prejoratively to the role of Jews in the revolutionary movements. To publish the letter in the *Morning Post* was a double affront since this paper was at the time championing the myth of a Jewish world conspiracy.[21] The 'Letter of the Ten' triggered off a storm of protest. It was rounded on by Greenberg, condemned in the Yiddish press and censured at a meeting of the Board of Deputies.[22] For a generation of Jews, a central segment of the old leadership had forfeited the trust or respect essential to preserve the ligaments of authority in a voluntaristic society.

[18] Cohen, *English Zionists and British Jews*, pp. 303–9.
[19] See D. Cesarani, 'Anti-Alienism in England after the First World War', *Immigrants and Minorities*, 6: 1 (1987), pp. 14–16; Holmes, *Anti-Semitism in British Society*, p. 146.
[20] S. Kadish, '"The Letter of the Ten": Bolsheviks and British Jews', ed. J. Frankel, *Studies in Contemporary Jewry* (Oxford, 1988), vol. IV, *The Jews and the European Crisis, 1914–1921*, pp. 92–107.
[21] L. Poliakov, *History of Anti-Semitism* (Oxford, 1985), vol. IV, *Suicidal Europe, 1870–1933*, pp. 197–8, 212; Holmes, *Anti-Semitism in British Society*, pp. 141–50; K. Wilson, '"The Protocols of Zion" and the "Morning Post", 1919–1920', *Patterns of Prejudice*, 19: 3 (1985), pp. 6–14.
[22] *JC*, 2 May 1919, pp. 14, 22; *Di Tsait*, 2 May 1919, pp. 1, 3; BOD, vol. 17, 29 April 1919. See Kadish, '"The Letter of the Ten"', pp. 103–4.

Yet, in spite of the upheaval of June 1917 and the rumpus in May 1919, the political constellation of British Jewry remained essentially unaltered. If the Zionists did not 'capture the community' in 1917, neither did the representatives of non-London Jewry or the Jewish middle class. The 1920s were marked by the persistence of the *ancien régime*.[23] Regardless of the head of steam behind calls for democratization, the eventual reform of the Board was limited and cautious. For the first time, representatives of non-synagogal institutions were admitted, but this was balanced by enlarged representation for the two London synagogue organizations. The nationwide Jewish friendly society movement – with around 50,000 members – was allotted fifteen seats, while the London-based United Synagogue Council acquired twelve deputies, whose nomination was virtually controlled by the honorary officers. The Federation of Synagogues likewise acquired two delegates, pocket nominees of its President, Lord Swaythling. The representation of the council for the Anglo-Jewish Association was also strengthened, to nine in all.[24]

The old social and political elite retained control of the commanding heights of British Jewry. In 1920, the Presidency of the Board of Deputies was held by Sir Stuart Samuel, a member of the circle of pre-1914 ruling families. He was flanked by two Rothschilds serving as vice-presidents. The only representative of non-London Jewry amongst the honorary officers was Nathan Laski, a Mancunian Jew of pre-war eminence. Out of nearly 100 places on the various committees of the Board, and discounting the two Rothschilds who represented northern constituencies *in absentia*, only seventeen were occupied by deputies from Jewish centres north of London. Of these, nine places were taken by the ubiquitous Nathan Laski and his son, Neville. The friendly societies managed to obtain only one authentic representative on a committee of the Board.[25]

At the Board, Samuel was succeeded by Cyril Henriques in 1922, to be followed four years later by Osmond d'Avigdor Goldsmid, who held office until 1933. The vice-presidencies were held by Lord Rothschild, 1918–33, Anthony de Rothschild, 1918–22, Joseph Prag, 1925–8, and Sir Isidore Salmon, who took office in 1929. All, except for Prag, were drawn from the social matrix which supplied the pre-war leadership and even though Prag was of more humble origin, he had been active in communal affairs since the 1890s and was virtually a part of the establishment. The other honorary officers represented continuity, too, with the post of treasurer being held by Nathan Laski, B. S. Strauss and Prag.[26] The Anglo-Jewish Association remained a fiefdom of the

[23] Cf. Cohen, *English Zionists and British Jews*, pp. 245–76.

[24] *Board of Deputies 67th Annual Report, December 1917–December 1918* (London, 1918), pp. 23–4; Cohen, *English Zionists and British Jews*, pp. 289–90. In 1925, the AJA was entitled to 9 deputies, the United Synagogue Council to 12, the Federation of Synagogues to 6, the Union of Jewish Women to 2, the Association of Jewish Friendly Societies to 3, with 11 seats apportioned among the individual orders. The Jewish students of Oxford and Cambridge each had one delegate, too.

[25] *Board of Deputies 69th Annual Report, December 1919–December 1920* (London, 1920), pp. 18–19.

[26] Data contained in the annual *Anglo-Jewish Year Book* (London, 1918 et seq.).

'Cousinhood' and was headed successively by Claude Montefiore, Osmond d'Avigdor Goldsmid and Leonard Montefiore, Claude's son. At the United Synagogue, another Rothschild, Lionel de Rothschild, held the office of President until 1942. Effective power was in the hands of Sir Robert Waley Cohen, one more figure from the pre-war Jewish plutocracy, who dominated its business in his capacity as vice-president from 1918 to 1942.[27] The same pattern was evident in the Board of Guardians. The only crack in this carapace of the old regime came at the Federation of Synagogues in the mid-1920s.

Louis Samuel Montagu, second Lord Swaythling, had virtually inherited the Federation from his father. A founding member of the League of British Jews, he was at odds with its East European immigrant membership on almost every conceivable issue. Swaythling was an outspoken anti-Zionist and had been a signatory to the 'Letter of the Ten'. On both matters he was taken to task by the Council of the Federation, but managed to face them down by threatening to resign if he was formally censured. His autocratic rule was exercised through a venally dishonest factotum, but confronted with the forfeiture of Swaythling's prestige and patronage, the council lost heart.[28] The *casus belli* of the revolt of 1925–6 lay with the use of Yiddish at council meetings. Yiddish had been banned, along with any mention of Zionism, by the first Lord Swaythling and was resisted with even more determination by his son. The demand for the use of Yiddish was symbolic of immigrant assertiveness around a cluster of long-standing grievances. The rebels, led by M. H. Davis, a local councillor, success-fully articulated the frustration of the Federation's immigrant membership, championing internal democratization and practical support for Zionism. After a series of calculated challenges to his authority, Swaythling again offered his resignation. This time it was accepted by the insurgent faction, which followed his deposition with a number of popular measures such as donations for Palestine.[29]

II

Aside from the Federation of Synagogues, throughout the 1920s the Jewish middle class, artisans and workers largely remained penned into the institutions which they had created – the B'nai B'rith, the Zionist Federation, the friendly societies and the Jewish trade unions. There was an obvious disparity between the size and competency of these bodies and their representation on the Board. There was a similar dysfunction between the changed nature of Jewish society in Britain and the character of its titular heads. These anamolies became the subject of renewed controversy when the tribulations of the post-war era exposed the failings of the erstwhile leadership.

[27] A. Newman, *The United Synagogue, 1870–1970* (London, 1976), pp. 212–13.
[28] C. Roth, *The Federation of Synagogues, 1912–1937* (London, 1937), pp. 9–11; G. Alderman, *The Federation of Synagogues, 1887–1987* (London, 1987), pp. 55–7.
[29] *Di Tsait*, 15 January 1926, p. 1; *Zionist Review* (*ZR*), 9: 10 (February 1926), p. 112; Roth, *The Federation of Synagogues*, pp. 15–16.

In the wake of World War I, Britain was swept by a wave of vindictive xenophobia.[30] Since Jews formed the largest immigrant population in Britain, they were bound to be amongst its chief victims. Immediately after the armistice, thousands of Galician Jews were threatened with deportation as former 'enemy aliens'. At the same time 'Conventionists' – Jews who had returned to Russia in 1917 – were denied re-admission to Britain. Large numbers of non-naturalized immigrant Jews settled in Britain became acutely vulnerable under the draconian Aliens Restriction (Amendment) Act of 1919, which gave unprecedented power to immigration officials, the police, magistrates and the Home Secretary to deny aliens leave to land in the country and to deport non-naturalized immigrants without any judicial proceedings or right of appeal. Under the Act, 'Conventionists' who re-entered Britain illegally, Jews who committed minor infractions of the aliens' regulations – such as failing to register a change of address – or Jews convicted of petty crimes were condemned to deportation. During the period 1919–29, central government and local authorities were also systematically discriminating against Jewish aliens in the spheres of education, welfare, housing and employment.[31]

These hostile currents might have been offset by the Balfour Declaration and British patronage of the Jewish National Home in Palestine. However, the potential legitimating effects were limited by the strong anti-Zionist forces in British politics. Between 1920 and 1924, the *Morning Post, Spectator*, Northcliffe, Rothermere and Beaverbrook presses mounted a sustained campaign against British involvement in the Middle East. The government's Palestine policy was debated repeatedly in Parliament and was the subject of heated controversy in the general elections of 1922, 1923 and 1924. The rhetoric of anti-Zionism veered frequently into anti-Jewish stereotypes, evoking themes of Jewish power and a Jewish world-conspiracy.[32]

The leadership of the Board of Deputies was constantly upbraided for the failure to oppose the Aliens Act effectively. The Board sent several deputations to the Home Office between 1919 and 1926, but these visits obtained only a few token modifications to the regulations. Nor was the Board apparently able to promote an effective opposition to the passing of the Act or its annual renewal in the House of Commons. Two of the most senior Jewish MPs, Sir Charles Henry and Sir Philip Magnus, were members of the League of British Jews which operated its own discrimination against alien Jews. Other Jewish MPs were reluctant to offend public opinion by standing against the measure, although there were some outstanding exceptions such as the Conservative MP Samuel Finburgh.[33] To the immigrant section of the Jewish population, the Board was not adequately performing its central role as intercessor and

---

[30] G. Webber, *The Ideology of the British Right, 1918–1939* (London, 1986), pp. 57–9.

[31] Cesarani, 'Anti-Alienism in England after the First World War', pp. 5–18.

[32] See D. Cesarani, 'Anti-Zionist Politics and Political Anti-Semitism in England, 1920–1924', *Patterns of Prejudice* 23: 1 (1989) and idem 'Joynson-Hicks and the Radical Right in England after World War One', in eds T. Kushner and K. Lunn, *Traditions of Intolerance* (Manchester, 1989), pp. 123–7.

[33] Cesarani, 'Anti-Alienism in England after the First World War', pp. 9, 16, 18, 19–21.

protector. Deputies sitting for the friendly societies, whose members were most affected by the aliens regulations, complained about the repeated failure to win any amelioration of the laws or the discrimination against foreign-born Jews. They blamed this on the neglect of friendly society and working-class interests, which they felt would not have been allowed if they had had a stronger presence at the Board. In 1925, the Annual Report of the Association of Jewish Friendly Societies commented that 'The totally unsatis-factory representation in the past had created a strong feeling in the movement and had begun to undermine sympathy for the Board, which was reflected at the Association.'[34]

The authority of the Board of Deputies was eroded in the eyes of the Zionist section of the Jewish population by its attitude towards the Jewish National Home. Despite the official sanction which Zionism had obtained as a result of the Balfour Declaration and the 1922 White Paper (which reiterated Britain's pledge to facilitate Jewish settlement in Palestine), the old families of Anglo-Jewry did little more than make token genuflections in that direction. When Zionist deputies tried to commit the Board to concrete action, they were habitually defeated. Although in 1924 the Board joined the Jewish Agency – an international body set up to enable non-Zionist Jews to contribute materially to Jewish work in Palestine – its officers refused to contribute what the Zionists most needed, their personal advocacy and their money.[35] Zionist frustration induced a return to the democratic rhetoric of 1917, and demands for further reforms of the communal power structure. Zionists condemned the 1917–18 revision of the Board's constitution as 'sheer oligarchy' and ran a slate of reform candidates in the Board's triennial elections in 1919.[36] They also opposed the reconstitution of the old Conjoint Foreign Committee by a 'treaty' between the Board and the AJA, a body which they regarded as undemocratic and anti-Zionist.[37] Zionist agitation provoked similar calls for democratization at the United Synagogue. Between 1921 and 1928, members of its council cam-paigned for the organization to donate money to Zionist causes or to allow funds to be raised through the constituent synagogues. These demands were rejected consistently by the honorary officers, of whom four out of eleven were members of the League of British Jews. On repeated occasions, the honorary officers simply ruled discussion out of order and threatened to close council

[34] *Association of Jewish Friendly Societies Annual Report, 1924–1925* (London, 1925). See also, *The Leader*, April 1923 and June 1923. The Order Achei Ameth proposed a boycott of the Board, at the Association's quarterly conference, May 1925. The friendly societies also voiced objections to their under-representation on committees of the Board and the Joint Foreign Committee, in particular, see *Leader*, June 1925.

[35] D. Cesarani, 'Zionism in England between the Two World Wars, 1918–1939', in ed. M. Kaufman, *Studies in Contemporary Jewry* (forthcoming); cf. G. Shimoni, 'From Anti-Zionism to Non-Zionism in Anglo-Jewry, 1917–1937', *Jewish Journal of Sociology*, 28: 1 (1986), pp. 19–47.

[36] *ZR*, 3: 1 (May 1919), p. 2; *JC*, 9 May 1919, pp. 10, 25 and *ZR*, 3: 2 (June 1919), p. 29; English Zionist Federation (ZF) Communal Organisations Committee, Minutes, 15 May 1919, Central Zionist Archive, Jerusalem (CZA), Z4/618 and Special Council Meeting, 15 July 1919, CZA, Z4/631.

[37] BOD, vol. 18, 19 February 1922.

meetings if such matters were raised again.[38] Despite the support of a majority of council members and overwhelming votes by several constituent synagogues, the honorary officers blocked any affiliation with or support for the Zionist movement. This, in turn, led to an unsuccessful attempt to amend the constitution. Several times after bruising council meetings, members complained that they were being 'muzzled'.[39]

Through their opposition to Zionism, the long-standing leadership of British Jewry appeared to be setting their faces against democracy in the defence of outworn ideas. Their methods were often high-handed and unscrupulous and the persistent assaults and criticism of the Zionist faction exposed the archaic and undemocratic nature of communal authority. Every clash highlighted the distance between the leadership and the rest of the Jewish population. Yet, during the 1920s, politics within Anglo-Jewry reached a stalemate. The Zionist Federation, the friendly societies and the B'nai B'rith were unable substantially to transform the power structure. This began to change in the early 1930s, when a combination of developments made the need for drastic change irresistible.

III

In January 1933, Neville Laski, KC, was elected President of the Board of Deputies, an appointment that promised much. Laski was a barrister who came from a prominent Manchester family long associated with work on behalf of Jewish settlement in Palestine. He thus appeared to personify all the elements in the 'revolt' of 1917. The Zionists, for example, assumed that he would be a natural ally and asked him to join the council of the Zionist Federation.[40] Yet Laski proved to be a huge disappointment.

Less than a month after he assumed office, Laski was confronted by the crisis of German Jewry. His response was formulated in close cooperation with Leonard Montefiore, the President of the AJA, with whom he was co-chairman of the Joint Foreign Committee (JFC). Both men had a substantial degree of power and authority; together they dominated the JFC, which presented policy to the Board. Initially, Laski and Montefiore counselled inaction.[41] In spite of anxious questioning at the Board, they were practically passive until March 1933, when there were raids on Jewish organizations in Germany, wholesale dismissals of Jews from public office, incidents of violence and the announcement of an anti-Jewish boycott. By the end of that month, there were demands in Jewish circles for a public protest and a boycott of German goods and services.

[38] See correspondence between the New Synagogue, Stoke Newington, and Philip Goldberg, secretary of the United Synagogue, United Synagogue Archive (USA), Permanent Folder (PF) 426A. For the move to alter the constitution, see *JC*, 5 November 1926, p. 17, 17 December 1926, pp. 17–18 and minutes of meeting of United Synagogue Honorary Officers, 23 November 1926, USA.

[39] See letters, *JC*, 3 March 1922, p. 17 and 17 December 1926, pp. 17–18.

[40] Paul Goodman, Hon. Secretary of the Zionist Federation, to Neville Laski, 27 January 1933, Board of Deputies Archive (BDA), E1/111.

[41] JFC Special Meeting, 1 February 1933, BDA.

However, Laski and Montefiore rejected all such initiatives and told the JFC, the Board and the Zionist Federation that demonstrations would be premature and, moreover, harmful to German Jews, who had advised against them.[42]

Laski's temporization aggravated the widespread impatience, which eventually exploded in a series of marches, demonstrations and an unofficial boycott.[43] In the midst of this welter, Laski appeared repeatedly before the JFC and the Board advising caution, assuring them that he was trying to arrange a suitable public demonstration and strongly deprecating spontaneous protests. He intervened vainly to prevent a march by Jewish trade unionists in May and persuaded Lord Melchett – Henry Mond – to withdraw his patronage of the boycott.[44] This led to a storm of criticism aimed at Laski, Montefiore and their respective institutions. Michael Levy, a respected friendly society worker and Zionist activist, complained that 'After 14 years as a member of the Deputies, I have arrived at the conclusion that the Board does not represent the opinion of Anglo-Jewry, although it may represent the opinion of a miserable minority who are always against coming to the front lest their social standing suffer.'[45] The friendly societies were outspoken in their criticisms, singling out the conservatism of the Board's hierarchy and Laski's divisive style of leadership. Two of the largest societies were reported to be contemplating the formation of a united opposition at the Board. The *Jewish World*, down-market sister paper to the *Jewish Chronicle*, commented that 'It is undeniable that ever since the crisis brought about by Hitlerism, the unity of the Board has been broken and the rupture seems to get more serious.'[46] Zionists, too, were prominent in the chorus of discontent. In early March 1934, the *Zionist Review* published a series of damning profiles of communal hierarchs. Sir Robert Waley Cohen, for example, was characterized as a 'dictator in the age of dictators'.[47]

The corrosive effect of this barrage on the legitimacy of the ruling circle was evident. The Board had difficulty imposing its authority on the Jewish population and a series of power struggles broke out at the apex of communal government. In May 1933, Simon Marks, one of 'the Family' which controlled Marks and Spencer and amongst the wealthiest backers of the Zionist movement, made a rare appearance at a meeting of the Board of Deputies to suggest that Laski and Montefiore withdraw in favour of Chaim Weizmann, the President of the Zionist Federation and former President of the World Zionist Congress. This plan was amended by the addition of Lord Rothschild and Sir

---

[42] Zionist Federation Executive Committee (ZFEC), Special Meeting, attended by Laski and Montefiore, 26 March 1933, CZA, Z4/3565–vii; *JC*, 24 March 1933, p. 28 for calls for a boycott.

[43] *JC*, 2 April 1933, p. 31, for the Workers' Circle-sponsored protest rally in the East End; *JC*, 21 April 1933, p. 26 and *Young Zionists (YZ)*, 7: 4 (May, 1933), p. 2, on the Youth Emergency Council; *JC*, 5 May 1933, p. 31, for the boycott.

[44] BOD, Vol. 26, 9 April 1933 and report *JC*, 14 April 1933, pp. 17–18. The march organized by the United Jewish Protest Committee was a great success, *JC*, 21 July 1933, p. 10, 28 July 1933, pp. 20–1 and 26. For Laski's opposition, see *JC*, 23 June 1933, pp. 4–5, 14 July 1933, pp. 24–5.

[45] *JC*, 31 March 1933, p. 43.

[46] *Jewish World*, 24 August 1933, p. 5.

[47] *Monthly Pioneer*, 5: 6 (March 1933), p. 4; *ZR*, 1: 1 (March 1934), p. 7, 1: 2 (April 1934), p. 20.

Herbert Samuel, so as to form a triumvirate, charged with the direction of Anglo-Jewry. Laski successfully parried this challenge, but other groups were crystallizing outside the Board and putting forward their claims to leadership.[48]

One was forming around Harry L. Nathan, the former Liberal MP for Bethnal Green and a member of the London County Council.[49] Nathan was instrumental in the creation of a Central Jewish Consultative Committee. He explained that 'Its authority derives from the men and women who compose it, for there have been brought together in this Council men and women not only representing every phase of Anglo-Jewish life, but holding outside the community positions of responsibility which entitle their possessors to respect.' The committee was intended as a 'clearing house' for ideas and plans by individual Jews, which would then be submitted to the overstretched Board and JFC.[50] Another grouping clustered around Henry Mond, a director of ICI. Mond came to prominence as a moving force and figurehead of the boycott movement. This item was taken up and developed by a newly formed Anglo-Jewish Council of Trades and Industry, which he headed along with Nathan.[51] They organized a conference in July 1933 to press for the extension and enforcement of the boycott, a gathering which was disclaimed publicly by Laski and Montefiore.[52] By September, control of the boycott had been centralized under the Jewish Representative Council for the Boycott of German Goods and Services. This body embraced Zionists and non-Zionists, trade unionists, friendly society activists, synagogue representatives and youth groups; its title was an obvious reproach to the Board of Deputies.[53]

The process of fragmentation was accelerated under the impact of Fascism and political anti-semitism in Britain. There had been sporadic verbal and physical attacks by Fascists on Jews since 1934, but during 1935 and 1936, the efforts of the British Union of Fascists (BUF) became concentrated on the Jewish districts of the East End. The area was saturated with loudspeaker vans and street corner meetings, the latter often degenerating into violence. Laski's approach to the threat posed by the BUF is well known. He advocated a pacific response, relying on the public authorities to protect Jewish persons and property. Laski argued that anti-Jewish currents were a social problem which could not and should not be fought in the realm of politics. To do so would politicize the 'Jewish question' and create an antagonism between the Jews and a political party. He recommended Jews to avoid confrontations with Black-shirts and advocated, instead, self-restraint combined with self-improvement. He repeatedly berated the Jewish population for stimulating anti-Jewish

---

[48] *Jewish Standard and Recorder* (*JSR*) 19 May 1933, p. 17.
[49] *JSR*, 19 May 1933, p. 15.
[50] *JSR*, 9 June 1933, p. 12. The Council included R. D. Blumenfeld, Fleet Street personality and former editor of the *Daily Express*, and two prominent Jewish lawyers, A. M. Langdon, KC, and A. M. Lyons, KC, MP.
[51] *JSR*, 9 June 1933, p. 12; 16 June 1933, p. 3.
[52] *JSR*, 7 July 1933, p. 9. Laski and Montefiore published a letter in the *Manchester Guardian* distancing the official bodies in Anglo-Jewry from the boycott.
[53] *JC*, 22 September 1933, pp. 6, 24; 29 September 1933, p. 21.

movements by their ostentation, their 'invasion' of certain occupations, their political radicalism and their physical engagements with Fascists.[54]

Jews who were the direct victims of Fascist harassment, many of them artisans and workers who were living in poor or modest circumstances, had little sympathy for Laski's palliatives.[55] In 1934, Jewish trade unionists, members of the Workers' Circle – an immigrant-based socialist friendly society – and left-wingers combined to form a Jewish Labour Council to combat Fascism and anti-semitism. Their aim was to unite Jews and non-Jews in the struggle against Fascism and to expose the political dimension of anti-semitism.[56] Jewish friendly societies also took issue with the policy of the Board of Deputies and demanded a more activist response. After meeting little success, in July 1936 they established a defence campaign on their own, organizing open-air meetings in East and North London to combat Fascist propaganda.[57]

The Jewish Labour Council was the progenitor of the Jewish Peoples' Council against Fascism and Anti-Semitism (JPC), set up in East London in July 1936. The JPC was dominated by Jewish leftists. Its approach was explicitly political, treating anti-semitism as a part of the extreme right-wing attack on democracy and the labour movement. The advent of the JPC deepened the fractures in the Jewish population. There was an instant and mutual hostility between the council and the Board, whose authority it challenged openly.[58] The repercussions of this rivalry spread widely as the JPC's stance on communal authority and its leftist complexion triggered splits amongst the friendly societies and the Zionists, who otherwise sympathized with its work.[59] Eventually the JPC secured the affiliation of over eighty Jewish organizations comprising a wide range of synagogues, friendly societies, trade unions, socialist societies, ex-servicemen's bodies and Zionist groups. Like the Jewish Representative Council it was a standing indictment of the traditional leadership and structures of communal authority. Yet even the pro-establishment Order Achei B'rith friendly society, which refused to join the council, could sympathize with the frustration caused by the Board's policy and conduct. Its

[54] G. Alderman, *The Jewish Community in British Politics* (Oxford, 1983), pp. 116–17 and 122–3; G. Lebzelter, *Political Anti-Semitism in England, 1918–1939* (London, 1978), ch. 7, esp. pp. 139, 143–51. Laski's views are set forth in *Jewish Rights and Jewish Wrongs*, (London, 1939), pp. 113–41, esp. pp. 135 and 138–41.

[55] Lebzelter, *Political Anti-Semitism*, p. 149.

[56] *Jewish Daily Post*, 5 February 1935, p. 12. See E. Smith, 'Jewish Responses to Political Anti-Semitism and Fascism in the East End of London, 1920–1939', in Kushner and Lunn, *Traditions of Intolerance*.

[57] *Association of Jewish Friendly Societies, Annual Report 1936* (London, 1936), pp. 4–5; *JC*, 31 July 1936, p. 20.

[58] *JC*, 31 July 1936, p. 22. In some of its publications, the Council actually called itself the Jewish Peoples' Council against Fascism and Anti-Semitism and the Board of Deputies.

[59] *The Leader*, December 1936, dubbed the council a 'rebel army' and castigated it for dividing Anglo-Jewry. The journal was also worried that it would lead to an identification of Jews with 'one party'. The ZFEC condemned the Federation of Zionist Youth for affiliating to the JPC: ZFEC, 11 January 1937, CZA, A295/6. For the debate on the JPC, see *YZ*, 12: 1 (January 1937), p. 8, 12: 3 (March 1937), p. 4.

magazine, *The Leader*, commented in August 1936 that 'There is no doubt that the hesitant and over-cautious attitude of the leaders is tending to make Jewry look elsewhere for the championship of Jewish rights.' In January 1937, it urged the reform of the Board to bring in the Jewish trade unions in order to end the necessity for their association with a 'political body', that is, the JPC.[60]

Popular dissatisfaction with the Board reached new heights at the time of Mosley's attempted march through the Jewish districts of Whitechapel and Stepney on 4 October 1936. The Board of Deputies and the 'semi-official' voice of Anglo-Jewry, the *Jewish Chronicle*, advised Jews to remain at home and avoid confrontations with the Blackshirts. Disregarding this warning, Jews in East London, led by the JPC, organized resistance in advance of the Fascist procession. At a late stage they received the official backing and formidable assistance of the Communist Party (CP).[61] Although Mosley's parade was blocked, violence against Jews in East London did not abate, nor did the fortunes of the BUF decline significantly. Violence continued and feelings of neglect ran high.[62]

The leadership of the Board of Deputies did not respond to the crisis until late July 1936, setting up a Co-ordinating Committee intended to bring together all existing anti-Fascist work. The committee also assumed a role in anti-defamation work and was responsible for a number of publications.[63] The policy and behaviour of the Jewish leadership may have been prudent and reasonable; in their eyes it certainly was the best that could reasonably have been expected given the resources of the Board and kindred bodies, and in the face of enormous demands at home and abroad. There is also evidence that they did have some success, particularly in terms of maintaining good relations with the authorities. However, much of this work was necessarily covert and fostered the impression that they were not doing enough. The fact that the Co-ordinating Committee did not change its title to Jewish Defence Committee until November 1938 and was persistently underfunded reinforced the appearance of complacency.[64] Addressing itself to the communal leadership, the *Leader* protested in November 1938 that 'While you play bridge in Golders Green, old people are living in the shadow of impending terror in Bethnal Green.'[65]

The mixed record of the Board on anti-Fascism and its lack-lustre defence of Jewish rights, such as Sunday trading, led rapidly to a questioning of the way

[60] *The Leader*, August 1936, January 1937.

[61] See J. Jacobs, *Out of the Ghetto: My Youth in the East End, Communism and Fascism, 1913–1939* (London, 1978), pp. 235–58 and, for the party line, P. Piratin, *Our Flag Stays Red* (London, 1980), pp. 17–27.

[62] See C. Thurlow, *Fascism in Britain: A History, 1918–1985* (Oxford, 1987), pp. 109–11 on 'Cable Street', and pp. 111–18 on its equivocal consequences.

[63] Lebzelter, *Political Anti-Semitism*, pp. 143–6; Alderman, *Jewish Community in British Politics*, p. 122.

[64] For examples of protests at the Board by Barnett Janner and Morris Myer, two tribunes of East End Jewry, see *ZR*, 19 January 1939, p. 6.

[65] *The Leader*, November 1938.

in which it functioned and its claim to be representative. Left-wing Jews attacked the Board because it did not adequately represent Jews in the East End, in the labour movement or in the broad Jewish lower-middle class. Demands were raised for the inclusion of the Jewish trade unions, the enlargement of the number of deputies alloted to the friendly societies and a review of the system of election based on the traditional synagogal constituencies.[66] The cumulative effect was to stoke the fires of disillusionment and the search for saviours from other quarters.

The Communist Party was one receptacle for Jewish discontent. It was the only party to adopt a militant anti-Fascist line and had organized opposition to the Blackshirts since the BUF's inception. Despite its prior equivocation, after the 'Battle of Cable Street' it became an instant myth that the CP had, virtually alone, defended the Jews of East London. The rewards were handsome, as large numbers of young Jews associated themselves with the party.[67] While the CP had always had a presence amongst East End Jews, during the 1930s its Stepney branch was swollen with Jewish recruits. A generation of gifted Jewish East End writers aligned themselves with the party and celebrated it in their novels of East End Jewish life.[68]

The Zionist movement was a casualty of the left's newly-won popularity, since both movements were competing for the same constituency of young, British-born Jews. Zionist youth groups were, consequently, the first to register the strength of communism in this section of the population.[69] The *Zionist Review*, organ of the Zionist Federation, ran a series of articles in 1935 on 'The Challenge of Communism'. The first article was prefaced with the comment that 'This subject is of growing importance, especially in the East End of London, where great difficulties are experienced in Zionist organizations, particularly among the youth, who, impelled by circumstance, regard everything only from the economic and material point of view.'[70] Early in 1933 the East London Young Zionist Association, which had been one of the strongest Zionist youth groups, was forced to merge with two other Jewish youth clubs in order to survive.[71] The senior Zionist movement noted in its annual report for that year that the East End was 'one of the greatest problems facing Anglo-Jewry'.[72] Explaining the situation in the area in 1934, the secretary of the

[66] *The Leader*, August 1936 and January 1937. 'Watchman' (Simon Gilbert), *JC*, 11 December 1936, p. 11. The Board discussed inconclusively the admission of trade unions, *JC*, 25 December 1936, p. 6. On Sunday trading, see *JC*, 22 May 1935, p. 62 and 1 May 1936, p. 14.

[67] For the views of contemporaries, see Piratin, *Our Flag Stays Red*, pp. 79–87, Jacobs, *Out of the Ghetto*, pp. 170–3, B. Sokoloff, *Edith and Stepney: The Life of Edith Ramsay* (London, 1987), pp. 69–82.

[68] The popularity of the CP can be inferred from its gains in Jewish districts of the East End in the national and local elections in 1945, Alderman, *Jewish Community in British Politics*, pp. 117–18 and Srebrnik, ' "Salud di Heldn!" ', p. 381. See also Smith, 'Jewish Responses'. For a similar pattern outside London, Williams, *Manchester Jewry*, p. 97. On this generation of Jewish writers, see K. Worpole, *Dockers and Detectives* (London, 1983), pp. 84–118.

[69] *YZ*, 6: 11 (December 1983), p. 137; *YZ*, 8: 8 (September 1934), p. 3.

[70] *ZR*, 2: 6:7 (August–September 1935), p. 89. The series, by J. L. Cohen, was later issued in pamphlet form by the Federation of Zionist Youth as *The Communist Challenge and the Zionist Reply* (London, 1936).

[71] *YZ*, 7: 2 (March 1933), p. 13.

[72] *Zionist Federation of Great Britain 34th Annual Report, 1933* (London, 1933), p. 75.

Association of Young Zionist Societies (AYZS) told the ZF executive that they 'were confronted in East London with the danger of Communism, which seemed to attract a good many young Jews'.[73] In fact, the Zionists had to fight to keep a foothold there. During 1935–9, the East End was the scene of fierce rivalry between the two ideologies, sometimes spilling over into street violence as the highly politicized, antagonistically oriented groups clashed with one another.[74]

The spread of a militantly anti-nationalist communism spelled a potential disaster for the Zionist movement which had always regarded East London as one of its strongest bases. Zionists were increasingly frustrated by the way in which the Board of Deputies seemed intent on propelling Jews into the ranks of the left.[75] Only an appreciation of this threat can explain the attitude of the Zionists towards the established communal authorities. It stimulated them to search for ways of reinvigorating the established Jewish communal organizations by making them more relevant to the Jewish population and added to their already strong inclination to launch an assault on the high points of communal government.[76]

IV

The compulsion which Zionists felt to reform communal authority merged with their historical antipathy towards the old Anglo-Jewish social elite and the leadership of the Board. Furthermore, it dovetailed with their urgent need to clear away a leadership which was not only a liability at home, but threatened to damage the Zionist project in Palestine. While the left had no interest in challenging the establishment's hegemony over communal institutions, the Zionists regarded the organized British Jewish community as important to their strategy. Anglo-Jewry served as a mediator between the British government and the Zionist movement. Since only British Jews could influence the electoral fortunes of the Members of Parliament and ministers of state who shaped the fortunes of Mandatory Palestine, it had a vital lobbying role that no other Jewish population could perform. All these elements conjoined to make the Zionist movement the single most determined and effective antagonist of the traditional authorities in Anglo-Jewry and accounts for their eventual replacement of the old regime by one that was not only more attuned to their ideology and aspirations, but was also dominated by a new leadership drawn from their own ranks.

Relations between Laski and the Zionist movement were at first cordial. He followed the example of his predecessor and involved himself in the work of the

[73] ZFEC, 3 October 1934, CZA, Z4/3565–ix.
[74] See, for example, *JC*, 1 February 1935, p. 24; *ZR*, 6: 2 (12 May 1938), p. 3; *JC*, 20 May 1938, p. 27 and 3 June 1938, pp. 32–3.
[75] For the *cri de coeur* of Moshe Rosetti, a leading Zionist, see *JC*, 24 August 1936, p. 28.
[76] *ZR*, 19 January 1939, p. 6 on Zionist efforts to reform Board.

enlarged Jewish Agency. However, it was not long before differences of approach to questions concerning Palestine began to divide him and his vice-president, Lionel Cohen, from the Zionist Federation. In 1933, Laski deflected a call by Zionist deputies for a protest about plans to deport Jews who were detected in Palestine without proper visas. Instead, he suggested that he and Cohen make a private visit to the Colonial Office. Once there, he told the Secretary of State, Sir Philip Cunliffe Lister, that 'their object was to discourage any idea of a formal deputation from the Board of Deputies'.[77] At the close of 1935, the government announced its intention to create a Legislative Council in Palestine that would have given Palestinian Arabs power to obstruct Jewish immigration. The Zionist movement was immediately up in arms and preparing public protests. They wanted the chief representative body of Anglo-Jewry to play a leading role in these demonstrations, but Laski told Waley Cohen privately that he hated the idea of 'all the paraphernalia of a raging, tearing campaign'.[78] Laski resisted and was only won round to a special protest conference on the condition that no other public activity should be organized. When Zionist deputies urged the Board to maintain pressure on the government they were stonewalled by Laski and Cohen.[79]

The next clash came over responses to the outbreak of rioting in Palestine in April 1936. The Board's Palestine Committee, which had a Zionist majority, drafted a resolution regretting the loss of life and damage to property and expressing support for the government's intention to uphold Jewish immigration and maintain the Mandate. Waley Cohen opposed this, putting forward an amendment which, among other points, called for round table talks to work out fundamental differences between Jews and Arabs. It was contested by the Zionist deputies and defeated heavily.[80] This was a severe blow to the prestige of Waley Cohen and the Board's officers, but it had more profound implications for the balance of power between the old leadership and the Zionist opposition and its allies. Since the Zionists controlled the Palestine Committee which formulated policy for the Board and now appeared able to muster a majority of deputies for that policy, Laski and his colleagues were virtually their prisoners. Henceforward, if they wished to promote the views of non-Zionist Jews in Britain and to combat Zionist initiatives with which they disagreed, they had to resort to private diplomacy – disclosure of which only further aggravated the Zionists.

[77] Joint Foreign Committee, Minutes, 15 November 1933, BDA; Memorandum on behalf of the Secretary of State, 23 January 1934, Public Record Office (PRO), C0733/255/5. Laski made a later offer to spy on the Jewish Agency, Laski to Cunliffe Lister, 31 July 1934, PRO, C0733/266/10.

[78] *ZR*, 2: 11 (January 1936), p. 167 for the Zionist reaction; Laski to Waley Cohen, 15 January 1936, BDA, E3/210. Waley Cohen concurred: Waley Cohen to Laski, 31 January 1936, BDA, E3/210.

[79] Laski to Waley Cohen, 5 January 1936, BDA, E3/210 and Board of Deputies Palestine Committee Board of Deputies Palestine Committee, Minutes, BDA (hereafter BDPC), 13 January 1936; BOD, Vol. 27, 15 March 1936.

[80] BDPC, 7 July 1936 and 16 July 1936; *JC*, 24 July 1936, p. 27; *ZR*, 3: 5/6 (July–August 1936), p. 80.

The private diplomacy of the non-Zionists reached its zenith during and after the deliberations of the Royal Commission appointed in May 1936 to investigate the causes of the violence in Palestine. Its report, published in July 1937, recommended the partition of Palestine into separate Jewish and Arab states. This conclusion threw British Jews who had always regarded a Jewish State as anathema into a dilemma since, as loyal citizens, they were compelled to accept government policy.[81] Their only recourse lay in either proving that the Mandate over a united Palestine was still viable or compelling the government to drop partition.

In pursuit of the former course, Laski obtained several memoranda on the Palestine question from Albert Hyamson and Norman Bentwich, former officials in the Palestine administration, who were equally dismayed at the prospect of partition.[82] Through these contacts, he was kept abreast of negotiations with various Arab figures and pro-Arab lobbyists.[83] While these interchanges were conducted initially with the consent of the Zionists and the Jewish Agency, the Jewish representatives went much further than was considered acceptable, agreeing to abrogate the right of free immigration into Palestine and consenting to a fixed percentage of Jews in the total population. The Zionists, disenchanted with their go-betweens and suspicious of their motives, dropped them. Lord Melchett complained typically to Weizmann that 'Hyamson is carrying on some secret intrigue with the Foreign Office independently, which he has not told me about.'[84]

With the second option in view, the Anglo-Jewish elite considered a public *démarche* in the style of May 1917, hoping to scuttle partition by the weight of their collective prestige. To this end a meeting was held in July 1937 in New Court, business headquarters of the Rothschild family, to draft a public declaration. The attendance was strikingly similar to the communal line-up twenty years previously: Anthony de Rothschild, Osmond d'Avigdor Goldsmid, Sir Robert Waley Cohen, Lionel Montagu, Leonard Montefiore, Sir Isidore Salmon and Neville Laski amongst other notables. Perhaps with the effects of the manifesto of 1917 in mind, no declaration was issued.[85] However, a further opportunity offered itself later in the year. In August 1937, Weizmann had hoped to placate Anglo-Jewish opposition to partition by inviting leading figures

[81] See the letters to Laski from Sir Isidore Salmon, 9 July 1937, Lord Bearsted, 12 July 1937 and Lionel Cohen, 12 July 1937, BDA, E3/236.

[82] 'Policy in Palestine', A. M. Hyamson, 12 November 1936, BDA, E3/234. Laski to Hyamson, 12 November 1936, and letters to Waley Cohen, Lionel Cohen, d'Avigdor Goldsmid and others, 23–4 November 1936, BDA, E3/234; 'Proposals for a Settlement of the Palestine Problem', A. M. Hyamson, 26 May 1937, BDa, E3/236.

[83] 'Memorandum on the Possible Basis for Arab-Jewish Negotiations', N. Bentwich, 14 July 1937, BDA, E3/237; Hyamson to Laski, 19 July 1937, BDA, B4/HU15; Bentwich to Laski, 20 July 1937, BDA, E3/237. 'Resumé of Correspondence and Documents in Connection with Palestine', A. M. Hyamson, and Hyamson–Laski correspondence, BDA, B4/HU15.

[84] Melchett to Weizmann, 20 December 1937, Weizmann Archive, Rehovot, Israel (WA). For the complex international context, see S. Dothan, 'Attempts at an Arab-Jewish Agreement in Palestine During the Thirties', *Zionism*, 2 (1980), pp. 213–38.

[85] 'Memorandum of Meeting at New Court', 19 July 1937, BDA, E3/237.

in Anglo-Jewry to join a Political Committee which would take part in policy discussions. Lord Reading, Lionel Cohen and d'Avigdor Goldsmid consented on condition that they could make their position known to the Colonial Office. They did so in a memorandum produced three months later that turned out to be a classic statement of the anti-Zionist case against a Jewish State. The document, to which the President of the Board had appended his name, too, was due for delivery at a time when it appeared that the British Cabinet's decision on partition hung in the balance and Weizmann was desperately trying to impress the government with evidence of Jewish enthusiasm for statehood. He was outraged when news of it reached him. His aides in London, the Jewish Agency and the Zionist Federation were pressed into action to crush what they perceived as treachery.[86]

Lionel Cohen, Waley Cohen, d'Avigdor Goldsmid and Laski were subjected to formal censure at a meeting of the British Section of the Jewish Agency. Laski and Cohen were later upbraided at a special meeting of the Board's Palestine Committee.[87] The Palestine Committee then adopted a resolution declaring the support of Anglo-Jewry for a Jewish State – in the form of a Dominion within the British Empire. This resolution, which was identical to one which had been formulated by the Zionist Federation, was then put before the Board of Deputies in January 1938 and passed by an overwhelming majority. Only the honorary officers stood against it; afterwards, Lionel Cohen resigned as vice-president.[88]

From this point, the Zionist bloc of deputies at the Board were ascendant. In the election to replace Cohen, they championed the candidacy of Dr Israel Feldman, the pro-Zionist chairman of the Palestine Committee, against Otto Schiff, a philanthropist from the old social elite. It was a contest unprecedented for its liveliness and dirtiness. Attitudes towards Palestine and communal democracy were pushed to the forefront as Schiff was smeared as an anti-zionist and an oligarch. Feldman won: his victory signified the decisive shift in power that had occurred over the preceding five years.[89] The JFC, which Laski and Montefiore still controlled, became the next target of the Zionist press and deputies who asserted that it was not being bold enough in respect of the claims for Jewish refugee immigration into Palestine. The

[86] 'Non-Zionist Memorandum to the Secretary of State for the Colonies', enclosure, Lionel Cohen to Arthur Lourie, 17 November 1937, WA; Weizmann to Arthur Lourie, Jewish Agency, 20 November 1937, ed. A. Klieman, *Letters and Papers of Chaim Weizmann*, vol. 18 (Jerusalem, 1979), pp. 246–7; for the Whitehall aspect, see ed. N. Rose, *Baffy. The Diaries of Blanche Dugdale*, (London, 1973), 8 December 1937, p. 69, 11 December 1937, p. 70.

[87] Jewish Agency for Palestine, British Section, Minutes, BDA, 23 November 1937; BDPC, 1 December 1937.

[88] BDPC, 10 January 1938; BOD, vol. 28, 16 January 1938; *JC*, 21 January 1938, p. 8, 28 January 1938, p. 30; *ZR*, 5: 1 (January 1938), pp. 7–9, 11–12. For the resignation of Cohen, *Board of Deputies 88th Annual Report*, 1938 (London, 1939), p. 32.

[89] For the campaign, see *JC*, 11 February 1938, pp. 8, 13; 18 February 1938, pp. 8, 17; and 25 February 1938, p. 8; *ZR*, 5: 2 (February 1938), pp. 19–20. For the lobbying by the Zionist group, see ZFEC, 6 March 1938, CZA, A159/6. Cf. G. Shimoni, 'The Non-Zionists in Anglo-Jewry, 1937–1948', *Jewish Journal of Sociology*, 28: 2 (1986), pp. 91–6.

campaign against the JFC was redolent with democratic rhetoric, linking it to the attack on the traditional communal elites. The *Zionist Review*, for example, declared that 'The JFC ... survives like an antediluvian relic ... Why then is it kept alive? Because it holds the fort for assimilationism. Because it keeps official Anglo-Jewry out of the integrities of Jewish life.'[90]

The figureheads of Anglo-Jewry – most notably Laski – continued their public criticism of Zionist policy during 1939. This fuelled the rage of the Zionists who regarded dissent as a betrayal of what was now, thanks to their control of the Board, 'official' communal policy.[91] However, the outbreak of war in September 1939 offered Laski and his allies a chance to put the lid on communal politics for the duration. They proposed the creation of a small wartime executive and a suspension of the Board's meetings. This expedient was strenuously opposed by the Zionists at the Board – it was the occasion for Brodetsky's maiden speech – and blocked. Instead, the Zionist faction put forward proposals for the enlargement of the JFC and the creation of a democratic executive that would dilute the influence of the honorary officers.[92] At the Board's meeting on 19 November, when these matters were due to come to a head, Laski announced unexpectedly that he was resigning from the Presidency.[93] In the lobbying to find a new official leader of British Jewry Laski promoted Anthony de Rothschild who was, however, unwilling to enter the electoral ring and suggested H. L. Nathan instead. The Zionists campaigned actively and powerfully for the choice of Brodetsky. Weizmann, Simon Marks and the Zionist Federation emerged as the kingmakers; they made it clear that they would not tolerate the appointment of either Rothschild or Nathan so, in the absence of a suitable alternative, Brodetsky was elected.[94]

Brodetsky's presidency was a formal acknowledgement of what had, in effect, been the case for the previous five years.[95] The Board and its leaders had ceased to represent the mass of British Jewry. During the 1920s there was a stalemate in communal politics that gradually evolved into a virtual system of 'dual power'. By the 1930s, the friendly societies and the Zionist Federation were making policy and implementing it autonomously. When they were able to, they imposed their line on the Board's reluctant leadership, but frustration and irritation with this haphazard system led them finally to assume direct control.

[90] *ZR*, 6: 35 (30 December 1938), pp. 10–11. The drive to reform the Board had continued unabated during 1933–7. The focus on the JFC was heightened in 1938, *ZR*, 6: 9 (23 June 1938), p. 13; and 6: 10 (17 July 1938), pp. 5–6.

[91] The *Evening Standard* cited Lionel and Anthony de Rothschild, Lionel Cohen and Leonard Montefiore as Jewish anti-Zionists, 10 March 1939. Laski published his reservations about Zionist policy and Jewish statehood in *Jewish Rights and Jewish Wrongs*, pp. 149–50 and 153–5.

[92] BOD, 12 September 1939; 1 October 1939; *ZR*, 6: 78 (19 October 1939), p. 11; 6: 78 (26 October 1939), p. 1; 6: 79 (9 November 1939), pp. 3–4.

[93] BOD, Vol. 29, 19 November 1939; *ZR*, 6: 81 (23 November 1939), pp. 2–3.

[94] Anthony de Rothschild to Weizmann, 1 December 1939, WA; Bakstansky to Brodetsky, 7 December 1939 and 8 December 1939, CZA, A82/89/1; ZF Public Relations Committee circular, 8 December 1939, CZA, A82/9/4; BOD, 19 December 1939.

[95] Cf. Shimoni, 'Selig Brodetsky and the Ascendency of Zionism', p. 125.

Yet the success of the insurgency would not have been conceivable without – was itself consequent upon – the restructuring of Jewish society in Britain.

V

World War I had a differential impact on particular sections of the Jewish population. The old families suffered a haemorrhaging of wealth through taxation, inflation and death duties. By contrast, the war years saw the enrichment of a stratum of the Jewish immigrant population that was active in sectors of the economy boosted by government contracts. Since the young male members of the old social elite were usually gazetted as officers, amongst whom casualties were the heaviest, they suffered disproportionately severe losses. The war eliminated from the ranks of the pre-1914 establishment capable young men who might have assumed the reins of communal government.[96]

Wartime prosperity accelerated the relocation of the Jewish population from the areas of first-settlement in the inner cities to the suburbs, a process which continued steadily during the inter-war years. Although the East End of London still contained over 100,000 Jews in the 1930s, there were now major centres in North-West, North, and North-East London comprising the more prosperous and, hence, socially mobile elements. In new districts like Hackney in London, Chapeltown in Leeds, Cheetham Hill in Manchester and Battle-field in Glasgow, first-generation British-born Jews established tightly knit ethnic neighbourhoods built around the synagogue – often serving as a community centre – the friendly society and the Zionist society. These institutions were bedded into the communities which they served; they became the local institutional foci and also the points of reference for a second-generation identity.[97]

The Zionist movement, the B'nai B'rith and the friendly societies followed the Jewish migration to the suburbs.[98] Their rank and file and leadership was reflective of the changed social composition of British Jewry. A majority of the council of the Zionist Federation, for example, were employed in the professions, manufacturing, financial or service industries. Nearly 10 per cent were women. Over half were immigrants and almost all were either first- or second-

---

[96] On the effects of taxation, Lucy Cohen, *Some Recollections of Claude Goldsmid Montefiore* (London, 1940), pp. 145, 198, C. Bermant, *The Cousinhood* (London, 1971), p. 326 and Finestein, 'Anglo-Jewry since 1933', p. 20; on the loss of sons, see Herbert Loewe, *Israel Abrahams: A Biographical Sketch* (London, 1944), p. 82. For the prosperity of the war years, see the annual reports of the Board of Guardians for the Relief of the Jewish Poor, 1915–1918. Bush, *Behind the Lines*, pp. 110–11, 185. Cf. Cohen, *English Zionists and British Jews*, pp. 267–8.

[97] See Lipman, *Social History*, pp. 168–70, 172; H. Pollins, *Economic History of the Jews in England*, (East Brunswick, NJ, 1982), p. 184; Williams, *Manchester Jewry*, p. 98; E. Krausz, *Leeds Jewry: Its History and Social Structure* (Cambridge, 1963), pp. 22–4; N. Kokosalkis, *Ethnic Identity and Religion: Tradition and Change in Liverpool Jewry* (Washington, DC, 1982), p. 156; Collins, *Aspects of Scottish Jewry*, p. 26.

[98] For the location of Zionist societies, see *Anglo-Jewish Year Books, 1918–39*; *Order Achei Brith 39th Annual Report, 1926–1927* (London, 1927).

generation British citizens. By contrast, the honorary officers of the Board of Deputies, the Anglo-Jewish Association and the United Synagogue between 1920 and 1940 were overwhelmingly British-born; there were no women in the hierarchies of any of these bodies.[99] The same phenomenon was evident in the rabbinate. In the 1920s, the Jewish press was prone to lament the ineffectuality of rabbis and their subservience to the lay leadership of the synagogues. This began to change in the late 1920s and 1930s with the appointment of rabbis who came from an immigrant background, but combined a British education with traditional *yeshiva* training. These young ministers, presiding over expanding suburban congregations, took an active part in communal affairs and Zionist politics. They articulated the increasing dissonance between the ethnic *Weltanschauung* of Jewish neighbourhoods and the denominational self-identity of the old leadership, most of which was domiciled either in fashionable, non-Jewish districts or in semi-rural retreats.[100]

A vital stage in the supersession of the old elite by the 'new men' and women of Anglo-Jewry was played out through the redrawing of patterns of philanthropy. The old leadership had always derived authority from its ability to finance the provision of welfare and education services. However, the effects of World War I and high levels of taxation in the inter-war years reduced their capacity for largesse. Many members of the old families derived their wealth from outmoded and declining sources of income, often living simply as rentiers. The *nouveaux riches* in the Jewish population were connected with waxing new enterprises: these men and their families, almost all of immigrant birth or first-generation British-born, identified themselves with the Zionist movement and with the insurgent faction in the Jewish middle class which chafed under the continued rule of the old families. They were also prepared to back up their convictions with their increasingly ample resources.[101]

In the 1920s, large sums were raised for traditional eleemosynary causes such as the Board of Guardians, the Jewish Religious Education Board and the London Jewish Hospital. The total amounts collected for these appeals ranged from £10,000 to £50,000, with substantial initial contributions from long-standing communal patrons. However, these sums were dwarfed by the munificence of Bernhard Baron, the immigrant cigarette magnate, who in 1925 alone gave away £70,000 followed by £50,000 in 1926 to the Keren Hayesod

[99] This analysis is based on lists of personnel contained in *Zionist Federation Annual Report, Anglo-Jewish Year Book*, 1920–40, and obituaries in the *Anglo-Jewish Year Book, Zionist Yearbook* (London, 1950 et seq.), *Jewish Chronicle*, 1950–70.

[100] For the lay leadership's objections to 'Pulpit Tirades' by Rabbis Louis Rabbinowitz (Cricklewood), Bernard Cherrick (Stoke Newington) and Saul Amias (Edgware), see United Synagogue Honorary Officers, Minutes, 24 April 1939, 8 May 1939 and appended letter, Hertz to Waley Cohen, 4 May 1939, USA.

[101] For example, Bernhard Baron (cigarette manufacture), Montague Burton (garment manufacture), Oscar Deutsch (cinema chains), Sigmund Gestetner (copying machines), Michael and Ephraim Goldberg (Glasgow department stores), Alfred and Henry Mond (chemical engineering), Simon Marks, Harry Sacher, Israel Sieff (chain stores), Isaac Wolfson (mail order). Pollins, *Economic History of Jew*, pp. 194–208 and *passim*.

(Palestine Foundation Fund).[102] The evidence of a shift in money power was accentuated by the massive fund-raising efforts to meet the crises of the 1930s. In the annual appeals for the Central British Fund (CBF) founded in 1933, for the relief and resettlement of German Jewish refugees, followed by the Council for German Jewry in 1936, the interrelated families of Simon Marks, Israel Sieff and Harry Sacher out-donated even the Rothschilds. The contributions of Claude Montefiore, Sir Robert Waley Cohen, the Sassoons and the Samuels paled by comparison.[103] In a Jewish society whose voluntary organizations depended upon princely donations, where authority and wealth were inter-mingled, this was more than symbolic. It was apparent that an alternative potential leadership stood in the wings; it had proved its administrative competence and demonstrated its capacity to support communal institutions. The awareness that there was less reason than ever before to cling to the old cadres underlay the confident move in 1939–40 to supplant the *ancien régime* with one closer and more congenial to the mass of British Jews.

VI

The transformation of communal authority in Anglo-Jewry can be understood as a shift of power from one section of the Jewish middle class to another. The years of World War I and the 1920s saw the growth and consolidation of the Jewish middle and lower-middle class, fractions of the bourgeoisie that had more in common with one another than with the upper-middle class social elite.[104] The political exclusion practised by the old hierarchy generated frustration and resentment, while its apparent incompetence threatened to benefit the left in the Jewish population, which was even more distressing. Although the left championed democracy, it was unacceptable as a vehicle for change because of its radical social doctrines and was, anyway, hardly interested in communal authority. The Zionists, by contrast, demanded and needed the democratization of communal institutions; they provided a coherent ideology which explained the crises which Jews faced and offered palatable solutions. Middle-class Jews in the suburbs were, therefore, able to rally behind the popular-democratic rhetoric of the Jewish national movement, which had the

---

[102] Major charitable donations were recorded in 'Notable Events', *Anglo-Jewish Year Book*, 1920–1927.

[103] The lists of donors were published in the *Jewish Chronicle* after each appeal. See also 'List of Subscriptions to the First Three Appeals of the CBF', CZA, A173/39.

[104] There is a persistent tendency in the historiography to label the elite as an 'aristocracy' and to employ the term 'Grand Dukes' coined by the Russian-born Zionist writer Nahum Sokolow. This is a fundamental error which distorts any reading of intra-communal Jewish politics. The elite was essentially an *haute bourgeoisie*: they were bankers, financiers, some of them manufacturers, who had been recently ennobled and their social outlook was that of the Victorian bourgeoisie rather than a feudal, landed ruling class. See J. Harris and P. Thane, 'British and European Bankers 1880–1914: An 'Aristocratic Bourgeoisie''?' in eds. P. Thane et al., *The Power of the Past* (Cambridge, 1984), pp. 215–34.

organization, the financial backing and the motivation to seize the reins of communal government.

The outcome was the displacement of the old leadership and the triumph of Zionism. This did not lead to an exodus of British Jews of Palestine: in practical terms the agenda of the Zionists in Britain was oriented entirely towards domestic affairs. The ideology of the movement, as in other countries, provided a viable Jewish identity which enabled Jews to remain in the Diaspora and a rhetoric of revolt for middle-class elements denied access to communal power.[105] The 'ascendancy' of Zionism was, thus, a phenomena which must be comprehended in a specific, local context. In this sense it was part of the renegotiation of Anglo-Jewish identity which occurred during the inter-war period as the meaning and content of that identity was adjusted to accord with the new Jewish social constellation. Zionism was the vehicle for a middle-class Jewish ethnic identity which first- and second-generation British Jews constructed through ethnic neighbourhoods, community organization and their immigrant heritage. This process of redefinition was bound to have an impact on patterns of communal authority. Before 1914, authority had rested on wealth, degree of Anglicization and duration of settlement in Britain. After the mid-1930s, it derived from wealth, ethnic identification via Zionism, and immigrant credentials.

Zionism was the ideological container for this transformation, since effective alternatives did not exist. Jewish religious orthodoxy had been eroded by prior phases of Anglicization and secularization; a secular Jewish identity drawn from the Jewish socialist, autonomist tradition of Eastern Europe could have little purchase on an upwardly mobile middle-class Jewish population. Since ethnicity as a fully developed political idea, the basis for a social movement, did not exist in Britain at this time, Zionism was its surrogate and shibboleth. As in British society, shifts in the ideological and political hegemony were conjunctural with processes of economic and social change. It is only through the integrated analysis of these forces that it becomes possible to understand the transformation of Jewish society in Britain and the forms of authority within it.

---

[105] D. Cesarani, 'Zionism in England, 1917–1939', D. Phil. thesis (Oxford University, 1986), pp. 416–21; Y. Shapiro, *The Leadership of the American Zionist Organization* (Urbana, Ill., 1971), p. 5; S. Poppel, *Zionism in Germany* (Philadelphia, 1977), p. 92.

8

Jews and Politics in the East End of London, 1918–1939

Elaine R. Smith

The years 1918 to 1939 are distinctive in the history of the Jewish community in the East End of London. The generation which came of age then consisted primarily of English-born Jews eager to participate in local politics. Indeed, the very Englishness of these Jews facilitated their ability to communicate with their non-Jewish counterparts. Although active in general political organizations, these East End Jews were also anxious to preserve their distinct ethnic identity. The present study is an inquiry into some of the major issues concerning the East End Jewish community and its involvement in politics in the inter-war years. Firstly, what was the socio-economic background of those Jews who became involved in politics? Together with the forces of migration, Anglicization and assimilation, socio-economic factors had an important impact on the class structure of the community and thus on its political affiliations. Secondly, did East End Jews have a collective identity as Jews? Thirdly, were there any specifically Jewish issues they addressed? Finally, did Jewish political activists experience any conflict between their Jewish interests and their general political interests?[1]

The inter-war period marked a new and important stage in the evolution of the East End Jewish community. Jews who became active in the political life of the area after 1918 were either the English-born children of the immigrant generation or had spent most of their lives in England. They had received their education at local London County Council schools where they had become Anglicized if not fully integrated into the local non-Jewish society. A further important point about the post-1918 East End Jewish community was that it

---

[1] For a full discussion of these issues see Elaine Smith, 'East End Jews in Politics, 1918–1939: A Study in Class and Ethnicity', Ph.D thesis (University of Leicester).

was almost entirely working-class. This was in sharp contrast to the situation before 1914 when the community had contained comparatively prosperous Jews who were able to set up their own small business or to buy cheap local housing as an investment.[2] As soon as it became practical for them to do so, these upwardly mobile Jews began to move away from the narrow confines of the ghetto to North-East and North-West London. Thus the East End Jewish community before 1914, with its upwardly mobile elements who had not yet moved out of the area, was marked by a far greater degree of social diversity than that which characterized the community after World War I. The social cohesiveness of the Jewish East End after 1918, as compared with the relatively diverse social and economic structure of the community before 1914, proved to bc of fundamental importance in shaping the community's political allegiances.

Despite the major changes which were taking place in the nature of the community, the Jewish East End remained in some senses an enclosed, ghetto community. Social and work contact, even for young English-born Jews who had received their education at local London County Council schools, continued to be conducted in a predominantly Jewish environment.[3] Yet, according to one contemporary observer, the most striking characteristic of the East End Jewish community, particularly of the youth, was the extent to which it had become assimilated into the English working class.[4] William Zukerman, an American journalist, attributed this advanced degree of assimilation to two factors. Firstly, the period of Jewish immigrant life in England was too short-lived and the number of immigrants who entered too small to leave a lasting influence on the second generation. Secondly, the young English-born Jews 'grew up in the midst of the English working class, and were assimilated to it'.[5] There is some evidence to indicate that young Jews, especially those inclined to radical left-wing politics, had become assimilated to the English working class.[6] However, Zukerman over-emphasizes the completeness of the process in denying the existence of a separate Jewish identity. It was not true to suggest 'that what goes under the name of the East End Jew is in reality no specific Jewish type at all. It is but the general East London Labour type with which the young East End Jew has assimilated so thoroughly that it is difficult to differentiate between the two.'[7] A more satisfactory analysis of the situation was provided by a prominent member of the Workers' Circle Friendly Society. Referring to the decline of Yiddish as a spoken language among young East

[2] C. Russell and H. S. Lewis, *The Jew in London: A Study of Racial Character and Present Day Conditions* (London, 1900), pp. 17, 57–60.

[3] Interview with Moshe Rosette (Tel Aviv, April 1987). The *East London Observer (ELO)* reinforced the community's sense of separateness by running a weekly column entitled 'Ghetto Gossip'. The column first appeared on 8 January 1927.

[4] W. Zukerman, *The Jew in Revolt* (London 1937), pp. 69–73. On the level of Anglicization among East End Jews see the *ELO*, 14 January 1928, p. 4.

[5] Zukerman, *The Jew in Revolt*, p. 70.

[6] See, for example, M. Cohen, *I was One of the Unemployed* (London, 1945). See also the novel by S. Blumenfeld, *Jew Boy* (2nd edn; London, 1986).

[7] Zukerman, *The Jew in Revolt*, pp. 72–3.

End Jews, Dr I. N. Steinberg concluded that, although these Jews were 'divorced from Jewish tradition, and as a consequence are removed from the Jewish masses' they could not assimilate themselves with the English working class because they did not possess a common tradition.[8]

The decline of Yiddish among the second generation separated young English-speaking Jews from the immigrant world of their parents.[9] Many young East End Jews also remained aloof from organized Jewish activities.[10] For example, the Jewish friendly societies movement which had originated in the East End showed a steady decline in membership during the inter-war years. This downward trend was attributed to the failure to attract Jewish youth in sufficiently large numbers.[11] It was, however, in the sphere of religious observance that young Jewish East Enders became most alienated from the culture and traditions of their parents. As early as 1919 a Zionist magazine argued that it was useless to attempt to shepherd young Jews into a synagogue.[12] Concern about the decline in religious observance among working-class Jews was frequently expressed by London Jewry's lay and religious leaders in the 1920s and 1930s. In 1928 the Independent Order of B'nai B'rith organized a symposium at which leading Anglo-Jewish communal figures expressed their concern at the way in which 'the East End had got right away from religion'.[13] This was attributed to the fact that young Jews felt alienated from the foreign, Yiddish-speaking rabbis who served the small Federation synagogues in the East End. Ernest Lesser, chairman of the United Synagogue's Welfare Committee, expressed this succinctly: 'the children grew up out of sympathy with the foreign atmosphere and ritual of the synagogue, and consequently the synagogue did not make the appeal it should make.'[14]

A number of initiatives were suggested to reverse the trend towards secularization. For example, a series of letters published in the *Jewish Chronicle* at the beginning of 1919 emphasized the need for resident ministers in the East End.[15] Rabbi Dr Meir Jung, Chief Minister of the Federation of Synagogues, felt that the answer to the decline in orthodoxy in the East End lay in more religious education.[16] To this end, he founded the Sinai League which aimed 'to preserve and promote traditional Judaism amongst Jewish young men and women'.[17] The League was based in Whitechapel and became the launching

---

[8] *The Circle*, October 1934, p. 2.

[9] On the decline of Yiddish see *The New Survey of London Life and Labour*, vol. VI (London, 1934), pp. 291–2; *The Circle*, November 1934, p. 5; *East London Advertiser* (*ELA*), 10 March 1934, p. 3.

[10] *Jewish World*, 11 January 1934, p. 8.

[11] *Zionist Review* (*ZR*), January 1935, p. 167; *Order 'Achei Brith' and 'Shield of Abraham': 46th Annual Report and Balance Sheet* (London, 1934).

[12] *Junior Zionist*, supplement to *Zionist Review*, April 1919, p. 9.

[13] *Jewish Graphic*, 3 February 1928, p. 3; *Jewish Guardian*, 3 February 1928, p. 5.

[14] Ibid. An article in *The Times* also drew attention to the decline in religious observance among second-generation English-born Jews. See *The Times*, 28 November 1924, p. 16.

[15] See, for example, *JC*, 14 February 1919, p. 6.

[16] Ibid., 28 February 1919, p. 22.

[17] The Sinai League (file), Moses Gaster MSS, University College London. See also *The Sinaist*, 3:1 (February 1919).

pad for a network of Sinai Associations throughout London.[18] Another serious attempt to deal with the problem was the Reconstruction movement which was initiated in 1919 by the Rev. Joseph Stern, minister of the East London Synagogue in Stepney Green.[19] The movement was supported by such communal luminaries as the Rev. A. A. Green, minister of Hampstead Synagogue, and Henrietta Adler who, as well as being the author of the Jewish study in *The New Survey of London Life and Labour*, was a well-known Jewish communal worker and granddaughter of a former Chief Rabbi. Reconstruction embodied the paternalistic idea that West End Jews should offer their services as voluntary workers in order to raise the spiritual standards of East End Jewry.[20] From the late 1920s, the idea began to circulate in the Jewish press that in order to attract young East End Jews to the synagogue a concerted effort should be made to 're-Judaize' the East End.[21] In 1935 there was even a suggestion that the social activities of the youth should be 'Judaized' by instilling in Jewish youth clubs a strong religious bias.[22] However, despite all the initiatives suggested and the attempts made to revive religion in the East End, young Jews continued to drift away from the synagogue and to reject traditional Jewish values. The *Zionist Review*'s conclusion in 1935 that 'religion does not dominate Jewish life in the East End' was therefore correct.[23] For example, one eyewitness has reported how Jews from the East End flocked to the West End on Friday evening at the start of the Jewish sabbath.[24] In addition, regret was expressed at the time by West End Jews that East End Jews sought amusement 'in such places as the dance hall, the billiard saloon, and similar places'.[25] Nevertheless, it has been pointed out that although young Jews were not practising their religion as much as their parents, and indeed were increasingly questioning the whole concept of religion, they still considered themselves to be Jews and were prepared to defend themselves against external threats such as anti-semitism.[26] This astute analysis encapsulates the important fact that East End Jews retained a sense of community even when they rejected their religious identity. This had important implications for the political activities and loyalties of East End Jews.

Although Stepney followed the rest of working-class London in its general political outlook, specific ethnic factors did have a unique impact on local political allegiances. This impact was not powerful enough to push Stepney in an opposite political direction from the rest of working-class London. It was,

[18] G. Alderman, *The Federation of Synagogues, 1887–1987* (London, 1987), pp. 48–9.
[19] *JC*, 31 January 1919, p. 6.
[20] *JC*, 14 February 1919, p. 6.
[21] See, for example, *Jewish Guardian*, 11 March 1927, p. 11.
[22] *Jewish Daily Post*, 5 June 1935, p. 6.
[23] *ZR*, January 1935, p. 167.
[24] J. Jacobs, *Out of the Ghetto: My Youth in the East End. Communism and Fascism, 1913–1939* (London, 1978), p. 119. For further accounts of the extent to which the Jewish sabbath was flouted by East End Jews see *ELA*, 8 January 1927, p. 6; 15 January 1927, p. 3.
[25] *Jewish Guardian*, 3 February 1928, p. 5.
[26] Jacobs, *Out of the Ghetto*, p. 190.

nevertheless, sufficiently strong to make a mark on the political landscape in the Jewish East End. There were, for example, distinct Jewish attitudes to both the Conservative and Liberal Parties. These attitudes explain why the Conservatives enjoyed so little support in the Jewish areas of the East End and why the Liberals continued to enjoy the support and loyalty of some East End Jews until relatively late in the period. As the party associated in the minds of working-class Jews with the anti-alien legislation of 1905 and 1919, the Conservative Party was deeply unpopular in the Jewish East End. At the 1922 general election, there was even an attempt to urge Jews not to vote Conservative. In an appeal published in the *Jewish Chronicle*, Shlomo Kaplansky, a Palestinian representative of the socialist Zionist party, Poale Zion, who was in London at the time, argued that a Conservative victory would mean an intensification of anti-foreign feeling and anti-alien legislation.[27] However, not all Jews accepted that Conservatism was incompatible with Jewish interests. Indeed, as late as 1938, one Jewish Conservative in Stepney believed that 'the principles of true Conservatism are the only principles to which as Jews they can adhere, for what more conservative religion based on heritage and historic custom is there than the Jewish religion?'[28] The participation of Jews in the local branches of the Conservative Party was confirmation that this analysis was not the preserve of an isolated individual.

Among the most prominent Jewish Conservatives in Stepney were Adolph Ludlow (formerly Ludski), Joseph Emden, Rabbi B. N. Michaelson, Lewis Beber, Lionel Franks and G. E. Abrahams. Ludlow twice stood unsuccessfully in London County Council (LCC) elections as a Municipal Reform candidate for Whitechapel.[29] He was connected with the Junior Imperial League, the forerunner of the Young Conservatives, and he was an executive member of the Union of Stepney Ratepayers, an anti-socialist alliance. In addition, Ludlow was, for a time, vice-president of the Whitechapel and St George's Conservative Association. As a rising star in the Zionist movement in England, he was honorary secretary of the English Zionist Federation (EZF).[30] Emden was a colourful character who frequently had letters published in the East London press espousing his beliefs as a Conservative trade unionist. He was a vice-president of the Mile End Conservative Association and was chairman of both the Mile End and East London branches of the Junior Imperial League.[31] In addition, he was vice-chairman of the London Federation of Conservatives.[32] Rabbi Michaelson, a communal worker who was attached to the Jewish Institute in Stepney, was chairman of the Mile End West ward Conservative

[27] *JC*, 10 November 1922, p. 13.
[28] *ELA*, 23 April 1938, p. 6.
[29] This was in 1919 and 1925. See *East London Handbook*, 1919, p. 11; *ELA*, 28 February 1925, p. 4.
[30] *ELA*, 28 February 1925, p. 4; *ELO*, 22 October 1927, p. 4. For additional information about Ludlow I am grateful to the late Percy Cohen, CBE, head of Library and Information at Conservative Central Office, 1928–48.
[31] *ELA*, 8 July 1933, p. 3; 2 March 1935, p. 2; 8 February 1936, p. 8; 15 February 1936, p. 3.
[32] *ELA*, 10 April 1937, p. 5.

Association. He was also a councillor in Mile End during the years 1928 to 1934.[33] Beber was chairman of the Mile End Conservative Association.[34] Despite the involvement of these individuals in local Conservative associations, the political loyalties of the East End Jewish community did not lie with the Conservative Party.

In contrast to the Conservatives, the Liberal Party in the East End retained the fidelity of sections of the Jewish community. This was despite the fact that after 1918 the Liberal Party had entered a period of irreversible decline at the national level and was rapidly becoming a political irrelevance. Three main reasons can be cited to explain the survival of Jewish support for the Liberals in the East End. First, as the party which had granted Jews political emancipation in the nineteenth century, the Liberals were still able to claim the support of a minority of Jewish political activists in the East End. Secondly, the Liberal Party enjoyed the patronage of a number of prominent local Jewish communal personalities. The presence of these individuals in the party created the impression that Liberalism was still a viable force in the area even though in fact the local party organizations were little more than hollow shells. Thirdly, the Whitechapel Liberal Party's election campaign for the parliamentary by-election of November 1930 and Barnett Janner's subsequent victory in Whitechapel in the 1931 general election inaugurated an impressive, albeit brief, revival in the local Liberal Party's fortunes.[35]

The importance of personalities in keeping Liberalism alive in the Jewish East End should not be underestimated. The *East London Observer* went so far as to comment in 1929 that Liberalism in the East End was moribund except in the areas controlled by two Jewish communal workers: Miriam Moses and Ida Samuel.[36] However, it was not only Jewish Liberals who helped to keep the party alive in the East End. James Kiley, a former mayor of Stepney and MP for Whitechapel between 1916 and 1922, was a noted philo-semite who championed Jewish interests in Parliament.[37] As far as the Jewish Liberals were concerned, there is evidence that some were popular because of their involvement in Jewish communal life rather than because of their participation in local politics.[38] This was certainly true of Miriam Moses, who was the best-known Jewish communal worker associated with the Liberal Party in Stepney. The daughter of Mark Moses, a prominent Liberal and synagogue worker in the East End, Miriam Moses was one of the stalwarts of Liberalism in Whitechapel and was for many years chairman of the Whitechapel Liberal Association. Through her work as a manager in local schools Miriam Moses came into contact with many Jewish

[33] *ELA*, 10 August 1929, p. 5; 15 November 1930, p. 3.
[34] *ELA*, 30 June 1928, p. 8.
[35] See, for example, *ELA*, 28 February 1931, p. 3.
[36] *ELO*, 25 May 1929, p. 6.
[37] *JC*, 10 November 1922, p. 13; *ELA*, 4 January 1919, p. 4; press cutting from the *Star*, n.d., United Ladies' Tailors' Trade Union Archive (ULTTU Archive), D/S/24/53/2; *East London Handbook*, 1918, p. 9.
[38] This was the view of the late Sam Klein, *JC* correspondent in the East End in the 1930s (Interview with Sam Klein, April 1985).

parents. In this way, she was able to build up a personal following in the local Jewish community. This has led one former political colleague to argue that she was associated in the Jewish community's mind with public and social rather than with political work.[39] Nevertheless, the popularity which Miriam Moses engendered in the Jewish East End was translated into support for her at the polls. Evidence of a personal following can be seen in the fact that in the five council elections which she contested in the predominantly Jewish Spitalfields East ward between 1921 and 1931, she always headed the poll by a significant majority.[40] In addition, the fact that Spitalfields East failed to return any Labour councillors until 1934, when Miriam Moses chose not to stand for re-election, provided further evidence of the personal following which she commanded among the local Jewish population.[41] Miriam Moses' involvement in Jewish organizations was exceptionally wide-ranging. In particular, she was the founder of the Brady Jewish Girls' Club and helped to run the Jewish Children's Country Holiday Home.[42] Her political career in Stepney reached a peak in 1931 when she was elected the country's first Jewish woman mayor.[43]

Another well-known Jewish Liberal personality in Stepney was Harry Kosky, a successful businessman who lived in Knightsbridge. Kosky represented the heavily Jewish Whitechapel East ward during the years 1904–28 and was mayor of Stepney in 1923.[44] Like Miriam Moses, his involvement in Jewish communal life gave him a high profile in the East End community. He was president of the Great Garden Street Talmud Torah and a vice-president of the Federation of Synagogues.[45] A committed Zionist, Kosky participated in the movement locally as a member of the East London Jewish National Fund Commission.[46] Jack Somper, who succeeded Kosky as mayor in 1924, was a man of considerable political experience. He had been Kiley's election agent in 1918 and held a number of positions in the local Liberal Party and on Stepney council.[47] In 1924 he was chairman of the Mile End Liberal Association and leader of the council.[48] Somper was largely responsible for the alliance between Liberals and Conservatives in East London which found expression in the Ratepayers' Party.[49] As a prominent exponent of the anti-socialist alliance

---

[39] Interview with Harold Altman (May 1985). I am also grateful to Monty Richardson, Lady Janner, Phyllis Gerson and the late Florrie Passman for providing me with detailed insights into the motivations and character of Miriam Moses.

[40] For Miriam Moses' electoral victories in Spitalfields East see *JC*, 8 July 1921, p. 34 (by-election); *ELA*, 4 November 1922, p. 5; 7 November 1925, p. 8; *ELO*, 3 November 1928, p. 5; *ELA*, 7 November 1931, p. 5.

[41] *ELA*, 10 November 1934, p. 3.

[42] *JC*, 2 July 1965, p. 37 (Obituary).

[43] Ibid., 13 November 1931, p. 23.

[44] *ELO*, 11 November 1922, p. 3; *ELA*, 11 November 1922, p. 5.

[45] *ELO*, 11 November 1922, p. 3; *ELA*, 30 June 1923, p. 3; C. Roth, *The Federation of Synagogues, 1912–1937: A Record of Twenty-Five Years* (London, 1937), p. 11.

[46] *ZR*, October 1918, p. 104. See also *English Zionist Federation* (EZF), *24th Annual Report* (1922–3). For Kosky's Zionist family background see *Jewish Guardian*, 28 May 1926, p. 7.

[47] *ELA*, 24 November 1923, p. 3.

[48] *ELA*, 24 March 1923, p. 5; *ELO*, 15 November 1924, p. 3.

[49] *ELA*, 26 December 1925, p. 5.

Somper was also a member of the executive council of the Union of Stepney Ratepayers.[50] In 1932 he was chosen as leader of the Ratepayers' Party, a post he held until he retired from municipal work in 1934.[51] Somper's political record suggests that it may be more accurate to describe him as an anti-socialist rather than a Liberal. Nevertheless, from 1919 to 1928 he represented the largely Jewish ward of Mile End West as a Liberal councillor. Although active in Jewish communal life in Golders Green where he lived, Somper was not noted for his commitment to Jewish affairs in the East End. Two Liberals in Stepney who were actively involved in East End Jewish communal life were Abraham Magen and Jack Rosenthal. Like Somper, Magen was a councillor for the Jewish stronghold of Mile End West ward. He was a member of the London Shechita Board, the London Talmud Torah Trust and the Federation of Synagogues, which he represented on the Board of Deputies. In addition, he was vice-president of the Philpot Street Great Synagogue.[52] Rosenthal was best known as the owner of the Pavilion Theatre in Whitechapel, which staged Yiddish plays and was the venue for many important meetings of Jewish interest. He represented Spitalfields West ward until 1925, when he joined Miriam Moses in Spitalfields East.[53]

No list of Jewish Liberals in the East End would be complete without the Rev. Joseph Stern, or the 'Jewish Bishop of Stepney', as he was referred to by non-Jewish East Enders.[54] Stern was Minister of the East London Synagogue from 1887 to 1927. As Minister of the only synagogue in Stepney belonging to the United Synagogue, Stern was acutely concerned with the Anglicization of immigrant Jews. In local politics, he represented the Mile End West ward on the council until 1928, and was chairman of both the Mile End Board of Guardians and the Committee of the LCC schools in Mile End. In Jewish affairs, he was one of the founders of the Stepney Jewish Lads' Club, secretary of the Stepney Jewish Schools and a member of the Jewish Education Board and the Jewish Board of Guardians.[55]

As events were to show, the apparent revival of East End Liberalism caused by the 1930 by-election in Whitechapel lacked substance, as it was based on a specific issue and relied on the personal popularity of Barnett Janner. As far as East End Jews were concerned, the single most important issue in the election was the Labour government's recent White Paper on Palestine, which imposed new restrictions on Jewish immigration. The advice given by the *Jewish Chronicle* to Jewish voters in the constituency was unequivocal: under no

[50] *ELA*, 27 January 1923, p. 5.

[51] *ELA*, 19 November 1932, p. 2; *ELO*, 19 November 1932, p. 6.

[52] *ELO*, 5 December 1931, p. 5; *JC*, 15 February 1963, p. 26 (Obituary).

[53] *JC*, 31 October 1919, p. 37. For profiles of Rosenthal see also *Jewish Guardian*, 22 April 1921, pp. 21–2; *ELA*, 7 January 1922, p. 3.

[54] *Jewish Guardian*, 12 April 1922, p. 9; *ELA*, 22 April 1922, p. 3.

[55] *ELA*, 7 July 1934, p. 5. See also I. Finestein, 'J. F. Stern 1865–1934: Aspects of a Gifted Anomoly', in ed. A. Newman, *The Jewish East End 1840–1939* (Leicester, 1981), pp. 75–92.

circumstances should Jews vote for the Labour candidate.[56] The issue was further simplified when the Whitechapel Liberal Party selected as its candidate Barnett Janner, a young Jewish communal activist and a prominent leader of the English Zionist Federation. The *Jewish Chronicle* commented: 'Now there is a Jewish candidate no Jewish vote need be lost.'[57] Janner's campaign was aided by the support of the Palestine Protest Committee which was formed by the East London Young Zionist League with the specific aim of opposing the Labour candidate and thus registering a protest against the government.[58] The result of the election was a narrow victory for James Hall, the Labour candidate. However, the Labour majority was drastically reduced, from 9,180 to 1,099.[59] The *East London Advertiser* had no hesitation in attributing the high Liberal poll to Janner's personal popularity.[60] The following year, Janner won the Whitechapel seat in the general election. Janner's energetic constituency work contributed to the false impression that the local party was now in a healthy condition. Any hope that the revival was genuine was shattered in 1935 when the Labour candidate, James Hall, won back the seat he had lost to Janner in 1931. Janner's defeat and subsequent departure from Whitechapel in 1935 signalled the irreversible decline of Liberalism in the East End. By 1937 David Goldblatt, the prospective Liberal parliamentary candidate for Whitechapel and St George's, could only appeal to Jewish voters on the basis of the Liberal Party's past record. The *East London Advertiser* commented: 'The large majority of the people of Whitechapel were of his own faith and his message to them was to harken back to the history of Liberalism, in which was embodied security, freedom, comfort and safety for them.'[61] This was just one indication of the Liberal Party's irrelevance to the East End Jewish community.

The primary reason for the East End Jewish community's abandonment of the Liberal Party was the fundamental shift which had occurred in the social and economic structure of the community. As has been seen, the dispersal of wealthier Jews to North-East and North-West London left a primarily working-class Jewish population in the East End. As far as the social and economic conditions of this population were concerned, *The New Survey of London Life and Labour* commented in 1929: 'The Jewish working-class community in East London is still on the whole a poor community, its proportion of poverty being slightly greater than that of the surrounding non-Jewish population (13.7

---

[56] *JC*, 31 October 1930, p. 27; 28 November 1930, p. 7. For analyses of the election see G. Alderman, *The Jewish Community in British Politics* (Oxford, 1983), pp. 112–13; D. Cesarani, 'The White Paper Crisis of 1929–1931', *Zionist Yearbook*, (*1984–5*) (London, 1985), pp. 25–8; G. Shimoni, 'Poale Zion: A Zionist Transplant in Britain (1905–1945)', in ed. P. Y. Medding, *Studies in Contemporary Jewry*, vol. II, (Bloomington, Ind., 1986), pp. 241–5.

[57] *JC*, 7 November 1930, p. 6.

[58] *JC*, 14 November 1930, p. 22; *ELA*, 15 November 1930, p. 4; *ELO*, 15 November 1930, p. 5.

[59] *JC*, 5 December 1930, p. 13.

[60] *ELA*, 6 December 1930, p. 5.

[61] *ELA* 16 January 1937, p. 4. See also *ELA*, 24 April 1937, p. 4.

per cent compared with 12.1 per cent).'[62] The primary reason for this poverty was unemployment or part-time and casual employment. Both part-time and casual employment were common features of the tailoring and furniture trades, which continued to employ considerable numbers of Jews. The seasonal nature of these trades meant that full-time employment throughout the year was virtually unknown. In 1933 Marcus Lipton, a Labour activist in Stepney, contended that unemployment among young English-born Jews in the East End was increasing. This trend was confirmed by the experience of the Jewish Board of Guardians, which was no longer able to support the Jewish poor without assistance from the public authorities. Lipton attributed the high level of unemployment among Stepney's Jewish population to the fact that occupations on which East End Jewry had previously depended for their livelihood, in particular tailoring, were badly hit by the depression.[63] In 1932, for example, over 75 per cent of the membership of one tailoring union in the East End were unemployed, while the remainder were underemployed.[64]

The effect of such social and economic conditions was to radicalize the Jewish East End, especially young Jewish East Enders who became profoundly alienated from the politics of the Liberal Party. However, it was not only young Jews who were attracted by the pull of the Labour Party. Abraham Valentine, the veteran president of the Whitechapel and Spitalfields Costermongers' Union and a Liberal councillor in Whitechapel since 1903, switched his allegiances to the Labour Party in 1919.[65] Marcus Lipton, who was elected Labour MP for Brixton in 1945, began his political career in the Liberal Party in Stepney. In 1928 he was adopted as a Liberal LCC candidate for Mile End.[66] Six years later he was returned as a Labour councillor in Mile End, where he had become chairman of Mile End Labour Party's East ward.[67] The attraction of the left meant that the normal political home of many working-class Jews became the Labour Party and, increasingly in the 1930s, the Communist Party.

At the inaugural meeting of the Stepney Labour Party and Trades Council in June 1918 there were delegates from most of the Jewish trade unions in the East End. In a sense this was not surprising because there was no rival political party to appeal for the support of the trade unions. After 1920, however, the Labour Party constantly had to compete with the Stepney Communist Party for the support of the trade unions. This was of particular importance for the Stepney Labour Party because most of the Jewish unions affiliated to it were more radical than non-Jewish unions. The Boot and Shoe Operatives, the Jewish Bakers' Union, the Cigar Makers' Trade Union, the National Amalga-

---

[62] *The New Survey of London Life and Labour*, vol. VI, p. 22.
[63] *JC*, 3 March 1933, p. 8; *Jewish World* (*JW*), 9 March 1933, p. 2.
[64] *ULTTU, 25th Annual Balance Sheet and Report* (London 1935), p. 6.
[65] J. Bush, *Behind the Lines: East London Labour 1914–1919* (London, 1984), p. 220. See also *ELA*, 18 February 1922, p. 3; *ELO*, 2 March 1929, p. 5.
[66] *ELA*, 3 March 1928, p. 5.
[67] *ELA*, 10 November 1934, p. 3; *Stepney Citizen*, October 1934, p. 1.

mated Furnishing Trades Association (NAFTA), the Hat and Cap branch of the United Garment Workers' Trade Union, the United Ladies' Tailors' Trade Union (ULTTU), and the Whitechapel and Spitalfields Costermongers' and Street Sellers' Union were all affiliated to the Stepney Labour Party.[68] As well as trade unions, the new Stepney Labour Party included among its affiliates the British Socialist Party (BSP) and the Independent Labour Party (ILP). Both of these bodies were represented by Jewish delegates.[69] The first secretary of Stepney Labour Party was a Romanian-born Jew named Oscar Tobin.[70] Tobin, a chemist by profession, played an instrumental role in the formation of the party.[71] Together with Sam Truman, who was also Jewish, Tobin helped to found the Mile End Labour Party in 1918 and was described by the *East London Advertiser* as the 'Father' of that party.[72] It would not be an exaggeration to credit Tobin with being the major force in the Stepney Labour Party in the immediate post-war period. He held virtually every important position in the local party. He was secretary of Stepney Trades Council, the first Labour Party whip on the council elected in 1919, and the first Jewish mayor of the borough in 1922.[73] In addition, Tobin was responsible for organizing Labour's campaign in the first council elections after the war in 1919 and must therefore take much of the credit for the Labour victory.[74]

Throughout the inter-war years most Jewish Labour councillors in Stepney belonged either to the Mile End Labour Party or to the Whitechapel and St George's Labour Party. These neighbourhood parties were both affiliated to the Stepney Labour Party. Mile End Labour Party was effectively all-Jewish. An examination of the names published in the *Stepney Citizen* reveals that the party consistently chose Jewish ward and section officers.[75] Among its founder members were those who were to become leading figures in the Stepney Labour Party. Alfred Kershaw, a teacher, served as secretary of Mile End Labour Party from its foundation until 1930.[76] In 1923 he was elected secretary of Stepney Trades Council and Borough Labour Party.[77] In addition, Kershaw edited the *Stepney Labour Times*, a newspaper produced by Mile End Labour Party.[78] He served as a councillor on the first Labour council elected in 1919 and in 1922 was elected an alderman.[79] Dan Frankel, a tailor by profession, started his political career in the ILP. He represented the Whitechapel and

[68] *Stepney Trades Council and Central Labour Party, Annual Report, 1919–1920* (London, 1920) p. 1; *ELO*, 1 June 1918, p. 3.
[69] *Stepney Trades Council and Central Labour Party, Annual Report, 1919–1920*, p. 1.
[70] *ELO*, 1 June 1918, p. 3.
[71] *ELA*, 6 March 1920, p. 5.
[72] *ELA*, 24 November 1923, p. 3. See also *ELA*, 6 March 1920, p. 5.
[73] *ELA*, 20 March 1920, p. 2; 26 November 1921, p. 3; *JC*, 25 November 1921, p. 18.
[74] *ELA*, 18 October 1919, p. 5; 26 November 1921, p. 3; 28 January 1922, p. 3.
[75] *Stepney Citizen*, 1929–39.
[76] Ibid., January 1930, p. 4; *ELA*, 25 January 1930, p. 3.
[77] *ELA*, 19 May 1923, p. 3.
[78] *ELA*, 23 March 1929, p. 7.
[79] *ELA*, 19 May 1923, p. 3.

Mile End branch of the ILP on the new Stepney Labour Party in 1918.[80] However, Frankel was not on the left wing of the Labour movement and he gradually moved into the mainstream of Labour politics in Stepney, becoming chairman of the Mile End Labour Party from 1925 to 1936.[81] In addition, he served as president of Stepney Trades Council and Borough Labour Party, and in 1928 was elected chairman of the Stepney Board of Guardians.[82] The following year he became mayor of Stepney and in 1934 was chosen as leader of the Labour group on the council.[83] Frankel's political career extended beyond the East End. He represented Mile End on the LCC (1931–9) and in 1932 he was elected to the executive committee of the London Labour Party.[84] His career reached a pinnacle in 1935 when he was elected the Labour MP for Mile End.[85] By this time, Frankel's popularity had plummeted among the more radical Jewish workers in the East End. He was increasingly disliked for his right-wing views and his opportunistic tendencies.[86] One Jewish voter in Mile End even wrote to the *East London Observer* prior to the 1935 general election calling on Jews not to vote for Frankel because he had done nothing in the fight against Fascism.[87] Although his record on this was poor, the claim was not entirely true because Frankel had recently spoken at a mass protest demonstration in Hyde Park against Nazi persecution.[88]

The professionalism of Mile End Labour Party owed much to the organizational skills of its full-time secretary and election agent, Israel Shafran.[89] Shafran ran the election campaigns of both John Scurr, MP for Mile End from 1923 to 1931, and Dan Frankel. He was a charismatic figure who was responsible for making the Mile End party the largest and most effectively organized branch of the Stepney Labour Party. At the annual meeting of the party in 1930, a record membership of just over 2,000 was reported.[90] In the same year, Mile End Labour Club, established in the Jewish neighbourhood of Stepney Green, was praised as the finest Labour Club in East London.[91] It offered social activities and free legal advice, and was responsible for the publication of the *Stepney Labour Times* and the *Stepney Citizen*.[92] Some of the party's activities were specifically aimed at a Jewish audience. For example, its

[80] *Stepney Trades Council and Central Labour Party, Annual Report, 1919–1920*, p. 1.

[81] *Tailor and Garment Worker*, December 1935, p. 11; *Stepney Citizen*, April 1936, p. 1.

[82] *ELA*, 21 April 1928, p. 4.

[83] *JC*, 21 December 1928, p. 26; *ELA*, 17 November 1928, p. 3; 10 November 1934, p. 5.

[84] *Stepney Citizen*, December 1932, p. 1.

[85] *ELA*, 16 November 1935, p. 5.

[86] A number of contemporaries have testified to Frankel's unpopularity, especially as a constituency MP. Interviews with Lady Janner (April 1985); Jack Wolkind (April 1985); Harold Altman (May 1985).

[87] *ELO*, 2 November 1935, p. 6.

[88] British Non-Sectarian Anti-Nazi Council circular, *Programme for Demonstration*, n.d., uncatalogued, Communist Party of Great Britain Library.

[89] *ELA*, 14 February 1925, p. 5.

[90] *ELO*, 18 January 1930, p. 5; *Stepney Citizen*, February 1930, p. 4.

[91] *Stepney Citizen*, January 1930, p. 1.

[92] Ibid., See also June 1930, p. 1.

League of Youth organized membership drives in Jewish streets.[93] In addition, the Women's Section, a vibrant body with over 600 members in 1935, was amply supplied with Jewish members.[94] Leading members of the Women's Section included the wives of Oscar Tobin and Dan Frankel, who were both political figures in their own right. Sarah Tobin was elected to the council in 1922.[95] Lily Frankel's political career was more wide-ranging. Elected a councillor in 1934, she served as secretary and chairman respectively of the Women's Section.[96] She was also a member of various school managing bodies, a co-opted member of the LCC and served as chairman of Stepney council's Maternity and Child Welfare Committee in the 1930s.[97]

The Whitechapel branch of Stepney Labour Party had no figure comparable to Shafran to galvanise the members into action. Another difference between the Whitechapel and Mile End branches was that the Whitechapel Labour Party contained a sizeable number of Irish-Catholic members. Nevertheless, the first secretary of the party, Harry Schwarz, was Jewish.[98] In September 1919, Schwarz and John Raphael were involved in fighting a number of eviction orders affecting tenants in Brick Lane, many of whom were Jewish. A series of highly successful open-air protest meetings was organized and Raphael bombarded the local press with letters publicizing the plight of the tenants.[99] As a result of the Labour Party's campaign the eviction orders were withdrawn.[100] Although the Whitechapel Labour Party never fulfilled its early promise, the branch did include two Jewish members who were to achieve considerable prominence in Labour politics in Stepney: Issy Vogler and Morris Davis. Vogler, who was a teacher in the East End, was regarded as one of the intellectuals of the Labour Party in Stepney. He rose quickly through the ranks of the Whitechapel Labour Party, which he joined in 1922, becoming a member of the executive committee in 1924. Two years later he became secretary of the Stepney Trades Council. In a council by-election in 1927 he fought Spitalfields East ward and won a seat there for Labour for the first time. The following year he was re-elected to the council for the predominantly Jewish St George's North-West ward. During the years 1930 to 1931 he was the leader of the Labour group on the council and in 1931 he was re-elected to the council for Mile End New Town. He was subsequently appointed both chairman and leader of the Labour opposition on the council. In 1935, at the remarkably young age of twenty-nine, he was elected mayor of Stepney.[101]

Morris, or Morry, Davis was a highly controversial politician who aroused the

[93] Ibid., September 1931, p. 1; October 1937, p. 1.
[94] Ibid., March 1935, p. 1.
[95] *ELA*, 4 November 1922, p. 5.
[96] *Stepney Citizen*, February 1930, p. 4; February 1934, p. 4; *ELA*, 10 November 1934, p. 3.
[97] *ELA*, 3 February 1934, p. 5.
[98] *ELO*, 20 September 1919, p. 3; *ELA*, 13 September 1919, p. 5.
[99] *ELO*, 20 September 1919, p. 3; 27 September 1919, p. 4; *ELA*, 13 September 1919, p. 5; 20 September 1919, p. 3.
[100] *ELO*, 20 December 1919, p. 2.
[101] *ELA*, 10 November 1934, p. 5; interview with Lily Gold, sister of Issy Vogler (February 1985).

strongest feelings of anger and resentment amongst East End Jewish radicals. One of the founders of the Whitechapel Labour Party, Davis was first elected to Stepney council in 1924.[102] He was simultaneously chairman and treasurer of the party.[103] From 1925 he represented Whitechapel and St George's on the LCC and served on virtually every committee of Stepney council. He became mayor of the borough in 1930 and was elected leader of the council in 1935.[104] It was during Davis's years as council leader in the mid-1930s that he consolidated his power on the council and extended his control over most political offices in the borough. He was a power broker *par excellence*. Unlike most Jewish Labour politicians in the East End, Davis was also active in Jewish communal life. He was a founder of the London Jewish Hospital, a manager of Jews' Free School, vice-president of the Talmud Torah Trust, a member of the Board of Deputies, and a vice-president of the Jewish National Fund, the Zionist fund-raising body which bought land in Palestine. However, it was as president of the Federation of Synagogues, a post to which he was elected in 1928, that Davis made his mark on the Anglo-Jewish communal scene.[105] Davis was a fervent Zionist and he used the Federation's campaign against the previous president, the aristocratic and anti-Zionist second Lord Swaythling, to champion the cause of the immigrant Jews in the East End.[106] Once in office, Davis's refusal to tolerate opposition, both in the Federation and on Stepney council, earned him many political enemies.

Despite his often dubious methods, Davis deserves credit for his work on behalf of East End Jewry. In particular, he led a Board of Deputies deputation in 1928 which asked the LCC to remove the restrictions on the award of its scholarships to the children of aliens.[107] The deputation was successful.[108] Davis was also instrumental in transforming the character of the Federation and in making it one of the most radical of the Anglo-Jewish institutions. Notably, in 1933 the Federation was in the forefront of the protests against Nazi persecution of Jews in Germany. This was in sharp contrast to the more passive stance assumed by the Board of Deputies' leadership. As early as May 1933 the Federation passed a resolution, which was communicated to the British government, protesting against the Nazi's treatment of German Jewry and urging the government to facilitate the admission of German Jews into Palestine and Britain.[109] Later in the year, the Federation played a major role in the

---

[102] *ELA*, 24 June 1924, p. 5; *JC*, 23 December 1927, p. 9.

[103] *ELA*, 22 November 1924, p. 3; *Jewish Graphic*, 30 March 1928, p. 2.

[104] For profiles of Davis see *ELO*, 15 November 1930, p. 5; ELA, 15 November 1930, p. 4; 28 December 1935, p. 3.

[105] On Davis's Jewish communal work see *Jewish Graphic*, 30 March 1928, p. 2; *ELA*, 15 November 1930, p. 4; *ELO*, 15 November 1930, p. 4. For a recently published account of Davis's career see Alderman, *The Federation of Synagogues*, pp. 56–68.

[106] Minutes of the Board of the Federation of Synagogues, 2 December 1925; 20 March 1928, Federation of Synagogues Archive (FSA).

[107] *JC*, 13 January 1928, p. 20.

[108] *JC*, 21 December 1928, p. 9; LCC Education Committee Minutes, Report of the Higher Education Sub-Committee, 28 June 1928, Greater London Record Office (GLRO).

[109] Board of Federation Minutes, 22 May 1933, FSA.

formation of the Jewish Representative Council which, in the Federation's own words, was formed because the Board of Deputies had 'declined to declare an official boycott of German goods and services'.[110]

Specifically Jewish issues were rarely discussed on the council. This was because many Jewish councillors, especially Jewish Labour councillors, had already become distanced from Jewish communal affairs. In 1926 even the Irish-Catholic mayor of Stepney, who was also vice-chairman of the Stepney Board of Guardians, said he had been very disappointed with some of the Jewish members of that body because they had taken no steps to make provision for the religious needs of the Jewish children in the Board's homes. He had therefore set up a home for Jewish children, the first of its kind in Stepney, where the dietary laws could be kept.[111] The *East London Observer* took a more sympathetic view of the Jewish members of the Stepney Guardians who, it reported, 'made a point of looking after the religious and other needs of their co-religionists'.[112] In addition, there is no doubt that Jewish communal causes could still attract the support of East End Jews from across the political spectrum. Thus, in March 1927 a mass meeting organized by the Society for the Promotion of Trades and Agriculture among Jews, known by the acronym ORT, was supported by both Labour and Liberal Jews. Prominent among those involved in ORT was the Liberal Kosky and the Labour activist Kershaw.[113] Thus, there were Jews who, as well as being active in municipal politics in the East End, continued to participate in Jewish institutional life and to be concerned with issues which affected Jews. Morry Davis is the most outstanding example of such a politician but there were others.

The most common form of communal involvement for politically inclined East End Jews was the Jewish friendly society movement. Most Jewish friendly societies had been formed in the East End in the second half of the nineteenth century during the period of mass immigration from Eastern Europe. The principal benefit offered by Jewish friendly societies was the death benefit.[114] For many Jewish activists in the Stepney Labour Party, the friendly societies provided them with their only contact with formal Jewish institutional life. They also fulfilled an important unintended function. Their rules and methods of procedure initiated many Jews into the world of associational politics. Experience in this field often served as the launching pad for a career in municipal

---

[110] Ibid., 21 December 1933. On the Federation's support for a boycott see also 19 July 1933, FSA.

[111] *Jewish Guardian*, 2 July 1926, p. 6.

[112] *ELO*, 28 April 1928, p. 6.

[113] Handbill advertising ORT mass meeting, 6 March 1927, ORT file, Gaster MSS. On East End Jews involved in ORT see also *Jewish Guardian*, 11 June 1926, p. 14.

[114] For short accounts of the history of the Jewish friendly society movement in the East End see L. P. Gartner, *The Jewish Immigrant in England, 1870–1914* (2nd edn; London, 1973), pp. 178–80; V. D. Lipman, *A Social History of the Jews in England, 1850–1950* (London, 1954), pp. 51, 119–20. For a more recent study of Jewish benefit societies and their cultural function in the Jewish East End in the late nineteenth century see D. M. Feldman, 'Immigrants and Workers, Englishmen and Jews: Jewish Immigration to the East End of London, 1880–1906', Ph.D. thesis (University of Cambridge, 1986), pp. 285–99.

politics. Alfred Kershaw and Israel Shafran were both prominently involved in friendly societies. Kershaw became president of the Achei Ameth Friendly Society in the 1920s, and in the 1930s he was elected chairman of the Association of Jewish Friendly Societies.[115] He represented the Association on the Board of Deputies.[116] Shafran also became chairman of the Association during the early 1930s.[117]

On the rare occasions when Jewish issues were raised on Stepney council, it was invariably by Jewish Labour councillors. For example, the deportation of alien Jews was a highly emotive issue in the East End Jewish community during the early post-war years. In April 1920 Stepney council adopted councillor Kershaw's resolution protesting against the 'alleged wholesale deportations of alien Jews in the East End of London' without trial.[118] Tobin dwelt at length on the issue in the 1919–20 annual report of Stepney Trades Council and Labour Party. He said that the action of the government in arresting and deporting alien trade union officials had been a matter of such 'grave concern' to the council that a deputation interviewed the Labour Party in Parliament with a view to drafting amendments to mitigate the worst features of the Aliens Restriction Bill. Tobin believed that the position of all trade unionists was threatened by the government policy which made it a criminal offence for an alien to incite or organize industrial unrest.[119] In this way, he related the specific difficulties of alien trade unionists to the labour movement in general, thus giving a broader socialist validity to the problem.

Another major concern of Jewish Labour councillors was the plight of Jews in Central and Eastern Europe who, after World War I, were the victims of famine and pogroms. In 1920 the Stepney Trades Council and Labour Party passed a resolution urging the setting up of a fund for the relief of distress in Central and Eastern Europe. Tobin brought the matter to the attention of the council and requested that a meeting be called to focus interest on 'Fighting the Famine'.[120] Nearer to home, Jewish Labour Party activists were confronted with discrimination against British-born and foreign-born Jews in a variety of areas including employment, housing and education. The LCC was a particular target for criticism, as has already been seen in the case of the educational scholarships.

Despite the extent to which discriminatory legislation affected the lives of many East End Jews, there is little evidence of protests from Stepney's Jewish councillors. One important exception was Jacob Fine, who was also secretary of the Jewish tailors' union the ULTTU. In 1935 Fine protested in the strongest terms against the LCC regulation excluding aliens from council housing

[115] *Jewish Guardian*, 27 February 1925, p. 10; *JC*, 4 January 1935, p. 19.
[116] *Jewish Guardian*, 9 November 1928, p. 4.
[117] *Association of Jewish Friendly Societies, Annual Report* (London, 1933), p. 22.
[118] Stepney Borough Council Minutes, vol. XX, 26 April 1920; *JC*, 30 April 1920, p. 28.
[119] *Stepney Trades Council and Central Labour Party, Annual Report, 1919–1920*, p. 5.
[120] Stepney Borough Council Minutes, 8 March 1920; 26 April 1920. For Jewish East End protests against pogroms in Poland in the immediate post-war period see Bush, *Behind the Lines*, p. 208.

estates.[121] There were occasions when Jewish Labour councillors actually opposed policies which would benefit Jews. In 1923, for example, a group of Labour councillors, including at least one Jewish councillor, objected to a proposal that Jewish patients in the Bancroft Hospital, Mile End, should be provided with kosher meat. Their justification for opposing the proposal was that Jewish patients would be receiving preferential treatment. In reality, the episode illustrated the extent to which some Jewish councillors had abandoned their religious beliefs in favour of a secular perspective on local affairs. The outcome of the controversy was that the Mile End Board of Guardians agreed to supply kosher meat to patients who requested it.[122]

Inevitably, there were numerous disagreements between Jewish Liberal and Labour councillors on a whole variety of issues. In 1933, for example, Dan Frankel attacked Miriam Moses' proposal for Jewish charitable endeavour to fund a housing programme 'as one asking rich Jews to house poor Jews'. He added that he strongly opposed 'any racial element being brought into the housing problem'.[123] Together with the provision of kosher meat in hospitals, the housing crisis indicated the extent to which some Jewish councillors were trying to exclude specifically Jewish issues from the local political agenda. This in turn was an indication of the new type of secular East Ender who had become fully assimilated into local political life. The Labour Party solution to the housing problem was articulated by Vogler, a councillor for the North-West ward of St George's, the most overcrowded ward in London. Vogler believed that only local authorities could solve the housing problem. He pointed out that Stepney council and the LCC were making progress but that much more could be achieved if the Jewish communal workers ceased to put their trust in large-scale philanthropy 'and supported wise public expenditure instead of supporting the economy ramp'.[124] Jewish Liberals remained unconvinced that local councils were the best institutions to manage housing estates. Jack Somper, for example, remained committed to private enterprise and appealed to 'big city companies' to help in the destruction of the slums.[125]

The unemployment issue served as a further source of conflict between Jewish Labour councillors and their Jewish anti-socialist opponents on the council. In 1933, a deputation from the Stepney branch of the Communist Party-backed National Unemployed Workers Movement (NUWM) made a number of demands at a council meeting. The three representatives of the branch were Jewish and its secretary was Nat Cohen, a fiery local Communist who was ordered out of the chamber by Miriam Moses. Vogler, by contrast, welcomed the deputation which, he said, proved how much suffering existed among people living in a distressed area. This provoked the response from Somper that the Labour government had not improved the lot of the working

---

[121] *JC*, 8 March 1935, p. 50; *ELA*, 9 March 1935, p. 7; *ELO*, 2 March 1935, p. 5.
[122] *Jewish Guardian*, 25 May 1923, p. 13; 25 April 1924, p. 19.
[123] *ELA*, 4 March 1933, p. 6.
[124] *JC*, 27 January 1933, p. 14.
[125] *ELA* 5 August 1933, p. 5.

class. Dan Frankel's reply to this attack was to say that the Labour government had not been responsible 'for cutting the unemployment benefit, and giving local authorities instructions and orders not to spend money on unemployment'. He added that it was not within the jurisdiction of local councils to deal with unemployment.[126] However, even a subject as controversial as unemployment could draw Jews of differing political persuasions together. In 1934, for example, both Somper and Vogler supported a request from the Stepney branch of the NUWM for the council to receive a deputation from the branch. The deputation asked the council to provide accommodation for the Hunger Marchers who were protesting against the Unemployment Bill. As a result of the deputation, both Vogler and Miriam Moses proposed that the council ask the Minister of Health for permission to incur expenditure in order to be able to comply with the request of the Stepney branch of the NUWM.[127] It therefore seems that where a humanitarian issue rather than a purely party political one was at stake, Jewish councillors were able to present a united front.

The major issue on which Jewish councillors of different political persuasions were never able to agree was the funding of local authority services. In practice, this was the rates question which dominated municipal politics in the East End in the 1920s. In Stepney, Jack Somper was in the forefront of the attacks against what he regarded as the first Labour council's extravagance. He was particularly incensed about the cost to the rates of Labour's milk scheme and its £4 minimum wage for council workers.[128] Tobin's response was that Stepney had no choice but to levy a high rate. He cited a number of reasons why the council had been forced to increase the rates. One of the most important reasons was that Stepney, in common with other poor boroughs, had a low rateable value. This meant that it was necessary to levy a high rate in order to get the same return as a richer borough which could levy a lower rate. Tobin added that Stepney would follow Poplar's lead in refusing to pay the LCC and Police precepts levied upon it and instead would use the rates to support the borough's unemployed. The Labour council's case thus rested on what it believed to be the basic unfairness of a system which placed a very heavy burden on the mainly poor people of Stepney. In this context, Tobin's call for the 'equalisation of the rates' was a reflection of events in other East End boroughs.[129] When a Ratepayers' council was elected in 1922 Somper, as chairman of the council's Finance Committee, seized the opportunity to propose a motion which abolished the £4 minimum wage.[130] He believed that this would save ratepayers £80,000 per annum.[131] Somper was also responsible

[126] *ELA*, 28 January 1933, p. 5.

[127] Stepney Borough Council Minutes, vol. XXXIV, 31 January 1934.

[128] *ELA*, 9 April 1921, p. 5; 27 January 1923, p. 5.

[129] *The East End Pioneer*, October 1921, p. 1; November 1921, p. 6. For a discussion of the rates protest movement in Poplar see N. Branson, *Poplarism, 1919–1925: George Lansbury and the Councillors' Revolt* (London, 1979).

[130] *ELA*, 28 April 1923, p. 5; Stepney Borough Council Minutes, vol. XXIII, 23 April 1923.

[131] *ELA*, 11 August 1923, p. 5.

for implementing a significant reduction in the rates.[132] It seems that he regarded rate reductions as a personal crusade. In an interview published in the *East London Advertiser* in 1923, Somper said that he considered the reduction of the high rates to be the most important aspect of council work.[133]

Such political disagreements provide good illustration of Jews challenging each other on political grounds rather than on an ethnic basis. The fact that the disagreements had nothing to do with Jewish or ethnic interests indicates the extent to which these Jews had integrated into local political life. However, despite their deep involvement in general political matters, Jewish political activists did not neglect the rise of political anti-semitism in the 1930s. This was, without doubt, the single most important political issue for East End Jews in that decade. However, left-wing Jews did not treat anti-semitism as a specifically Jewish problem but as a threat to democracy in general.[134] This analysis was shared by Jewish trade unionists, Jewish Communists and the Jewish People's Council against Fascism and Anti-Semitism. The Jewish People's Council (JPC) was formed in the East End in July 1936 by a group of trade unionists, Communists and Workers' Circle activists.[135] In contrast to the Board of Deputies' anti-defamation campaign, the JPC conducted a vigorously political campaign, believing that anti-semitism could not be fought effectively without attacking Fascism. These diametrically opposed policies in the important matter of communal defence inevitably led to many bitter clashes between the Board and the JPC. In line with its belief that Fascism posed a threat to democracy in general, the JPC cooperated with a number of non-Jewish anti-Fascist bodies, especially the National Council for Civil Liberties.

Jewish trade union leaders in the East End continually urged Jewish workers to join a trade union as the best means of fighting Fascism. In November 1934 a Jewish Labour Council had been formed in the East End from a conference of Jewish trade unionists with the specific aim of 'combating Fascism and anti-semitism'. Aaron Rollin, an official of the National Union of Tailors and Garment Workers who was appointed by the union to take control of its East End branch, was the main driving force behind the Jewish Labour Council. The East End branch of the union put forward a resolution at the conference urging 'all Jewish workers to enter the recognised trade unions, and to fight along with their English comrades against capitalism and reaction'.[136] In a similar tone, the predominantly Jewish Houndsditch and Whitechapel Branch of the Shop Assistants' Union commented in 1936 that the growth of the branch offered the most effective means of fighting Fascism.[137]

---

[132] *ELA*, 4 August 1923, p. 5.

[133] *ELA*, 11 August 1923, p. 5.

[134] For a fuller discussion of the issue see my article 'Jewish Responses to Political Antisemitism and Fascism in the East End of London, 1920–1939', in eds K. Lunn and T. Kushner, *Traditions of Intolerance* (Manchester, 1989).

[135] *JC*, 31 July 1936, p. 22.

[136] 'The Provisional Committee of the Jewish Labour Conference to Combat Fascism and Anti-Semitism'. Typescript, n.d., Rollin Papers, Modern Record Centre, University of Warwick.

[137] *The Shop Assistant*, 23 May 1936, p. 432.

It was often the case that Jewish trade union leaders were more radically inclined than the official leaders of the Stepney Labour Party. This was particularly true in the 1930s, when the party increasingly came under the influence of a few right-wing individuals such as Dan Frankel and Morry Davis. These politicians had little in common with the radical leaders of the furniture and tailoring trade union branches. The East London branch of the National Amalgamated Furnishing Trades Association (NAFTA), which was Jewish in all but name, was especially noted for its militancy. The long-serving secretary, Sidney Fineman, was a Communist, as was the branch chairman Morris Jacobs and his son Julius.[138] Julius Jacobs was prominently involved in the JPC. East End tailors joined the relevant union for their section of the industry. In ladies' tailoring this was the United Ladies' Tailors' Trade Union and in gents' tailoring the East End Sub-Divisional Workers Branch of the National Union of Tailors and Garment Workers (NUTGW). For a time, there was also a Communist breakaway tailoring union in the East End, the United Clothing Workers' Union. The leadership of the United Clothing Workers was composed of East End Jewish Communists and its outstanding personality was Sam Elsbury. Elsbury was a brilliant orator who commanded a huge personal following among East End tailors. He was a founder member of the Communist Party in 1920 and had been secretary of its Electoral Committee. He had also been active in local politics in the East End in the 1920s as a Bethnal Green borough councillor and as chairman of the militant South-West Bethnal Green Labour Party.[139] The crucial event which led to the formation of the United Clothing Workers' Union was the unofficial strike at the giant Rego factory in Hackney which began in October 1928.[140] The executive board of the NUTGW refused to sanction the withdrawal of labour requested by Elsbury and he was subsequently expelled from the union in March 1929.[141] Elsbury believed that the sole reason for his expulsion was his membership in the Communist Party.[142] At the time of his expulsion, he was the prospective Communist Party parliamentary candidate for South-West Bethnal Green. His election agent, J. Valentine, who was also Jewish, published a letter in *The Garment Worker* stating that Elsbury had no intention, if elected, of surrendering his union activities. This sealed Elsbury's fate with the NUTGW.[143] The United Clothing Workers' Union initially won over most of the London membership of the national union including the Jewish tailors in the small East End workshops and Elsbury claimed that, at its peak, the London membership reached 5,000. However, this success was short-lived. Following a number of disastrous strikes the union swiftly collapsed. The most severe blow to the

[138] Interview with Morry Lebow (June 1986).
[139] *The Garment Worker*, August 1926, p. 5; *Workers' Life*, 22 February 1928, p. 5.
[140] *The Garment Worker*, November 1928, pp. 6–7.
[141] Ibid., March 1929, p. 3.
[142] S. Elsbury and D. Gershon, *The Rego Revolt: How the United Clothing Workers Trade Union was Formed* (London, 1929), p. 3.
[143] *The Garment Worker*, March 1929, p. 3.

union was Elsbury's expulsion from the Communist Party for refusing to implement the party's policy involving the indiscriminate calling of strikes. As the man on the scene, he was aware of the damaging effect which this policy was having on the morale of the membership.[144] The grass-roots membership had no say in the disastrous policy which the Communist Party pursued. The collapse of the United Clothing Workers' Union therefore rested ultimately with the Communist Party and not with the Jewish members and leaders of the union in the East End.

This conflict between the interests of Jewish tailors in the East End and the demands of a non-Jewish trade union was not unique. It also appeared in the debates in the United Ladies' Tailors' Trade Union (ULTTU) concerning the relative merits of amalgamation with the national union as opposed to a federation with the master tailors. The ULTTU had been formed in 1909 from an amalgamation of smaller Jewish tailoring unions and functioned as an independent Jewish union until 1939.[145] Throughout this time, the union served as the forum for a wide spectrum of left-wing views. Anarchists, Bundists, Communists and Labour Party activists all had the opportunity to air their views at union meetings. Although left-wing and internationalist in outlook, the membership nevertheless took a lively interest in Jewish questions and in the welfare of Jews both in England and abroad. In the immediate post-war period, for example, the union participated in the relief of Jews from pogroms and famine in Central and Eastern Europe through its involvement in the Federation of Ukrainian Jews and the Federation of Polish Jews.[146] The Communists in the union continually argued that the only way forward for the union was to amalgamate with the NUTGW. However, powerful voices in the union managed to block at least one attempt at amalgamation, fearing that it would lead to a loss of the union's Jewish identity. Amalgamation was finally achieved in 1939, after the Communist Mick Mindel was elected chairman of the ULTTU. Mindel had actively campaigned for amalgamation during his election addresses and his personal victory was also a victory for those favouring unity with the national union.

The Workers' Circle Friendly Society, founded in Stepney in 1909 by a group of Russian Bundists, served as the meeting place and forum for all left-wing Jews in the East End. Individual branches of the Circle were organized along ideological lines. Thus, Branch 10, most of whose members lived in the East End, was known as the 'Communist branch'.[147] However, the Circle was much more than a political forum serving a group of ideologically committed left-wing Jews. The organization's headquarters at Circle House in Alie Street, Stepney, which was opened in 1924, became a focal point for Jewish social and

---

[144] *Daily Herald*, 24 December 1929, p. 6.
[145] M. Stewart and L. Hunter, *The Needle is Threaded: The History of an Industry* (London, 1964), p. 179.
[146] ULTTU Executive Committee Minutes, 8 April 1926, 15 April 1926, ULTTU Archive, file D/S/24/4.
[147] Interview with Louis Appleton (January 1985).

cultural activities in the East End. Its Sunday concerts were particularly popular and in the 1930s the Circle ran a Yiddish School.[148]

During the inter-war years the working-class Jewish community in the East End produced a locally based political leadership. These leaders were not, on the whole, represented on the Board of Deputies or active in established communal institutions. Nevertheless, they devoted much of their energy to various initiatives on behalf of East End Jewry and were acutely concerned with the fate of Jews abroad. Specifically Jewish issues could normally be tailored to coincide with party political interests. Thus, for example, in 1920 Jewish socialists saw no conflict between their opposition to the deportation of foreign Jews and their commitment to the ideals of the British Labour Party. In the Whitechapel by-election of 1930 the situation was more complicated, with Labour Zionists having to choose between the British Labour Party and Palestine as a National Home for the Jewish people. From contemporary accounts, it seems as though active Poale Zion members grudgingly voted for the Labour candidate in the hope that government policy towards Jewish immigration to Palestine would eventually be changed. Other examples of conflict between Jewish interests and general political interests occurred in the local Jewish trade union branches. Here, Jews were often reluctant to submit to the control of outside influences, whether from the Communist Party or from the wider trade union movement.

The fact that local Jewish politicians were able to raise Jewish issues in a secular political context marked a new stage in the development of the East End Jewish community. However, even though East End Jewish leaders functioned inside general political organizations, much of their contact continued to be with other Jews. This situation was conducive to fostering a strong sense of collective identity, particularly among radical left-wing Jews. Class and ethnicity, rather than religion, were thus the key factors in uniting second-generation East End Jews.

---

[148] *The Workers' Circle Friendly Society, Diamond Jubilee, 1909–1969* (London, 1969), pp. 5–7.

9

Jewish Refugees, Anglo-Jewry and British Government Policy, 1930–1940

Louise London

On 31 August 1938, a year before the start of World War II, Joseph P. Kennedy, the United States Ambassador in London, called on Lord Halifax, the British Foreign Secretary, to discuss the Jewish refugee problem. Kennedy suggested that the two countries and France 'should agree to take and place somewhere so many Jews and should then approach the German Government, and invite them to give such assistance as they could, saying that, if they were unwilling to do this, they must choose between keeping or killing their Jews.'[1] The next day a British official predicted, 'The German Government will no doubt choose the latter part of the second alternative, by "suicide" and starvation.'[2]

There was a third alternative. From the start of the German refugee problem in 1933, France, Britain and the United States had the option of opening their doors. Until Jewish emigration from German-held territory was finally forbidden by the Nazis on 31 October 1941, Jews had a good chance of escape by finding a place of refuge abroad. Yet the plight of Jews was perceived as a problem of immigration rather than a duty of rescue. It was for this reason that flight became such a restricted and elusive option. This essay shows that the immigration-based approach dominated British responses to the question of admitting Jewish refugees to the United Kingdom. This approach classified them primarily as immigrants, and only secondarily as refugees. Jews leaving Europe were seen by British policy makers as problematic immigrants rather than refugees with a claim to asylum; as transmigrants – 'birds of passage' – rather than permanent residents.

Moreover, Jews were seen as the responsibility – above all the financial

[1] Halifax to Lindsay, 31 August 1938, PRO FO 371/21636/422ff (C9002/1667/62).
[2] Ibid., Creswell, minute, 1 Sept. 1938.

responsibility – of the Jewish community rather than of the British people. Anglo-Jewish leaders consequently played a crucial and unprecedented role in the evolution of government policy towards Jews seeking admission. They were driven to this role in part by their own insecurities. Most Jews in Britain were immigrants or the children of immigrants: many long-standing residents were still classified as aliens. The passage of numerous Jewish transmigrants from Eastern Europe through Britain in the 1920s helped to keep alive the Jews' uncertainties about their position in British society. The refugee problem of the 1930s consequently exacerbated their anxieties. Although their own prejudices were important, the refugee agencies and policy makers in the Jewish community also had to contend with the spectre of anti-semitism. Taken together, these anxieties within, as well as anti-semitism without, explain why Jewish leaders accepted a restrictive British government policy as correct.

This essay is thus a chapter in the politics of Anglo-Jewish assimilation as well as part of the history of Jews fleeing Nazi persecution. It traces the triangular relationship between the British government, the refugees and, in a secondary but crucial role, Anglo-Jewry – its communal organizations, leaders and refugee bodies. It focuses primarily on the administrative mechanics of refugee immigration and the close involvement of the Jewish community in immigration procedures. But it also provides insights into British policy makers' reactions and casts light on the responses of different sections of the Anglo-Jewish community – not only their reactions to the refugees, but the impact of the crisis on their Jewish identity and on their perceptions of the role of Anglo-Jewry in British society.[3]

I

In 1933 Britain did not have a refugee policy: any such matter fell under the heading of alien immigration.[4] To the British government, Jewish refugees fleeing Nazism and seeking entry to Britain were first and foremost an immigration problem complicated by anti-semitism. Britain's laws gave no rights of entry or asylum to refugees. British traditions of giving asylum were a matter of secondary importance and possessed no legal force – asylum was merely a privilege conferred by a sovereign state.[5] Freed from any legal obligations to refugees, British policy makers were able to decide refugee

---

[3] The development of British policy on refugees is chronicled in A.J. Sherman, *Island Refuge; Britain and Refugees from the Third Reich, 1933–1939* (London, 1973); See also Bernard Wasserstein, *Britain and the Jews of Europe, 1939–1945* (Oxford, 1979), pp. 1–133, and 'The British Government and the German Immigration 1933–1945', in ed. Gerhard Hirschfeld, *Exile in Great Britain* (London, 1984), pp. 63–81; for refugee organizations, see Norman Bentwich, *They Found Refuge: An Account of British Jewry's Work for Victims of Nazi Oppression* (London, 1956).

[4] In English law there had been no formal distinction between refugees and other aliens since 1919. See Ian A. Macdonald, *Immigration Law and Practice in the United Kingdom* (London, 1987), pp. 7–8, 276.

[5] Wasserstein, 'British Government and German Immigration', pp. 69–70.

admissions within the terms of existing immigration policy, which was already highly restrictive.[6] Yet, like other Western European countries, Britain still valued its liberal tradition of asylum, and sometimes acted in accordance with it.

The bulk of the immigration occurred in the nine months preceding World War II, when over 40,000 Jewish refugees entered Britain; only 11,000 or so came before November 1938.[7] Most refugees from Nazism were admitted to Britain on a strictly temporary basis, pending eventual re-emigration; others might remain only if they posed no threat to British jobs.[8] The determinants of this policy were not only fears of the impact of job-hungry immigrants on British unemployment figures, but also the fear of enlarging the Jewish population. British policy makers ruled out the admission of large numbers of Jews to Britain. The invariable explanation for this policy was the threat of an unacceptable increase in anti-semitism at a time when it was feared that Nazi-style anti-semitism might take root in Britain.[9] This argument was endlessly re-used by the Home Office to disarm its critics, and to discipline those in the Jewish community who cooperated in the management of Jewish immigration.[10]

British policy started from the position that anti-semitism was at least in part caused by Jews and hence must be contained by limiting total Jewish immigration to Britain, carefully selecting those who came.[11] If they were obviously 'foreign' and unassimilated, the problem was greater.[12] The major groupings

[6] When Nazi persecution began to bite in 1933, the countries of potential refuge were already entrenched behind highly restrictionist immigration policies. See Herbert A. Strauss, 'Jewish Emigration from Germany – Nazi Policies and Jewish Responses (I)', *Leo Baeck Institute Year Book*, XXV (London, 1980), pp. 313–61, esp. pp. 346–58. Jewish immigration from Eastern Europe to Britain had been restricted since 1905. See Bernard Gainer, *The Alien Invasion: The Origins of the Aliens Act of 1905* (London, 1972); Todd M. Endelman, 'Native Jews and Foreign Jews in London, 1870–1914', in ed. David Berger, *The Legacy of Jewish Migration: 1881 and its Impact* (New York, 1983), pp. 109–29. Britain restricted Jewish immigration to Palestine for political reasons, linking it with the country's 'economic absorptive capacity'. H. A. Strauss, 'Jewish Emigration from Germany: Nazi Policies and Jewish Responses (II)', *Leo Baeck Institute Year Book*, XXVI (London, 1981), pp. 343–409, esp. pp. 343–57.

[7] Strauss, 'Jewish Emigration (I)', Table X, pp. 354–5. See statistics for 1933–9, and warning about their unreliability, Sherman, *Island Refuge*, Appendix I, 'Migration Statistics', pp. 269–72.

[8] See, for example, statement by Osbert Peake, Parliamentary Under-Secretary for Home Affairs, 19 June 1939, Hansard, House of Commons Debates (H.C. Deb.) 1829, vol. 348, col. 189.

[9] For the impact of governmental concern about the rise of domestic Fascism on refugee policy, see Tony Kushner, *The Persistence of Prejudice: Antisemitism in British Society during the Second World War* (Manchester, 1989) pp. 134–62, 174–80.

[10] The authorities tolerated a high level of anti-Jewish prejudice and were tardy in the defence of Jewish people living in Britain, then used the persistence of this hostility as a rationale for denying refugee Jews access to the UK. See the Home Secretary's remarks to a deputation from Board of Deputies, 1 April 1938, PRO HO 213/42, quoted below, p. 176.

[11] Vyvyan Adams, MP, argued that, to avoid 'fanning the embers of Fascism' by letting unlimited numbers of Jewish refugees into Britain, the gates of Palestine should be opened. *JC*, 8 July 1938, p. 30.

[12] Even persons who sympathized with persecuted Jews could blame the sufferings of 'good' Jews on the misconduct of 'bad' Jews, particularly immigrants. See Sir Horace Rumbold, 28 March and 13 April 1933, Documents 5 and 30, *Documents on British Foreign Policy, 1919–1939*, Second Series, vol. V (London, 1956), pp. 3–6, 38–44.

within the Anglo-Jewish community either did not challenge these assumptions and the consequent restrictions or supported them. In Britain, as in most European countries, Jewish bodies accepted that the best deal they could get for most refugees would be temporary refuge followed by re-emigration to countries of permanent settlement. Moreover, government policies of containment and selection received support in certain sections of Anglo-Jewry. Neither of the warring factions within Anglo-Jewry – the Zionists who advocated settlement in Palestine or the 'assimilationists' who championed emigration to other countries – desired or expected large-scale or permanent movement of refugees to Britain: they shared the assumption that the impact at home would be very limited and easily contained.[13]

In 1922 there was no major controversy over the plans for the refugees: a select few could come from Germany; with the help of the Jewish organizations, the majority would soon re-emigrate; the bulk of the emigration from Germany would be an orderly transfer of the younger generation to overseas destinations, particularly Palestine. When the refugee emergency intensified in 1938–9, British Jews attacked and defied the government over restrictions on immigration to Palestine, but – unlike many non-Jewish critics – were restrained in their criticisms of government policy on admissions to Britain.

Anglo-Jewish leaders shared the government's unwillingness to increase Britain's Jewish population, fearing likewise an anti-semitic backlash – a threat to both refugees and residents. Moreover, Jewish immigrants brought with them problems and burdens. The old-established Anglo-Jewish community had endured much discomfiture at the foreignness and poverty of the immigrants who arrived in Britain from Poland and Russia in 1880–1914. This 'old' community dominated the Jewish refugee organizations and did not challenge the Home Office principle of carefully selecting new immigrants. They fell in with the government's approach, and Jewish refugee organizations assisted the Home Office in the selection of 'desirable' refugees – whose 'desirability' seemed greater the less they resembled the Eastern European Jewish immigrants who had entered Britain a generation earlier.

The initial reactions of Anglo-Jewish leaders to the refugee crisis showed their humanitarian concern. Early in 1933 Anglo-Jewish representatives made their single most crucial intervention in the British response to Jewish refugees from the Third Reich: communal leaders asked the government to admit refugees from Germany, and undertook that the Jewish community would ensure that no refugee would become a charge on public funds. This all-important guarantee was signed by three senior officers of the Board of Deputies, conferring on it the weightiest assurance of communal concern.[14]

---

[13] For conflicts within Anglo-Jewry see chapter 7 by David Cesarani. For tensions between Zionists and non-Zionists over work for German Jewish refugees, see Cesarani, 'Zionism in England, 1917–1939'. D.Phil. thesis (University of Oxford, 1986), pp. 355–69.

[14] 'Proposals of the Jewish Community as Regards Jewish Refugees from Germany', appended to memorandum by Sir John Gilmour, Home Secretary, 6 April 1933, PRO CAB 24/239, C.P. 96/33. The signatories were Neville Laski, KC, President of the London Committee of Deputies of

The leadership's initiatives on refugee matters continued the community's established pattern of assistance to Jewish immigrants, most of whom still emanated from Eastern Europe, via the Jews' Temporary Shelter (JTS) in Whitechapel. The work of the JTS involved meeting Jewish migrants as they arrived in Britain at docks and at the railway termini. Most were transmigrants, passing through Britain on their way overseas. Some stayed at the Shelter, mostly for under seven days, until they could proceed on their journey. In the early and mid-1930s the majority of these visitors to the Shelter were Polish transmigrants.[15] The Shelter helped these impoverished immigrants by providing sufficient hospitality and financial backing to guarantee their admission for the purpose of a brief stop-over in Britain.[16]

Destitute immigrants were a reproach and an embarrassment to the community in its struggle for acceptance in Britain.[17] The Shelter repeatedly emphasized the valuable service rendered by its Advisory Bureau, 'the "safety valve" of the Community, inasmuch as, by the guidance and advice it affords, it saves many of the alien population of this country from committing breaches of the Home Office Aliens regulations and keeps them out of the Police Courts.'[18] Their connections with the Shelter initiated members of the Anglo-Jewish establishment into protecting poor Jewish immigrants and keeping them 'under proper supervision' – especially as regards compliance with immigration controls.[19] This experience facilitated their prompt and practical reactions to the new crisis and helped to mould the response at the level of policy.[20]

The responses of Anglo-Jewish leaders to the German refugee problem were also influenced by the broad pattern of Jewish emigration from Europe. In

British Jews (the Board of Deputies), Lionel L. Cohen, KC, Chairman of the Board's Law, Parliamentary and General Purposes Committee, Leonard G. Montefiore, President of the Anglo-Jewish Association, and Otto M. Schiff, of the Jews' Temporary Shelter and founder of the Jewish Refugees Committee. Laski and Montefiore were *ex officio* joint chairmen of the Board's Joint Foreign Committee.

[15] For nationalities and destinations of Jewish emigrants, see Jews' Temporary Shelter Annual Reports, Annual Reports, 1930–39 (London, 1931–40). The Shelter's year ran to the end of October. See Eugene Black, *The Social Politics of Anglo-Jewry, 1880–1920* (Oxford, 1988).

[16] Regulations limited residence in the Shelter to a maximum of fourteen days.

[17] An episode illustrating both the immense social gulf between the recipients of JTS charity and its organizers, and the contribution this charitable activity made to the preservation of self-respect took place in 1934, when the Secretary of the JTS, Erich Turk, went to Ostend, and 'arranged that any transmigrant en route for Dover who did not look particularly clean should be prevailed upon by the Port Authorities to undergo a cleansing process before embarking for England' – thereby halting an epidemic of refusals on health grounds, based on the allegedly unclean condition of Jewish passengers disembarking at Dover. JTS Annual Report for 1934, pp. 9–10.

[18] JTS Annual Report 1931, p. 9. the Home Office's appreciation of the Shelter's work was expressed by the Home Secretary, J. R. Clynes, at a JTS Appeal dinner in June 1930. JTS Annual Report, 1930, pp. 6–7. Publicizing its 1937 appeal, the Shelter claimed: 'This work is approved by the Authorities. It is important to note that the Shelter protects the honour and prestige of Anglo-Jewry by seeing to it that no transmigrant becomes a charge upon British Public Funds or competes with or displaces British Labour.' *JC*, 1 January 1937, p. 27; and see interview with Otto Schiff, ibid., p. 24.

[19] JTS Annual Report, 1934. p. 9.

[20] Prominent individuals connected both with the Shelter and with committees for refugees from Nazism included Otto Schiff (the Shelter's President), Erich Turk, Leonard Montefiore, Lionel and James de Rothschild, James Layton and the Chief Rabbi, the Very Rev. J. H. Hertz.

1930–40, Jewish emigrants from Europe, whatever their destination, were neither primarily refugees, nor primarily from Germany. JTS statistics gave evidence of this pattern, recording over 25,000 Jewish emigrants annually.[21] The typical Jewish emigrant of the 1930s was from Poland, and saw Britain only as a staging post. This pattern was repeated in Palestine. In the first four years of Nazi rule, the growth of Palestine's Jewish population resulted mainly from emigration from Eastern Europe, although many immigrants were now refugees from Nazi Germany.[22] Thus, the destinies of the Jews of Eastern Europe loomed behind discussions of the destinations of the Jews of Germany. Tortuous diplomatic moves were made by Western governments and international bodies to discourage the governments of Poland, Romania and Hungary from driving out their Jewish populations.[23]

The Board of Deputies saw the admission of refugees to Britain as a subsidiary aspect of the German crisis. Its leaders' approach to the refugee problem mirrored that of Western governments – the solution was the cessation of persecution, rather than the provision of refuge. In pursuit of this policy the Board focused on the need to counter anti-semitism and Nazi propaganda, and held meetings to protest against Nazi outrages. Persecution of Jews by Central European governments was taken up by the Board's Joint Foreign Committee (JFC) at a diplomatic level through representations to governments and the League of Nations.[24] The continuing need for places of refuge led the JFC to take an initiative in calling a conference to plan and co-ordinate Jewish relief efforts for German Jewry. The conference affirmed the pre-eminent position of Palestine among countries of permanent settlement.[25] For Anglo-Jewry, Britain's importance in relation to the refugee problem was perceived less as the holder of the keys to the United Kingdom than as the guardian at the gates of Palestine.

The Board's officers and committees kept formally behind the front line of the refugee effort, but an elaborate network of cross-memberships and co-options linked the Board with the Jewish committees responsible for refugee relief and funds.[26] Relief work for immigrants was seen as a necessary part of sustaining Jewish dignity: a tribute to the Jews' Temporary Shelter in 1937 praised its 'work in palliating suffering and in helping to maintain the prestige of the Jewish community in this country'.[27] This tribute came from the Board's Aliens Committee, which kept close contact with efforts on behalf of Jewish

---

[21] See n. 15 above.

[22] See Strauss, 'Jewish Emigration (II)', pp. 343–57; Werner Rosenstock, 'Exodus 1933–1939: A Survey of Jewish Emigration from Germany', *Leo Baeck Institute Year Book*, I (London, 1956), pp. 373–90. Probably one in five refugees from Germany to Palestine in 1934–5 was Polish or stateless. Bentwich, *The Refugees from Germany, 1933–5* (London, 1936), p. 145.

[23] See Sherman, *Island Refuge*, pp. 108–10, 115–16, 227–42 for responses to the plight of Jews in eastern Europe in 1938–9.

[24] Ibid, pp. 36–9.

[25] See Board of Deputies Annual Report for 1933, pp. 30, 63–65.

[26] Sir Osmond d'Avigdor-Goldsmid, just retired from the Presidency of the Board and chair of the CBF's Allocations Committee, was one of 14 members co-opted by the JFC in 1933.

[27] Board of Deputies Annual Report for 1937, p. 57.

refugees.[28] The Aliens Committee received regular reports from the Chairman of the Jewish Refugees Committee, Otto Schiff.[29] Having satisfied itself that the refugees' needs were being taken care of, the Committee maintained a diplomatic distance from them. It merely issued regular reminders about the consequences of failure to comply with the Aliens Registration rules and emphasized the importance of harmonious relations with the authorities. The leadership of the Board interpreted its role primarily in terms of a duty to represent the interests of the resident Jewish community, and generally focused on the wider task of fostering good relations between Jews and non-Jews in Britain. Officers of the Board and their families participated in refugee work as private individuals. When the Board did deal with refugees it usually confined itself to single interventions aimed at specific problems. As the émigré community expanded, the Board, in conjunction with the German Jewish Aid Committee, published a pamphlet for refugees, designed to minimize friction in the encounter between alien and native.[30]

The main task of negotiating with the Home Office on refugee policy was left to the fourth signatory of the Board of Deputies' guarantee, Otto Schiff, the representative of Anglo-Jewry's work with Jewish immigrants.[31] A German-born City stockbroker, Schiff had done voluntary work for refugees during and after World War I. Since 1922 he had been President of the Jews' Temporary Shelter, where relief efforts for refugees from Nazism began. Schiff inspired and led the work for refugees in Britain, and made crucial contributions to the evolution of government policy.

II

The British Cabinet first discussed Jewish refugees on 5 April 1933. Before this, in anticipation of government thinking, the Jewish organizations took several steps. They had already felt the impact of German Jews seeking refuge. Some of the new arrivals had turned to the Shelter. Schiff, the Shelter's principal officer, met the need for a new organization, starting the Jewish Refugees Committee (JRC) in March 1933.[32] The Central British Fund for German Jewry (CBF), the JRC's funding body, was set up later, after a meeting at the Rothschild bank's City headquarters.[33] Schiff, in conjunction with other

[28] Board of Deputies Annual Report for 1933, p. 37.

[29] Schiff was not elected to the Board, but was co-opted onto the JFC in 1933. See Board of Deputies Annual Report 1933, p. 26; 1934, p. 45; 1935, p. 39; 1936, p. 48; 1937, p. 57; 1938, p. 44; 1939, p. 30.

[30] See Sherman, *Island Refuge*, pp. 218–19; Gisela Lebzelter, *Political Anti-Semitism in England, 1918–1939*, (London, 1978), pp. 136–54. When administrative chaos overwhelmed the refugee bodies in late 1938, the Board investigated to satisfy itself that deficiencies were being made good.

[31] Otto Moritz Schiff (1875–1952). See obituary, *The Times*, 17 and 18 November 1952; *Jewish Chronicle*, 21 November 1952. p. 9; tributes, ibid. 28 November 1952, p. 9; Appreciation by H. Oscar Joseph, ibid., 2 May 1975, p. 9.

[32] The Jewish Refugees Committee became the German Jewish Aid Committee (GJAC) in January 1938; two years later the old name was resumed. Bentwich, *They Found Refuge*, p. 50.

[33] See Bentwich, *They Found Refuge*, esp. pp. 14–29; Joan Stiebel (Schiff's private secretary), 'The Central British Fund for World Relief', *Transactions of the Jewish Historical Society of England*, 27 (1982), pp. 51–60.

Anglo-Jewish leaders, now promised the government that the community would shoulder the burden of this new influx. The government was presented with a memorandum which guaranteed that 'all expense, whether in respect of temporary or permanent accommodation or maintenance, will be borne by the Jewish community without ultimate charge to the state'.[34]

The Jewish guarantee was designed to help refugees over the requirement in the Aliens Order that immigrants should demonstrate that they could support themselves and their dependants. Even affluent refugees would run out of funds sooner or later and want the chance to earn their living, but Schiff and his co-signatories did not ask that refugees be permitted to work. The government was told of the formation of the new Jewish Organization, but no financial evidence was put forward to show that the guarantee was a practical proposition – the CBF did not yet exist. The Cabinet set up a small committee to consider whether this guarantee by the Jewish community justified a relaxation of the provisions of the Aliens Order.[35]

The guarantee became the cornerstone of British refugee policy and the Jewish community was held to its promise until after the outbreak of World War II. Initially, the role of the Jewish bodies was conditioned by three interlocking elements: a firm promise of finance, unspecified plans for re-emigration, and belief that the total number of refugees would be small. The explicit reassurance given by the leadership to the government that they would limit the scale and the financial burden of the influx was based on a more far-reaching but less explicit understanding established at the same time – that the Anglo-Jewish community would itself control and contain the impact of the new arrivals on the host community, as in the past – through hospitality, guidance and dispersal. The offer of the financial guarantee was linked with plans for re-emigration: 'Negotiations are in progress with a view to the ultimate transmigration of refugees to countries other than England.' No mention was made of any future limitation on the community's capacity to honour the guarantee. According to Schiff, the numbers of arrivals would be perhaps three or four thousand, the bulk of whom would be of the professional classes. The determination of the Jewish leadership to maintain contact with the refugees – and to make sure the government was aware that they were doing so – was shown in the one restriction asked for in the Jewish memorandum: it should be a condition of leave to land in Britain that refugees register at the Jews' Temporary Shelter, whose representatives would meet all continental trains. Further reassurance as to the community's containment of the impact of the refugees was supplied by mention of a Hospitality Committee. In return for their pledge to finance and manage the influx, the Jewish representatives asked the government to grant temporary asylum to all refugees from Germany. Those arriving at the ports should be admitted 'without distinction'. Those

---

[34] See n. 14 above.
[35] Report of Cabinet Committee on Aliens Restrictions, 7 April 1933, PRO CAB 24/239, C.P. 96/33; ibid., Appendix I, memorandum by Home Secretary, 6 April 1933; Sherman, *Island Refuge*, pp. 29–32; Wasserstein, 'British Government and German Immigration', pp. 66–8.

already admitted 'should be allowed during the present emergency to prolong their stay indefinitely'.[36]

This request for asylum was rejected. The Cabinet, in line with the Committee's recommendations, decided to subject refugees to a requirement of immediate registration with the police, and otherwise to maintain existing entry arrangements.[37] Decisions at the ports had already made entry conditions for refugees stricter than for most aliens: refugees admitted in the first three days of April had been subjected both to a time condition (generally one month) and a condition forbidding employment.[38] The scale of the influx was not yet alarming, but the Committee did not accept Schiff's low estimate, noting that 'pressure to emigrate' was likely to increase.

However, the Cabinet decided to accept the Jewish guarantee. The Committee assumed the Jewish community had 'ample financial means to implement the guarantee', while the promise of re-emigration was welcomed as a safety valve against the accumulation of refugees in Britain.[39] The guarantee covered only Jews of German nationality: no commitment was made to ease the entry of non-German Jews fleeing Germany, who were largely excluded. Polish, Hungarian and stateless Jews all needed visas, which were not yet thought necessary for German refugees.[40] British policy was to refuse visas to Jews of Polish and Hungarian nationality who were suspected of being refugees. Poles and Hungarians were expected to return to their own country; stateless Jews were already virtually excluded under existing policy – the fact that many were now potential refugees was seen as an added reason for maintaining the ban.[41]

The Government was thus armed with extensive powers of control. Its refugee employment policy was calculated to confer benefits on Britain while displacing the financial risk onto the Jewish community. The Cabinet would not give general permission for refugees to take employment – this was seen as a potentially explosive issue – but Ministers were alerted to the potential benefit to the nation of allowing Jewish refugees who had already achieved distinction to continue their careers in the UK.[42] Some refugees offered opportunities which could only be realized by letting them work: 'There may be a certain

[36] See n. 14 above.

[37] Sherman, *Island Refuge*, pp. 32–3.

[38] Normal practice was to impose no conditions at the ports, unless some suspicion existed about an alien's future conduct; see Report, n. 35 above.

[39] Ibid.

[40] A visa was applied for abroad, and no alien requiring a visa could expect admission without one. Agreements for the mutual abolition of visas had been concluded in 1927 with both the Austrian and the German governments. See note of conclusions of interdepartmental meeting, 17 March 1938, PRO FO 372/3282/32ff (T 3605/3272/378) (which gives an incorrect date for the agreement with Germany).

[41] Ibid. 'There has been a certain number of applications by such persons to visit friends or relatives in this country but in such circumstances which indicate that the real motive is a desire to escape from Germany: these, on present practice, are refused.'

[42] See Sherman, *Island Refuge*, pp. 32–9, 42–4, 270; statements by the Home Secretary, 12 April 1933, 276 H.C. Deb., 2557–8, and Foreign Secretary, 13 April 1933, 276 H.C. Deb., 2807–12; Herbert Loebl, 'Refugee Industries in the Special Areas of Britain', in *Exile in Great Britain*, pp. 219–49.

number who could usefully be absorbed by this country ... some of the fur trade which has hitherto been centred in Leipzig may be, at least temporarily, transferred to London, and if so there would be room for a certain number of Jewish fur traders here.'[43] Henceforth the government discreetly encouraged selective immigration of refugees in certain desired categories. The rest had to qualify in the ordinary way, along with other foreigners.[44] Aliens who could not demonstrate the ability to support themselves and their dependants were normally excluded by the immigration authorities, but here the guarantee came to the rescue. An alien who was in possession of a Ministry of Labour permit could be admitted for employment, but no permit would be granted if this might take a job from a British resident.

The government did not engage in formal recruitment of refugees, but its policy of 'benevolent laissez-faire rather than vigorous direction' towards intellectual *émigrés* created a space for the development of voluntary initiatives, such as the Academic Assistance Council (AAC).[45] In May 1933 the AAC began to help scholars and scientists who had been forced out of university posts.[46] The AAC's approach to assisting displaced academics was cautious and highly selective, and it fostered re-emigration. There was a corresponding emphasis on emigration overseas in the work of the German Emergency Committee of the Society of Friends, set up in April 1933 by British Quakers, which primarily helped baptized Jews and non-Jewish refugees.[47] The Home Secretary praised the refugee organizations for these careful selection policies.[48]

[43] By 1939 the contribution of refugees had turned London into the most important fur market in the world. See Home Secretary's speech, n. 48 below; Sir John Hope Simpson, *The Refugee Problem: Report of a Survey* (London, 1939), p. 343.

[44] This dual aspect of the immigration authorities' approach was evident even prior to the Cabinet's decision. A few impecunious refugees had already been turned back, but the rules had not been applied strictly in all cases. The Committee's report mentioned three such cases: two were refused leave to land, but an 18-year-old apprentice tailoress, in possession of £2, was allowed to land for a limited period 'on purely compassionate grounds'. Report, see n. 35 above.

[45] Quoted from Wasserstein, 'Intellectual Émigrés in Britain, 1933–39', in eds Jarrell C. Jackman and Carla M. Borden, *The Muses Flee Hitler: Cultural Transfer and Adaptation, 1930–1945*, (Washington, DC, 1983), pp. 249–56.

[46] For the work of the AAC, see Bentwich, *The Rescue and Achievement of Refugee Scholars: The Story of Displaced Scholars and Scientists, 1933–1952* (The Hague, 1953) and *They Found Refuge*, pp. 16–19; Esther Simpson, Tape 4469, 'Britain and the Refugee Crisis 1933–47', Imperial War Museum. The AAC was set up by leading non-Jewish academics. Jews and non-Jews cooperated closely in refugee work, but non-Jews were seen as more effective advocates for Jewish refugees in Britain.

[47] Out of 7,000 persons assisted, 5,000 had emigrated by 1939; Hope Simpson, *Refugees: A Review of the Situation Since September 1938* (London, 1939), pp. 72–3.

[48] Sir Samuel Hoare spoke for the Society for the Protection of Science and Learning (as the AAC was now known) at a meeting on 6 February 1939. Welcoming the 'opportunity of attracting to these shores brains and experience of immeasurable value to our people', Hoare said, 'We must act cautiously, but none the less sympathetically. We must give no cause for any anti-Semitic or anti-refugee reaction in this country. The refugee organisations, to which I pay a most sincere tribute today, are fully alive to the need of careful enquiry and selection. So careful indeed have they been in insisting that no immigrant should displace British labour that 11,000 immigrants have provided work for 15,000 British workers who would not otherwise be employed. This result has been due above all things to very careful selection.' Hoare, *Refugees: Their Contribution to English National Life* (London, 1939), pp. 4–5; *JC*, 10 February 1939, pp. 7–8, 17.

III

From the start, the expenditure of the CBF reflected plans made by the Jewish Agency in 1933 to direct German Jews, particularly the young, to Palestine, and provide training or retraining for emigration.[49] The Fund embarked on a task of reconstruction rather than relief, undertaken in partnership with the community in Germany. Only £30,000 of the £100,000 raised in the first year was spent for maintenance of needy refugees admitted to the UK – the first charge on the fund. A large part of the remainder in this and subsequent years went to projects supporting emigration to Palestine, including the construction of housing. In 1936, the Council for German Jewry (CGJ) was formed after it was realized that the problem was greater than had been foreseen.[50] The CGJ incorporated the leadership of British, American and Continental Jewry, and adopted a stepped-up programme, largely implemented, of permanent emigration from Germany to overseas destinations. In its first year the CGJ raised £800,000 in Britain alone, more than three times the CBF's total in 1933–5. In 1933–6, 41,000 German Jews emigrated to Palestine: under 10,000 came to Britain.[51]

In the early phase, the migration of refugees from Germany and Austria to Britain was a movement of individuals who did not need visas. When they arrived they were admitted for a limited period and restricted from taking employment without permission. A large proportion of the new arrivals were directed to the JRC. Most refugees needed help with employment, training, finance, hospitality or emigration. Consciousness of the importance of emigration led to the formation of an Emigration Department of the JRC long before the Immigration Subcommittee came into existence.[52] Among many steps and projects to help refugees, it is possible to single out two in which Otto Schiff was involved.

The first illustrates Schiff's management of an existing body to help refugees, and the pressure on the JRC to help refugees already in Britain, rather than encourage further immigration. The Jewish Ecclesiatical Advisory Committee had been formed in 1932 at the request of the Home Office, to advise congregations and the Home Office on appointments of rabbis and chazanim from abroad. Schiff was chairman of this committee. In early 1934 Schiff had threatened to resign, expressing his anger that the committee had become a vehicle for unscrupulous synagogue officials to bring over unsuitable relatives from Eastern Europe, one of whom had recently been deported.[53] The

---

[49] Bentwich, *They Found Refuge*, pp. 19–29 and *Refugees from Germany*, pp. 121–2; Strauss, 'Jewish Emigration (II)', pp. 343–4.

[50] Bentwich, *They Found Refuge*, pp. 30–4.; Hope Simpson, *Refugees: Preliminary Report of a Survey* (London, 1938), p. 63.

[51] Strauss, 'Jewish Emigration (I)', Table I, p. 346; 'Jewish Emigration (II)', Table X, pp. 354–5.

[52] Bentwich, *They Found Refuge*, p. 51.

[53] *JC*, 16 February 1934, p. 18.

threatened dissolution of the committee had been averted after the Chief Rabbi and Schiff attended a meeting at which the Home Office pressed the case for continuing its work.[54] In November 1934, Schiff presided over a meeting which asked congregations with vacancies, rather than bringing over a chazan from abroad, to consider chazanim who were refugees from Germany, four of whom were now on the hands of the JRC.[55]

Schiff's work on a new scheme also illustrates his confidential relationship with the Home Office. Schiff regularly met with officials over refugee cases and policies. He developed a close working relationship with E. N. Cooper, Principal and later Assistant Secretary in the Aliens Department of the Home Office. Cooper was helpful and sympathetic to refugees, but the Aliens Department had its own agenda of limiting numbers. This was demonstrated in 1937. Schiff proposed a new scheme for the temporary admission of refugees to learn English before emigrating to Australia: Cooper agreed to the scheme, but linked the admission of additional arrivals with the embarkation of previous entrants.[56] Cooper also seized this opportunity to include thirty refugees already in Britain in the numbers emigrating, in order to avoid 'the difficulties connected with their establishment in this country'. A report evaluating the potential emigrants on behalf of the CGJ shows the anxiety that 'desirable' Jews should be chosen for emigration. These negotiations also show the beginnings of what was to become an important area of work for Anglo-Jewry – the selection of German refugees for emigration. The emigrants for the scheme were to be chosen by the JRC, which sent emissaries to Germany for this purpose, including some of the many friends and associates whom Schiff had recruited into his refugee work, such as Julian Layton.[57]

IV

Involvement of Anglo-Jewish refugee workers in the task of approving refugees for admission increased after the Anschluss in March 1938. Immediate and unprecedented pressure on Austrian Jews to emigrate led to the blocking of crucial paths of escape before more than a handful could depart. Britain responded with the reintroduction of visas for holders of Austrian and German passports in order to stem the flow of refugees to British ports. Anglo-Jewish representatives played a key part in these moves to restrict Jewish emigration. This will be dealt with in detail below, but the episode needs also to be related to attempts by the German government to avert the reimposition of visas for all German citizens by several countries – Britain, Switzerland, Sweden and

[54] *JC*, 2 March 1934, p. 18.
[55] *JC*, 16 November 1934, p. 13.
[56] 'German Refugees: Australian Immigration', PRO HO 213/250.
[57] Julian Layton, Tape 4382, Imperial War Museum; Interview, 20 April 1988. Norman Bentwich mentions having 'sifted' Australian candidates in several German cities in the summer of 1937, in N. Bentwich, *Wanderer between Two Worlds* (London, 1941), p. 270.

Australia. Britain's introduction of visas helped pave the way for Germany's decision to introduce the *J-pass* – a passport for Jews which carried the distinguishing mark of a letter 'J' – a means for the countries of refuge to pick out Jewish refugees.

By early 1938, the dimming prospects of a reduction in the numbers of refugees in Britain, and the likelihood of a new wave of refugees from Austria, led to discussions of ways to reduce the number of refugees entering the country. The Home Office wished to avoid the worry, extra work and public pressure which would result from an increase in port refusals and was aware that re-introducing visas for holders of Austrian and German passports would increase control over arrivals. The rationale for making this change was that once refugees had reached British shores it was usually too late to try to get rid of them: 'The proper course is to select our immigrants at leisure and in advance, and this means the institution of a visa system, for Germans and Austrians... The real point is to prevent potential refugees from getting here at all.'[58]

The Anschluss, and the prospect of a big influx of Jews fleeing persecution in Austria, elicited prompt action by Jewish representatives to establish some control over admissions, and gave Home Office discussions on visas a new urgency. By 12 March – within hours of Austria's occupation by Germany – someone, probably Schiff, had already told the Home Office that the Jewish refugee organization could no longer be financially responsible for any further Jewish refugees admitted to Britain.[59] This position was modified two days later, to indicate that an exception might be made for refugees admitted after consultation with the GJAC. As German forces marched into Vienna, the Home Office demanded the reintroduction of visas, using the reservations of the GJAC as part of its case.[60] Home Office anxiety was not merely about numbers, but also the types of Jews who might seek asylum in Britain: 'small traders and businessmen of limited means ... who may not be individually undesirable but may create social and labour problems'. The Home Office prevailed, but the decision was officially secret until late April.[61]

Weeks before the public learned of the new policy, it was discussed with a deputation to the Home Secretary from the Board of Deputies, in which Schiff took a leading role.[62] He indicated that his organization was also urging greater control of entry through visas. The reasons he gave showed the extent to which he endorsed the Home Office principle of careful selection of Jewish refugees, and of linking admissions to re-emigration prospects. It was 'very difficult to get

[58] McAlpine, memorandum, 1 March 1938, PRO HO 213/94.

[59] Strang, minute, 12 March 1938, PRO FO 372/3282/2ff (T 3272/3272/378); Bentwich, *They Found Refuge*, p. 45.

[60] Pimlott to Harvey, 15 March 1938, PRO FO 372/3282/21ff (T 3517/3272/378). See Sherman *Island Refuge* p. 87.; Wasserstein, 'British Government and German Immigration', p. 71.

[61] A reference to visas was cut from a statement on refugee policy by the Home Secretary, Sir Samuel Hoare, in the House of Commons on 22 March 1938, see minutes and correspondence, 21 March 1938, PRO FO 372/3282/56ff (T 3807/3272/378).

[62] Minutes of meeting with deputation, 1 April 1938, PRO HO 213/42.

rid of a refugee . . . once he had entered and spent a few months in this country. the imposition of the visa was especially necessary in the case of Austrians who were largely of the shopkeeper and small trader class and would therefore prove much more difficult to emigrate than the average German who had come to the United Kingdom.' Schiff's argument for visas reflected the financial worries of the GJAC, yet also mirrored class prejudices within the community. The contrast with the open-handed response of Anglo-Jewry to the plight of German Jews in 1933 reflected not only the greater scale of the crisis, but the greater social and personal distance from Austrian Jewry.[63] Instructions later issued to officials reiterated Schiff's prejudices by stating that among visa applicants 'those who must be regarded as prima facie unsuitable will be . . . small shopkeepers, retail traders, artisans and persons likely to seek employment.'[64] The Home Secretary warned, with the consensus of those present:

It would be necessary for the Home Office to discriminate very carefully as to the type of refugee who could be admitted to this country. If a flood of the wrong type of immigrants were allowed in there might be serious danger of anti-semitic feeling being aroused in this country. The last thing which we wanted here was the creation of a Jewish problem. The Deputation said they entirely agreed with this point of view.

Later, the support of the refugee organizations for the reimposition of visas was cited by Ministers facing critical questions in Parliament.[65]

The Germans reacted to the impending reintroduction of visas by putting intense diplomatic effort into getting this change reversed. The German Chargé d'Affaires put forward proposals for collusion between British and German officials to prevent unwanted *émigrés* from leaving Germany.[66] The proposed collaboration would operate through controls by German passport officials: unless Britain had previously approved the entry of particular would-be emigrants, they would either be denied passport facilities or their passports would be made invalid for travel to the UK.[67] The Head of the Foreign Office's Treaty Department, Sir Nevile Bland, saw no objections of principle to British collusion with the Nazi regime to keep unwelcome Jewish refugees in Germany. He commented that 'Under their proposals it is *we* who pass the refugee and the Germans only let him go when we have chosen him.'[68] Despite Bland's

---

[63] See the vivid comparison of German and Austrian refugees by William Zukerman, 'Refugees in England', *Quarterly Review* (April 1939), pp. 206–20.

[64] Foreign Office, Passport Control Department, Circular, 'Visas for Holders of German and Austrian Passports entering the United Kingdom', p. 3, 27 April 1938, PRO FO 372/3283/329ff (T 6705/3272/378), discussed by Sherman, *Island Refuge*, pp. 90–91.

[65] Butler, 4 May 1938, 335 H.C.Deb., 843–4; Hoare, 21 July 1938, 338 H.C.Deb., 2400–1.

[66] See minutes and correspondence in April and May 1938, PRO FO 372/3283/193ff (T 5565/6053/6352/6620/6718/3272/378); For the Home Office side of these discussions, see PRO HO 213/95.

[67] Cf. Sherman, *Island Refuge*, p. 89; Strauss, 'Jewish Emigration (I)', p. 361

[68] Bland, minute, 19 May 1938, PRO FO 372/3283/304ff (T 6620/3272/378).

warm recommendation of the German scheme, the Home Office was unimpressed.[69]

Like the German *J-pass*, Britain's new visa requirement was one of many obstacles initiated by the countries of refuge, which impeded flight and increased the pressure to emigrate illegally.[70] Many refugees did not wait for a decision, but fled without documents.[71] The scope for illegal entry to Britain was far more limited than to countries on the European mainland, but attempts were made by stowaways, people who rowed across the Channel in small boats, and other clandestine entrants. Those discovered entering illegally could expect deportation or expulsion: the Home Office felt it necessary to deal strictly with blatant evasion of immigration controls, and the Jewish community dared not protest loudly.[72] In general, evasion of British immigration controls took the form of attempts to mislead the immigration authorities. Passport Control officers tried to judge whether visa applicants who claimed to be coming to Britain on tourist or business visits were really potential refugees.[73] The authorities experimented with various methods of detecting inconsistent statements by applicants from Germany and Austria, including writing coded signals into their passports.[74]

V

In the summer of 1938 a crucial shift in refugee policy commenced within the Home Office. The immigration-based approach was modified to put greater

[69] Although forgotten in Britain, the German proposals had serious repercussions elsewhere. For German negotiations with Switzerland, see Joseph Tenebaum, 'The Crucial Year 1938', in *Yad Vashem Studies II* (Jerusalem, 1959), pp. 49–77; Carl Ludwig, *Die Fluchtlingspolitik der Schweiz seit 1933 bis zur Gegenwart* (Berlin, 1957), pp. 78–83, 124–9. For German negotiations with Sweden, see Helmut Müssener, *Exil in Schweden – Politische und Kulturelle Emigration nach 1933* (Munich, 1974), p. 65.

[70] For Nazi victimization of Jews outside the British Consulate in Vienna, see *JC*, 29 April 1938, p. 18; for arrests of Jews outside the Vienna Consulate early on 10 November 1938 (*Kristallnacht*), see Arthur D. Morse, *While Six Million Died* (London, 1968), p. 224.

[71] The problem of illegal immigration grew with the intensity of the persecution Jews faced. Eliahu Ben Elissar, *La Diplomatie du IIIe Reich et les Juifs, 1933–1939* (Paris, 1969), pp. 244–5; Hugo Rank made a clandestine flight from Austria to Switzerland, tape 4342, Imperial War Museum.

[72] For stowaways, see *JC*, 22 July 1938, p. 20; 29 July 1938, p. 22. For deportation of two Jews who had rowed across the Channel, *JC*, 4 August 1939, p. 21; For treatment of clandestine entrants see Sherman, *Island Refuge*, pp. 125–7; *JC*, 26 August 1938, p. 8; *JC*, 2 September 1938, p. 10. For port decisions see T. W. E. Roche, an ex-immigration officer, *The Key in the Lock: A History of Immigration Control in England from 1066 to the Present Day* (London, 1969), pp. 126–8.

[73] The Passport Control Officer in Budapest wished to prevent applicants from obtaining visas in case they should need them later. He told his superiors, 'The type of Jew found in Central Europe, no matter what his status or position, is notoriously untruthful and consequently statements must be examined with the utmost reserve.' Farrell to Director, Passport Control Department, 25 April 1938 and see also 9 July 1938, PRO HO 213/97.

[74] The detailed instructions for deciding visa applications issued in April 1938 (see above n. 64) were amended twice in the next four months: Foreign Office, Passport Control Department, Circulars, 'Visas for Holders of German and Austrian Passports entering the United Kingdom', 10 June 1938 and 30 August 1938, PRO FO 372/3284/8ff (T7056/3272/378). See arguments against re-introducing visas, Creswell, minute, 12 March 1938, PRO FO 372/3282/4ff (T3272/3272/378).

emphasis on rescue, but for months it seemed as if the change existed largely on paper. The immediate impact of the change was the build-up of a mountain of unresolved casework. The Home Office increased the burden of casework twice, first with the new visa restriction in May, then with a liberalized admissions policy in July. It failed twice to invest in administrative expansion to process the resulting mass of applications. Nor would it give the voluntary organizations the funds to do the work. Instead, it shifted more of the casework burden onto the overstretched voluntary bodies, involving them more closely in the work of selection. Accumulations of casework defeated the combined resources of the government and the voluntary bodies. The speed-up of admissions had to wait, until developments later in the year pushed the Home Office to make some exceptions to the full rigours of the visa system it had been so keen to re-erect a few months before.

During the period of restriction from mid-March to July, the administrative burden of the refugee problem had already expanded alarmingly. Visas were obligatory for Austrian passport holders from 2 May 1938 and for German passport holders from 21 May. Chaos ensued after visas were reintroduced – especially in Vienna. The impact of the reintroduction of visas in May had been to increase restriction, piling the cumbersome formalities of preliminary investigation on top of new narrowed-down guidelines for selection. The Home Office had succeeded in shifting part of its problem to Foreign Office outposts, but it was far from solved. There were not enough people to deal with the work. Hopes of eliminating the backlog and reducing delays were dashed by antiquated communications and ever-increasing numbers of would-be émigrés.[75]

Now the Home Office made a second fateful change in policy. The forthcoming Evian conference on refugees obliged the Home Office to address itself to the possibility of a more generous refugee policy. In the month before the conference, the new approach was formulated. At Evian, it formed part of the policy statement of the British delegation.[76] The major change was that 'on the grounds of humanity' the Home Office would now adopt a liberal attitude in the matter of admissions.[77] Certain additions to the categories of admission were also outlined, particularly for training with a view to emigration. The professional lobbies dictated that strict limits on doctors and dentists had to stay, but the only absolute limitation on numbers would now be the amount of hospitality, maintenance and employment the voluntary organizations could arrange. In the ensuing weeks the government stood by its new attitude, and decided to reveal to the new Inter-Governmental Committee on Refugees, which the Evian conference set up, that it had 'for some time past' been

[75] Sherman, *Island Refuge*, pp. 132–4; See Mary Ormerod's complaints about delays caused by bad communications, June–July 1938, PRO FO 371/21751/190ff (C 5809/2311/18).

[76] See Sherman, *Island Refuge*, pp. 95–122. The Home Office was under pressure to humanize policy from the Co-ordinating Committee, a representative body set up by the refugee organizations in April 1938, apparently at the Home Office's request. See ibid., pp. 99–100; Schiff, 1 April 1938, see n. 62 above; Hope Simpson, *Refugee Problem*, pp. 338–9.

[77] Sherman, *Island Refuge*, pp. 108–9.

recruiting refugees with capital to set up new factories.[78] Ministers stressed that there could nevertheless be no indiscriminate admission of refugees and that this policy had the support of the private refugee organizations.[79]

Being short of funds, the voluntary organizations had already set up financial hurdles for sponsors. They were now maintaining many jobless domestics and other refugees whose jobs or guarantees had fallen through. The spectre of yet more dependants was alarming. They warned the Home Office that they could not take financial responsibility for refugees whose circumstances they had not previously checked. They were already being used by the Home Office to sift applications, including those of prospective domestics.[80] Now the Aliens Department added to their administrative responsibilities. Refugee employment matters were removed from the Ministry of Labour, and the Co-ordinating Committee was authorized to investigate domestic applicants – the Home Office undertook to issue visas to those who were approved. This role gave the refugee bodies a measure of control, but they lacked both the funds and the administrative capacity to cope with the caseload.[81] Financial constraints hampered their efforts to expand the limited supply of maintenance and jobs available for refugees. They became more apprehensive about people whom they had not themselves approved. Their new powers to authorize the grant of visas gave them a greater appetite for control over admissions and reinforced their demands for funds. In October 1938 they alleged 'a complete breakdown, on the official side, of the policy of selected immigration through the voluntary organisations', objecting to admissions not previously authorized by them.[82] This elicited an illustration of the partial reversal of roles which had taken place, as Lord Winterton defended the right of the Home Office to admit persons not approved by the refugee committees.[83] Schiff's long-mooted plan for an office in Vienna never materialized. Casework delays multiplied. After another unsuccessful appeal to the government for funds, the Co-ordinating Committee staged a withdrawal from the task of assisting the Home Office with casework. The Committee's piles of unsifted visa correspondence were deposited at the Aliens Department. Next the Committee rejected the task of investigating visa applications for the Home Office. The GJAC, in a state of increasing alarm about finance, tried to limit its commitments – Schiff requested a temporary halt on admissions, and said his committee could not undertake responsibility for the new refugees from Czechoslovakia.[84]

[78] Cooper to Under-Secretary of State, 9 September 1938, PRO FO 371/22534/1 (W 12173/104/98); Sherman, *Island Refuge*, p. 131; Loebl, 'Refugee Industries', p. 221.

[79] See Lord Winterton, 29 July 1938, 338 H.C.Deb., 3565; House of Lords debate, 27 July 1938, Sherman, *Island Refuge*, pp. 122–3. Viscount Samuel said 'Emigration, if it is gradual and if it is of persons carefully selected, would not embarrass, but would enrich the country which accepted it.' 27 July 1938, 110 H.L.Deb., 1216–24.

[80] Sherman, *Island Refuge*, pp. 99–100.

[81] Ibid., pp. 124–5, 131–2, 155–6.

[82] Ibid., pp. 155–6, quoting Ormerod to Winterton, 18 October 1938.

[83] Ibid., pp. 155–6, quoting Winterton's remarks to deputation (Schiff, Mary Ormerod, Viscount Bearsted), 20 October 1938.

[84] Ibid., pp. 157–8.

As the urgency of rescue grew, many voices in the Jewish community criticized the chaos which reigned at Woburn House, headquarters of the Jewish refugee bodies. The Home Office had aggravated the problem by ruling that all refugee applications should in the first instance be made to the Jewish bodies: 'The effect has been that the passage through Woburn House has become a "bottleneck" from which an ever-growing army of refugees and their friends struggle to emerge.'[85] An urgent overhaul of refugee headquarters was set in motion. Sir Henry Bunbury, formerly Comptroller and Accountant-General of the General Post Office, was brought in as unpaid administrative head of the GJAC.[86] Schiff carried on as Chairman. Defending his organization's record, he pointed to the disruptive impact of the year's crises, and equivalent problems of delay at the Home Office.[87]

VI

After *Kristallnacht* in November, the urgent demand for places of temporary refuge was pursued by a host of Jewish and non-Jewish voices.[88] The CGJ launched an appeal to 'save all whom it is possible to rescue, especially the young.'[89] On 15 November the Prime Minister, Neville Chamberlain, was visited by a high-ranking CGJ deputation, led by Viscount Samuel, a former Home Secretary, and asked to facilitate the temporary admission of young people to age seventeen, for training and education. The deputation offered a guarantee on behalf of the young people – and made a plea for extra staff to help reduce the visa backlog.[90] As the Cabinet discussed the issue the next day, the Prime Minister asked a hesitant Home Secretary to consider allowing Jewish refugees to come to Britain as a temporary refuge.[91]

At this juncture, a new phase opened in refugee admissions. The rate of admissions was transformed. From an estimated 11,000 refugees admitted before November 1938, the numbers climbed until perhaps 55,000 refugees from Germany, Austria and Czechoslovakia had arrived in Britain by the outbreak of war on 3 September 1939.[92] This expansion was largely due to the

[85] *JC*, 9 December 1938, pp. 7, 21. Cf. Bentwich, *They Found Refuge*, pp. 54–5, who does not deal with the problems over visas.

[86] *JC*, 23 December 1938, pp. 8, 26–7; 13 January 1939, p. 23.

[87] *JC*, 13 January 1939, pp. 23–4, reacting to a refugee's criticisms made *JC*, 6 January 1939, p. 27; see women's criticisms, ibid., p. 36.

[88] *JC*, 4 November 1938, p. 20; 11 November 1938, p. 24; 18 November 1938, pp. 7, 24; 25 November 1938, p. 31.

[89] *JC*, 18 November 1938, p. 31.

[90] Record of meeting, 16 November 1938, PRO FO 371/22536/250ff (W 15037/104/98). For role of Helen (Mrs Norman) Bentwich in persuading Samuel to make this intervention, see Bentwich, *Wanderer Between Two Worlds*, p. 283. For reactions to *Kristallnacht* in Britain, see Sherman, *Island Refuge*, pp. 170–222, esp. pp. 171–6 and 213–14. The visa backlog stood at about 10,000 cases.

[91] Cabinet Conclusions, 55(38)5, 16 November 1938, PRO CAB 23/96.

[92] See n. 7 above.

increased use of transmigration as a category under which refugees could be admitted with less selectivity – albeit on a strictly temporary basis. They were not to be granted permanent asylum, but would be granted permission to come to Britain on condition that they either stay off the labour market or emigrate overseas. Children and young people would be expected to leave after completing their education or training, while adults were tied more closely to arrangements for onward emigration to the USA and elsewhere. The announcement of this new policy was made by the Home Secretary in the House of Commons on 21 November 1938, during a historic debate on the refugee question.[93] Working closely with the Home Office, Jewish communal workers presided over this new phase of transmigration.[94]

The Home Office now acted to by-pass some of the red tape it had created in the spring. A speed-up was achieved through procedural changes which partially dismantled the visa system. Decision-making on the bulk of applications for entry was shifted from the authorities to the voluntary bodies. They could now approve several more categories of refugee, and the Home Office relied on their assessments, without making inquiries of its own. For certain cases the Home Office dispensed with individual visa applications altogether, substituting a system of block visas, based on lists of names (known as 'nominal rolls') and serially numbered cards in coded colours. This procedure covered children's transports and certain closely defined categories of adult refugees: emigrants in transit, trainees, domestics, persons over sixty years of age, Czechs, and men bound for the Richborough transit camp.[95] The selection of individuals to receive visas could also now be made on the Continent by bodies linked to the Co-Ordinating Committee.

As concern for refugees spread among Jews and non-Jews, the main obstacle within British control, lack of resources, diminished.[96] The principle that private finance must be guaranteed was unshaken, except for refugees from Czechoslovakia, who were regarded differently.[97] The continuing role of the voluntary bodies in determining the limits of admissions – temporary or

---

[93] Sherman, *Island Refuge*, pp. 179–82; 341 H.C.Deb. 1428–1483, esp. 1471–2. The Jewish members present kept silent by collective agreement, and were complimented for their restraint in 'refraining from taking up the role of special pleaders'; the Chief Rabbi watched from an upstairs gallery. Ibid. Col. 1477; *JC*, 25 November 1938, p. 32.

[94] On 23 November 1938 the Commons was told that discussions with the Inter-Aid Committee for Children had produced an agreed scheme 'to eliminate all delay so far as His Majesty's Government are concerned' in the entry of children under the committee's auspices. Lloyd, 341 H.C.Deb., 1734–5. This mixed Christian and Jewish committee had been in existence since 1936, and had already brought 471 boys and girls to Britain: Bentwich, *They Found Refuge*, p. 65.

[95] Cooper to Brooks, 28 Mar. 1939, PRO FO 371/24076/210ff (W 5248/45/48); Hope Simpson, *Refugees: A Review*, pp. 68–74, esp. p. 69.

[96] Sherman, *Island Refuge*, pp. 183–5; Bentwich, *They Found Refuge*, pp. 65–85, and see pp. 38–9 for the Lord Baldwin Fund; two informative articles by J. L. Cohen, *JC*, 10 February 1939, pp. 14–16, and 17 February 1939, pp. 28–9.

[97] The Government committed £4,000,000 to help refugees from the Sudetenland after Munich. See Hope Simpson, *Refugees: A Review*, p. 40; for summary of refugee policy see ibid., p. 68; see Home Office policy statements on 24 November 1938, 341 H.C.Deb., 1971–2; 6 December 1938, 342 H.C.Deb., 1012–4.

permanent – was underlined by the Prime Minister on the morning of the crucial refugee debate. Numbers were 'limited by the capacity of the voluntary bodies dealing with the refugee problem to undertake the responsibility for selecting, receiving and maintaining a further number of refugees'.[98]

Admission for temporary asylum was linked to re-emigration – an issue which assumed great significance in 1939. The chance of rescue could depend on good prospects of re-emigration – although few people could maintain a refugee indefinitely, many could envisage doing so for one or two years. Thus the pleas for financial support which appeared in the *Jewish Chronicle* often included estimated emigration dates. The following appeared consecutively on 17 February 1939:

Urgently seek for uncle (55) in daily danger fearing return to Dachau, generous rescuer providing short-term guarantee until emigration overseas.

Urgent appeal, old couple (63 and 60). American visas 1940, to be expelled from Germany 1.4.39., threat concentration camp. Maintenance 1 year in England needed.[99]

The Jewish bodies expanded their work within the limits of their finances and the impermanence of their solutions.[100] The Jewish community also established an emergency transit camp at Richborough, Kent, for refugee transmigrants who could not proceed directly to a place of permanent settlement. Opened in February 1939 under the auspices of the CGJ, Richborough camp was 'a place of transit and training for men between the ages of 18 and 45, who had a definite prospect of emigration and had to be taken out immediately to save them from the concentration camps'.[101] The CGJ took the exceptional course of allocating funds to maintain these emergency cases. It sent representatives to Germany to pick out men who lacked private financial guarantees. In the offices of the surviving Jewish organizations in Berlin and Vienna, Julian Layton conducted interviews to choose people for Richborough: 'I would select young people to come out ... who were artisans or who would be useful to whichever country they went to.'[102] The Home Office would not help financially, but agreed to use its new procedures to speed the entry of men bound for the camp, on condition that they remained there until they re-emigrated, although for many their prospects of emigration were remote or fictitious. Werner Rosenstock, then a caseworker in the *Reichsvertretung*

---

[98] Chamberlain, 21 November 1938, 341 H.C.Deb., 1314.

[99] See also next item, *JC*, 17 February 1939, p. 3.

[100] See Central Council for Jewish Refugees (CCJR) – the CGJ renamed – *Annual Report of the Council for 1939* (London, 1940), pp. 5–6; for the rescue work of Rabbi Solomon Schonfeld, see eds David Kranzler and Gertrude Hirschler, *Solomon Schonfeld – His Page in History*, (New York, 1982); *JC*, 9 December 1938, p. 17; 16 December 1938, p. 31. For fund-raising pressures, see Lord Rothschild, letter, *JC*, 2 December 1938, p. 13, and speech, *JC*, 27 January 1939, p. 33.

[101] CCJR, *Annual Report*, p. 5, see n. 100 above; For Richborough, see Sherrman, *Island Refuge*, pp. 196, 215; Bentwich, *They Found Refuge*, pp. 102–14; Cooper, report of visit to camp, 2 May 1939, PRO FO 371/24100/59ff (W 7673/3231/48).

[102] for Layton, see n. 57 above.

office in Berlin, has described how, if the men 'had no direct chances of re-emigration then we worked on the fiction that they would go to Shanghai'.[103]

Although prospects of re-emigration enabled refugees like the Richborough men to enter Britain, the rate of actual re-emigration remained static.[104] By late April caseworkers realized that the holders of 50,000 refugee visas granted since May 1938 had not yet arrived, but could theoretically appear at any time.[105] In practice it proved impossible to keep short- and long-term residents in separate compartments. Admissions of temporary residents were affected by fears of increasing the numbers of long-term refugees. These fears were partly grounded in the fact that the same dwindling pool of private funds was expected both to guarantee the support of refugees in Britain and to finance onward emigration. The pre-war months of 1939 saw both Home Office and refugee bodies pursuing conflicting goals. A massive effort was made to speed up entries and save those who were eligible. Yet increasingly moves were made to tighten up admissions, in order to conserve funds and limit the numbers who might be stranded in Britain when war broke out.[106] By the summer of 1939 the prospect of rapidly finding permanent havens abroad for refugees temporarily in Britain had receded. The disappearance of this vital ingredient of the policy of temporary refuge inspired the Home Office to try, without success, to persuade the Colonial Office to reconsider its recent decision to suspend Jewish immigration to Palestine in order to make it possible to decant refugees from Britain.[107] As re-emigration became more elusive and had less impact on numbers, the government made a break with precedent on the question of refugee finance. Having doggedly stuck to its rule that the costs of German refugee immigration must be met from private sources, it finally agreed in July to commit public funds, but solely to finance refugee emigration from Britain.[108]

In December it was announced that Schiff was compelled on medical advice to cut down his refugee work.[109] By now the movement of refugees to Britain

---

[103] Interview, 19 April 1988; For Shanghai as a refuge, see David Kranzler, *Japanese, Nazis and Jews: The Jewish Refugee Community of Shanghai, 1938–1945* (New York, 1976).

[104] Hope Simpson, *Refugees: A Review*, p. 71. Cooper to Brooks, 28 March 1939, PRO FO 371 24076/210FF (W 5248/45/48).

[105] Jeffes to Randall, 27 April 1938, PRO FO 371/24100/49ff (W 7031/7321/48).

[106] For GJAC policy see Dixon to Layton, 10 May 1939, PRO HO 294/52; Hope Simpson *Refugees; A Review*, pp. 73–4; Wedgwood, 18 April 1939, 346 H.C.Deb., 190–2. For 'rigorous selection' of domestics, see Instructions to Passport Control for Paris, 2 June 1939, PRO HO 213/105; Russell to Schiff, 5 June, ibid. For clampdown on transmigrants bound for the USA, see minutes and correspondence, January–April 1939, PRO HO 213/115, and files 116 and 117, esp. Home Office, Aliens Department, Circular: 'Refugees desiring to come to the United Kingdom temporarily while waiting for United States visas', April, 1939, PRO HO 213/116.

[107] See Sherman, *Island Refuge* pp. 242–3. Cooper to Hibbert, 27 July 1939, PRO FO 371/24093/72ff (W 11321/1369/48); 300 men at Richborough had been selected for Palestine by the Jewish Agency in Vienna, but were stuck in Britain because of Colonial Office restrictions. Cooper to Schiff 12 July 1939, Bentwich to Cooper, 21 July 1939, ibid. For Palestine immigration policy and refugees, see generally Sherman, *Island Refuge*, and Wasserstein, *Jews of Europe*, esp. pp. 1–39.

[108] Sherman, *Island Refuge*, pp. 242–50.

[109] *JC*, 22 December 1939, p. 10; 29 December 1939, p. 13.

had largely ceased, with the consent of the exhausted refugee bodies.[110] The work of rescuing Czech refugees, subsidized by public funds, was not cut off so abruptly. In the winter of 1939–40 the Home Office was still authorizing visas for refugees from Czechoslovakia who had fled the German advance eastwards through Poland.[111] As the Polish refugee problem exploded, the new Home Secretary, Sir John Anderson, was 'somewhat alarmed' by a Foreign Office suggestion that a liberal line be taken on the admission of Polish refugees to Britain and hoped 'that no pressure would be brought for any relaxation of the existing practice'.[112]

VII

For Anglo-Jewry in the 1930s, the rise of Nazism and the refugee crisis produced new conflicts over identity and politics. The growth of 'Jewish' politics challenged the adherence of Jews in Britain to the politics of assimilation, but assimilationist responses to the question of Jewish survival remained important. Both assimilationists and Zionists offered solutions to the problem of anti-semitism, and of refugees. The refugee crisis presented Jewish identity as a handicap. The assimilationist response was to dilute the impact of Jewish refugees on the countries of refuge. Conversely, Zionists and supporters of the World Jewish Congress (WJC) tried to transcend the refugee problem by making Jewish identity a source of strength.

Anglo-Jewish leaders facilitated Britain's role as a haven for refugees by containing and controlling the influx.[113] The pressures to assimilate made them distinguish between different groups of refugees. Their belief that Jewish identity stood in the way of emigration incorporated knowledge of real barriers confronting would-be *émigrés*, but often mirrored anti-Jewish prejudices.[114] Such prejudices were held by many in Britain who disclaimed anti-semitism. It was assumed that in choosing which Jews to admit, it was preferable to limit the import of distinctive, uncompromising Jewishness. Refugees whose Jewishness had been blunted – for example through inter-marriage or lapsed observance – were seen as correspondingly less problematic candidates for assimilation or

[110] Sherman, *Island Refuge*, pp. 255–8, 263; Wasserstein, *Jews of Europe*, pp. 81–2; Cooper to Randall, 18 September 1939, PRO FO 371/24100/120ff (W 13792/3231/48); Grant to Under-Secretary, 10 October 1939, PRO FO 371/24101/140 (W 14595/3231/48).

[111] See correspondence with Czech Refugee Trust Fund, November 1939–January 1940, PRO HO 294/46; See Michael R. Marrus, *The Unwanted: European Refugees in the Twentieth Century* (Oxford, 1985), pp. 198–9, for the role of Vilna as a crossroads for refugees, especially Jews, until June 1940.

[112] 13 October 1939, extract from War Cabinet Conclusions 46(39) PRO FO 371/24102/269ff (W 14740/13884/48); see also notes for Parliamentary answers on the Polish refugee problem, 17 October 1939, PRO FO 371/24102/334ff (W 14983/13884/48).

[113] Both the Home Office and Jewish representatives preferred to play down the numbers of Jewish refugees actually admitted. See Sherman, *Island Refuge*, pp. 175–6; record of interdepartmental meeting, 16 December 1938, PRO FO 371/22537/296ff (W 15119/104/98).

[114] See Makins to Strang, 11 October 1938, PRO FO 371/21583/224 (C 12181/11896/12); For the advantage of being non-Jewish for gaining entry to Canada, see Irving Abella and Harold Troper, *None Is Too Many* (Toronto, 1986), pp. 48–50.

re-emigration. Thus, for their own reasons, the government and Jewish leaders had similar priorities, favouring Jewish refugees who would assimilate easily. Zionists, who needed suitable labour in Palestine, took a lead in helping refugees with emigration potential. Ease of emigration and assimilation generally depended – for the majority who did not possess movable wealth – on youth and manual skills, or the potential to acquire them. These preferences reflected not merely the respective immigration requirements of the countries of refuge, but also global immigration barriers which made Jewishness almost synonymous with inassimilability, and in which Jews were caught between 'the Scylla of persecution and the Charybdis of assimilation'.[115] Cooper thought the Home Office's role was to ensure that any substantial additions to the alien population of the United Kingdom were 'composed of desirable elements, easily assimilated'.[116] The many refugees, mostly women, who were prepared to adapt themselves to escape through domestic service encountered many misgivings about their desirability and assimilability.[117]

Conscious of these prejudices, Jews in Britain debated the emigration prospects of their co-religionists. It had not been hard to sympathize with German Jews, displaced despite their advanced assimilation. However, the notion that the 'kaftaned Jews of Poland' might try to emigrate was disturbing, because these Jews seemed to lack adequate consciousness of the need to assimilate, and would not even realize that they would be wise to 'discard their distinctive attire, although they cannot shed their Jewish features'.[118] The reluctance of CGJ leaders to become involved in the emigration of refugees from countries other than Germany illustrated the grim awareness in Anglo-Jewish circles that the vast dimensions of the emigration problem entailed harsh choices about who could be saved.[119] Norman Bentwich regarded Jews in Germany as 'not fitted for emigration' if aged over forty-five, 'although a certain proportion of them may find a home in other countries through a guarantee of their relations'.[120] Fearful of alarming the British with the prospect of too many

[115] Cecil Roth, *JC*, 25 November 1938, p. 27; see use of 'unassimilable' in substitution for the words 'of Jewish or partly Jewish origin, or have non-Aryan affiliations' (compare April regulations mentioned n. 64 above): Foreign Office, Passport Control Department, Circular, 'Visas for holders of German and Austrian passports entering British Colonies &c; Union of South Africa and South West Africa', 25 July 1938, PRO FO 372/3284/144ff (T 8648/3272/378).

[116] Cooper, memorandum, 29 June 1939, PRO FO 371/24077/134ff (W 10231/45/48).

[117] Parkin, Memorandum, 'Visas for United Kingdom granted to refugees', 8 May 1939, PRO FO 371/24100/63ff (W 7740/3231/48); Martelli (Governor of Jersey) to Holderness, 16 June 1938, PRO HO 213/281. For domestics, see Jillian Davidson, 'German-Jewish Women in England', paper given in Cambridge, September 1988; Antony Kushner, 'Asylum or Servitude? Refugee Domestics in Britain, 1933–45', *Bulletin of the Society for Labour History* (Winter 1988).

[118] 'Watchman', *Jewish Chronicle*, 28 October 1938, p. 11.

[119] See Viscount Bearsted, 'A Memorandum on the Jewish Situation on the Continent', 9 June 1938, PRO FO 371/21749/461ff (C 5681/2289/18); Bunbury, 'The Problem of Jewish Refugees from Czechoslovakia', 5 April 1939, PRO HO 294/39; Bentwich to Porter Goff, 15 December 1938, Papers of Mrs Leslie Edgar, Anglo-Jewish Archive, AJA 398.

[120] Bentwich to Porter Goff (as n. 119). In February 1941 Bentwich wrote, 'When the iron wall of war was raised between us and Germany, 200,000 men and women, largely past middle-age, were left to be crushed to dust. It was some consolation that less than 50,000 were under forty years of age.' Bentwich, *Wanderer Between Two Worlds*, p. 29.

burdensome refugees – even from Germany – the CGJ left the rescue of the old to private initiative, although not without agonized debate with the Jewish community,[121] and dissenting voices in the Cabinet.[122]

Selectivity was central to traditions of planned Jewish emigration prior to 1933, as well as to the Zionist programme in Palestine, whose 'centre of gravity' was 'colonisation, education, immigration and the maintenance of decent relations with the Mandatory power'.[123] Zionists, under the leadership of Chaim Weizmann, opposed 'the creation of a refugee problem in Palestine itself', through indiscriminate admission of refugees, and maintained an immigration-based, selective approach.[124] The 'constructive relief' offered to refugees in Palestine was 'only for part of the German Jews, notably the essential part, the Jewish youth whom we wish to help there to a new life, normally stratified, in the free air of Eretz Israel.'[125] Palestine offered more than mere refuge in 'an over-night asylum', but in its emphasis on the demographic, social, economic and political needs of the receiving community the Jewish Agency was offering a haven mainly to those who were more than mere refugees.[126]

The cumulative effect of immigration-based policies – Zionist policy for Palestine, plus British preferences for emigratable and assimilable immigrants – heightened the emphasis on selectivity in admissions to Britain, many of which were seen as preparatory to onward emigration to Palestine. It was hoped that many children and young people admitted to Britain in 1938–9 for education and training would soon go on to Palestine.[127] To save young people from

[121] See report of speech by Lord Rothschild, *JC*, 28 October 1938, pp. 17–18; see also *JC*, 18 November 1938, p. 7, for editorial acceptance that the settlement of older refugees was a secondary matter.

[122] 'The Secretary of State for Home Affairs referred to the older men and women who presented an almost insoluble problem. The Jewish Committee was not attempting to deal with the older people. It was concentrating on the younger people.' Cabinet discussion, 16 November 1938, see n. 91 above. For Lord Halifax's concern for the elderly on this occasion, see Sherman, *Island Refuge*, pp. 176–7. The ratio of old people in the Jewish population of Germany more than doubled between 1933 and July 1941, while that of those under 40 decreased by 80–83 per cent, Strauss, 'Jewish Emigration (I)', p. 327.

[123] Weizmann, *Trial and Error* (London, 1949), p. 417. For refugee settlement in Palestine up to 1936, see Bentwich, *Refugees from Germany*, pp. 144–56.

[124] Weizmann to Comité d'Aide et d'Assistance aux Victimes de l'Antisémitisme, Brussels, 26 April 1934, Letter 262, *The Letters and Papers of Chaim Weizmann*, Series A, vol XVI (Jerusalem, 1978), pp. 278–9. Zionist policy was to grant refugee certificates to 'suitable elements' – candidates who were 'outstanding craftsmen or young people who have received *adequate* training in agriculture or in a craft and who, in addition, are spiritually prepared for Palestine.' Ibid.

[125] Ibid., pp. 316–18; Weizmann to Zionist Federations and Refugee Committees, 28 May 1934, Letter 291.

[126] See interview with Chaim Arlosoroff, Director of the Jewish Agency's Political Department, 23 May 1933, Strauss, 'Jewish Emigration (II)', p. 343. Dr Werner Senator of the Jewish Agency feared German plans to set up a central organization for Jewish emigration would upset arrangements for export of refugee capital to Palestine, creating an imbalance between capitalist and labour emigration: Pinsent to Chargé d'Affaires, 22 November 1938, PRO FO 371/22537/174ff (W 15431/104/98).

[127] See Mrs Rebecca Sieff on the 'hard pioneering life for which they were intended'. *JC*, 2 December 1938, p. 10.

Germany, Jewish bodies organized projects and rescue missions whose priorities reflected the character of the organization concerned. The Polish Refugee Fund brought to England children of Polish Jews expelled from Germany.[128] Orthodox Jewish children were the particular object of missions of rescue led by Rabbi Solomon Schonfeld.[129] The arrival of large numbers of unaccompanied children and the susceptibility of the young to the assimilation process led to sectarian divisions within the community.[130]

The refugee issue was incorporated into the political goals and rivalries of Zionists and non-Zionists in Britain. While both factions agreed that Britain should have a minor and temporary role as a refugee haven, and both had sound reasons for working together for refugees, their cooperation was marred by mutual suspicion, power struggles and Zionist uncertainty as to whether the partnership constituted too great a compromise.[131]

To the advocates of Jewish politics, the need to establish legitimate representation of the Jewish people in the international arena was fundamental. The claims of the World Jewish Congress (WJC) to a supra-national mandate aroused the enmity of the Anglo-Jewish leadership, who questioned the legitimacy of 'Jewish' politics and the validity of the concept of 'International Jewry'. Fearful of the menace of Fascist politics and anti-semitism at home, and haunted by their need to prove their loyalty to Britain, the assimilated Jews who constituted the established leadership feared that a specifically Jewish response to anti-semitism would play into the hands of the persecutors, calling into question the reliability of Jews as citizens and undermining the real cure for anti-semitism, continued assimilation. The official stance of Neville Laski and his allies was one of resolute non-alignment with political positions, Jewish or otherwise, and a reluctance to stress 'the racial element in Jewish affairs'.[132]

Rival claims to represent Jewish concerns led to disputes between the

---

[128] *JC*, 17 February 1939, p.32; 4 August 1939, p.21.

[129] A Joint Orthodox Committee to deal with Orthodox refugees from Germany and Czechoslovakia was set up in the summer of 1939, *JC*, 4 August 1939, p.21. It has been suggested that the refugee committees 'ignored' the rescue of Orthodox children because of the consensus of the Jewish establishment in Britain that children who came to Britain should ultimately go to Palestine – the Zionists because they saw Palestine as the solution to anti-semitism; the non-Zionists who controlled the GJAC because this was preferable to the children remaining in England to aggravate Britain's Jewish problem'. See Kranzler et al., *Solomon Schonfeld* p. 23. The same authors provide a similar explanation for the alleged tendency of the refugee committees to overlook the rescue of Jewish religious functionaries who were considered 'unproductive and largely unassimilable'. In marked contrast to those who played down the Jewishness of the refugees, Schonfeld exulted in the Jewish spirituality of the souls he snatched from Nazi persecution. *JC*, 30 September 1938, p.28.

[130] 'Educating the Refugees', by 'Scholasticus', *JC*, 23 December 1938, supplement, p.2. The children were also subject to assimilationist pressures for their dispersal. See letter from Mrs Helen Bentwich, Hon. Secretary of the Movement for the Care of Children from Germany, hoping 'to spread our children as far over the British Isles as possible. We do not want too great numbers of them in any one place.' *JC*, 19 December 1938, p.32.

[131] See Cesarani, 'Zionism in England', n. 13 above.

[132] Quotation from a 1935 exposition by Leonard Montefiore of the assimilationist credo, ed. Leonard Stein and C.C. Aronsfeld), *Leonard G. Montefiore In Memoriam 1889–1961* (London, 1964), p.14.

old-established JFC and the new WJC. Laski, who was joint Chairman of the JFC, having led the opposition to the WJC's formation in 1936, tried repeatedly in 1937–9 to persuade the Foreign Office to have no dealings with the WJC's British Section or its Chairman, the Rev. Maurice Perlzweig.[133] Laski concentrated his covert and informal approaches on Sir Robert Vansittart, who was sympathetic.[134] However, Vansittart was increasingly isolated, and Foreign Office sceptics saw no reason to rule out potentially useful contact with the WJC or stop Perlzweig from calling to ask for British intervention on behalf of beleaguered Jews in Central Europe. But although the doors of the Foreign Office remained open, uncertainty remained as to the WJC's ability to speak for persecuted Jews.[135] The WJC and the JFC took up similar issues in similar ways, lobbying the British government to intervene to protect Jewish political rights in Europe, and launching rival petitions to the increasingly moribund League of Nations.[136] The pleas of both Jewish bodies were treated dismissively by the Foreign Office, which was reluctant to take up cudgels for the Jews, as it clung, with a sense of growing helplessness, to appeasement in Europe.[137] Nevertheless, a few minor postponements of dispossession and denationalization were achieved.

The sense of betrayal, impotence and apprehension Jews felt after the Munich Agreement led to a call to end the policy 'of *schnorring* [begging] for a crumb at this or that Foreign Office', and for Jews to abandon the old kind of politics and come together for mutual protection.[138] Nevertheless, Laski's antagonism to the WJC continued, provoking him in the summer of 1939 to try to dissuade the Foreign Office from facilitating Perlzweig's trips to Central

---

[133] Laski and Montefiore, memorandum, 'The World Jewish Congress', 6 January 1937; Laski to Sargent, 19 January 1937, PRO FO 371/20825/1ff (E 506/506/31);

[134] Laski to Vansittart, 4 March 1937, PRO FO 371/20825/9ff (E 1590/506/31), 21 February 1938, PRO FO 371/21887/52ff (E 1347/381/31) and 7 July 1939, PRO FO 371/24084/112 (W 10719/520/48). For mixed Foreign Office responses see subsequent minutes, and discussions on Upper Silesia in May–September 1937 with both Perlzweig and Nahum Goldmann of the WJC, PRO FO 371/20744/24ff (F 3719/4532/5257/5919/6305/372/18). Vansittart was Permanent Under-Secretary until the start of 1938, when he was made to relinquish the helm of the department – he became Chief Diplomatic Adviser: see Norman Rose, *Vansittart, Study of a Diplomat* (London, 1978), pp. 188–253. R. A. Butler had known Perlzweig at Cambridge and considered him trustworthy.

[135] See reactions to Perlzweig's efforts to obtain British intervention on behalf of Jews in Austria, minutes 21–23 March 1938, PRO FO 371/21748/172 (C 2908/2289/18) and minutes, 29–31 March 1938, PRO FO 371/22349/109ff and 144ff (R 3403/4032/4032/67).

[136] See minutes etc. on Romania and Hungary, March–May 1938, PRO FO 371/22349 (R 3403/4366/4397/4433/4481/4502/4506/4517/4032/67). For rivalry over which Jewish representatives might meet King Carol of Romania if he visited Britain, see Laski to Vansittart, 7 March 1938, PRO FO 371/22454/283ff (R 2266/153/37).

[137] See Cadogan, Permanent Under-Secretary, Diary entries, 15 and 21 February, 12 March and 20 April, ed. David Dilks, *The Diaries of Sir Alexander Cadogan, 1938–1945* (London, 1971), pp. 47, 55, 62, 69. Dilks comments (p. 69) that Cadogan had concluded 'that Britain could do nothing effective against the Reich's absorption of German minorities or even against a German attempt to take a stranglehold on little countries.'

[138] Editorial, *JC*, 7 October 1938, p. 7.

Europe[139] – when Perlzweig was embarking on a trip to investigate the plight of Polish Jews expelled from Germany.[140]

Although real unity was remote, Jewish leaders succeeded after *Kristallnacht* in mounting a deputation of prominent Zionists and non-Zionists to press the Prime Minister for concessions to Jewish refugees.[141] Weizmann's efforts on this occasion and in the following weeks to persuade Britain to admit or guarantee the admission of more refugees to Palestine were unsuccessful.[142] Nevertheless, the government's readiness to offer temporary refuge in Britain reflected not only the changed climate in Europe, but Weizmann's achievement in sensitizing some of Britain's rulers to the humanity of Jews.[143] There was now even a Zionist sympathizer in the Cabinet – Walter Elliot, the Minister of Health who implored his Cabinet colleagues to make an immediate offer of temporary refuge, to alleviate 'the terrible suffering and humilation which had been inflicted on many Jews'.[144]

This essay has shown how much refugee policy owed to the involvement of representatives of Anglo-Jewry, and how the readiness of Anglo-Jewish bodies to participate in the immigration process and cooperate with Home Office controls played a vital part in persuading the government to take the risks attendant on some liberalization of its admissions policy. It has also demonstrated how fears of anti-semitism, of demands on their charity, and their own prejudices, led Anglo-Jewish leaders to seek controls on the quality and quantity of Jews entering Britain. Their intercessions managed sufficiently to contain British hostility towards refugees from Germany to permit the admission of many more than Jewish leaders had expected or desired. Through its work for the refugees the Jewish community also contributed to its own assimilation. Initiation into the ways and spaces of the wider British community took place in innumerable encounters with non-Jewish sympathizers, whose motives also mixed charity with containment. By late 1939, the Jewish identity of the refugee organizations had become diluted and Anglicized. They shared

---

[139] Laski, 7 July 1939. See n. 134 above. Laski had been stung by Zionist gibes which contrasted the bravery of one of Perlzweig's diplomatic missions to Central Europe with the attitude of the JFC, 'whose monthly reports become more and more like the mutterings of a body seized by a sense of impotent despair'. The article went on to emphasize that Perlzweig's visit had been made 'with the warm approval of the British Foreign Office'. 'Commentator', *Zionist Review*, 6 July 1939, p. 8.

[140] For Perlzweig's planned visit to Warsaw, and Laski's hostile intervention see Laski, 7 July 1939 (n. 134 above) and minutes and correspondence, 7–14 July 1939, PRO FO 371 24084/73ff (W 10441/520/48).

[141] See n. 90 above. The members of the deputation were Samuel, Bearsted, the Chief Rabbi, Laski, Lionel de Rothschild and Weizmann. On the eve of *Kristallnacht* Weizmann failed to convince the Foreign Office to rush 'some prominent non-Jewish Englishman' to Germany, in the hope that this might avert the pogrom. See Strang to Ogilvie-Forbes (Berlin), 9 November 1938. PRO FO 371/21636/77ff (C 13660/13661/1667/67).

[142] See Blanche Dugdale, entries 15 and 17 November, 11, 12 and 15 December 1938, in ed. Norman Rose, *Baffy: the Diaries of Blanche Dugdale, 1936–1947* (London, 1973). MacDonald, 'Conversation with Dr Weizmann on the 12th December 1938', PRO FO 371/21868/374ff (E 7548/1/31).

[143] See Rose, *Baffy* and idem. *The Gentile Zionists* (London, 1973).

[144] Cabinet discussion, 16 November 1938, see n. 91 above.

premises and operated jointly with non-Jewish bodies, had non-Jewish administrators and were subject to the bureaucratic controls which accompanied a state subsidy. Both refugees and action on their behalf were thus incorporated into a process of assimilation.

The Home Office reluctantly kept most of the refugees in Britain for the duration of the war although its policy was to get rid of as many as possible, and many thousands departed.[145] After victory, very slowly, the Home Office resigned itself to accepting the unlooked-for permanent addition of perhaps 40,000 Jewish refugees to the population. Thus, a small number of Jews, who had the good luck to clear the immigration hurdles Britain placed in their path, were finally permitted to end their journey, and call Britain home.

---

[145] See Wasserstein, *Jews of Europe*, pp. 81–133 for internment, emigration and deportation of Jewish refugees during the war.

10

The Impact of British Anti-semitism, 1918–1945

Tony Kushner

Historians and observers of modern anti-semitism have often assumed that Britain, like the United States, is 'different'.[1] If there has been any anti-semitism, then it has been trivial, 'confined to music hall humour and a form of upper-class joking' in the words of one scholar, and leaving 'only a faint and delicate odour in the records' according to another.[2] Some admit that there is a golf-club variety of discrimination, but Philip Howard and John Gross insist that in practice this English-type anti-semitism 'is a little more than a minor nuisance' for Anglo-Jewry. Anti-semitism is regarded as a foreign disease; as one magistrate in the 1930s stated, it was 'very un-English and very unfair.' There could be no real anti-semitism in Britain, wrote a weekly paper in 1942, for 'the thing is too preposterously contrary to British character.'[3]

There is thus strong resistance to accepting the idea that Britain has experienced a tradition, or traditions of anti-semitism. This is reflected in the historiography of the subject, or until very recently, the absence of one. The religious philo-semite G. F. Abbott, highlighted the anti-semitism associated with the Eastern Crisis in the 1870s and the anti-alien campaign at the turn of the century, in a book published in 1907.[4] However, most historians who were

---

[1] B. Halpern, 'America is Different', in ed. M. Sklare, *The Jew in American Society* (New York, 1974), p. 72. See also E. H. Flannery, *The Anguish of the Jews: Twenty-three Centuries of Anti-Semitism* (New York, 1965), pp. 193–4; and *The Jewish Encyclopedia*, vol. I (New York, 1916), pp. 648–9 for statements that there is no anti-semitism in Britain.

[2] The first quote is from Christopher Sykes, *Two Studies in Virtue* (London, 1953), p. 135 and the second by John Vincent, *Times Higher Education Supplement*, 16 November 1979.

[3] See Philip Howard, 'Thanks Moses, You Were a Real Brit', *Times*, 19 October 1984; John Gross, 'Is Anti-Semitism Dying Out?', *20th Century*, 172 (Spring 1963), pp. 18–26; *JC*, 7 February 1936; *New English Weekly*, 25 June 1942.

[4] G. F. Abbott, *Israel in Europe* (London, 1907).

Abbott's contemporaries, both Jewish and non-Jewish, ignored the issue of anti-semitism in Britain. In the first half of the twentieth century the Jewish Historical Society of England did not touch the subject, and it was left to Nazis, such as Peter Aldag, and refugees from Nazism, particularly Caesar Aronsfeld, to carry out the pioneer work in the study of British anti-semitism.[5]

Outside the Wiener Library Bulletin this research received little attention and it was not until the publication of two books in the late 1970s that there was real academic interest in the subject of British anti-semitism. *Political Anti-Semitism in England 1918–1939*, by a young German scholar, Gisela Lebzelter, and *Anti-Semitism in British Society, 1876–1939*, by Colin Holmes, a British social historian, take differing views on the nature of British anti-semitism. Holmes concludes that throughout the years 1876 to 1939 there was a clear tradition of anti-semitism in Britain. Lebzelter, whose study is narrower both in scope and chronology, takes the opposite view, claiming that Fascist groups failed in this country because of 'the absence of a historical tradition of anti-semitism in Britain'.[6] Both authors concentrate on organized or political anti-semitism, although Holmes also covers what he calls 'its more amorphous, less ideologically based forms'.[7]

The discussion that follows will concentrate less on political anti-semitism, and will put emphasis on more widely based hostility to Jews in Britain, defining anti-semitism broadly as a hostility to Jews *as* Jews. It will suggest that non-organized forms of anti-semitism are not necessarily amorphous, and that indeed they can have strong ideological roots and make a large impact on Anglo-Jewry. Furthermore, it will argue that British anti-semitism persisted after 1939. This essay will concentrate on World War II, not because, as Lebzelter has suggested, it marked 'a renewed wave of anti-semitism', or as Aaron Goldman has likewise commented, 'there was a resurgence of antisemitism in Britain' during the war, but because in many ways the years 1939–45 witnessed a climax of the forms of anti-semitism that had existed in Britain in the inter-war period.[8]

The continuation of British anti-semitism in the war shocked contemporary

---

[5] See P. Aldag, *Das Judentum in England* (Berlin, 1943); and C. Aronsfeld, 'Anti-Jewish Outbreaks in Modern Britain', *Gates of Zion* (July 1952), pp. 15–21.

[6] Colin Holmes, *Anti-Semitism in British Society, 1876–1939* (London, 1979), p. 233; and G. Lebzelter, *Political Anti-Semitism in England, 1918–1939* (London, 1978), p. 27.

[7] See particularly Holmes's comments in the foreword to Robert Singerman, *Antisemitic Propaganda: An Annotated Bibliography and Research Guide* (New York, 1982), p. xxii; and also his *John Bull's Island: Immigration and British Society, 1871–1971* (London, 1988), p. 145; Geoffrey Field, 'Anti-Semitism with the Boots Off', *Wiener Library Bulletin*, Special Issue (1982), pp. 25–46, in which Field describes non-organized hostility to Jews in Britain but again regards it as amorphous, as does T. Endelman, 'Anti-Semitism in War-Time Britain', *Michael*, 10 (1986), pp. 75–95; S. Almog, 'Anti-Semitism as a Dynamic Phenomenon: The 'Jewish Question' in England at the End of the First World War', *Patterns of Prejudice*, 21 (1987), pp. 3–18; D. Cesarani 'Anti-Alienism in England after the First World War', *Immigrants and Minorities*, 6 (March 1987), pp. 5–29; and essays by Cesarani, Cheyette and Kushner in eds T. Kushner and K. Lunn, *Traditions of Intolerance: Historical Perspectives on Fascism and Race Discourse in British Society* (Manchester, 1989) move away from a narrow institutional approach to the study of British anti-semitism.

[8] Lebzelter, *Political Anti-Semitism in England*, p. 46; and A. Goldman, 'the Resurgence of Antisemitism in Britain during World War II', *Jewish Social Studies*, 46 (Winter 1984), pp. 37–50.

and modern commentators. Throughout 1938 and 1939, Tom Harrisson's social survey unit, Mass-Observation, had been carrying out a detailed analysis of anti-semitism, based largely in the East End. The project had been funded by the Board of Deputies of British Jews, and at the outbreak of war Harrisson curtailed the study. Harrisson wrote to the Board's President, Neville Laski, stating that 'all our work points to the present conflict as pointing away from antisemitism'. Three years later Mass-Observation would be appealing to the Board for more funds to continue their anti-semitism survey.[9] Harrisson's belief that war against the anti-semitic Nazis was bound to end domestic hostility to Jews is still widely held today. Alan Brien, recently reviewing an anti-semitic thriller first published in this country in 1940, was shattered to find his 'cherished beliefs about a Britain united in detestation of Nazi racialism' destroyed. Similarly recent work by David Rosenberg and the Beyond the Pale Collective has been inspired by the shock of discovering that there was 'antisemitism on the home front'.[10] These quotes are included simply to illustrate again the strength of the myths that Britain is a country free of anti-semitic traditions, and that any anti-Jewish antipathy would disappear in an anti-Nazi war.

The tradition of British anti-semitism that is easiest to trace and has consequently received the greatest attention is the organized or political form. However, historians and commentators are in general agreement that groups such as the Britons, the Imperial Fascist League and the British Union of Fascists (BUF) failed to make any impact on British society. They have thus been labelled as a 'wretched crew of fanatics', 'miserable movements', 'anonymous figures with double-barrelled names and half-baked ideas', and as 'obscure groupuscules of squalid fanatics'.[11] Two recent major studies of British Fascism by Gerry Webber and Richard Thurlow follow this line. Webber suggests that the far-right movements were totally marginal, and Thurlow comments that 'British fascism was small beer'.[12]

In terms of electoral impact there is little doubt that political anti-semitism and British Fascism failed totally. This was well illustrated in 1940 when the BUF fought its only national elections. In three by-elections Mosley's organization polled only 1,291 votes, doing best at Leeds North-East, where it managed 722 or just less than 3 per cent of the total vote. Local election results were also disastrous, although the BUF did well in the London County Council elections in East London in 1937.[13]

[9] See BDA, C6/10/26 for the Mass-Observation correspondence.

[10] Alan Brien, 'Popular Prejudice', *New Statesman*, 13 July 1984; David Rosenberg, 'Antisemitism on the Home Front', *Jewish Socialist*, January 1987; 'Beyond the Pale Collective', introduction in G. Seidel, *The Holocaust Denial* (Leeds, 1986), pp. xi–xiii.

[11] For these quotes see Kenneth Morgan, *Guardian*, 20 February 1987; Nigel Fountain, *New Statesman*, 20 February 1987; Colin Welch, *Spectator*, 21 February 1987.

[12] G. Webber, *The Ideology of the British Right, 1918–1939* (London, 1986), pp. 138–9; and R. Thurlow, *Fascism in Britain: A History, 1918–1985* (Oxford, 1987), p. 303. D. S. Lewis, *Illusions of Grandeur: Mosley, Fascism and British Society* (Manchester, 1987) also minimizes the impact of British Fascism.

[13] F. W. S. Craig, *Minor Parties at British Parliamentary Elections, 1885–1974* (London, 1975), p. 12 has details of the BUF vote in 1940. Holmes, *Anti-Semitism in British Society*, p. 194, covers the 1937 campaign.

However, it must be suggested that political anti-semitism in Britain has a greater importance than simply acting as a theoretical model of 'what might have been' had the situation been different – the approach of Gisela Lebzelter. Although a sense of proportion is vital in this matter, it is possible to trace the impact that extremist anti-semitism has made in Britain, both as an innovative and as a reinforcing factor in hostility to Jews in the period 1918 to 1945.

It was clearest in the East End and in other areas of Jewish concentration such as Manchester and Leeds. The impact of the anti-semitic campaign of the BUF on the Jewish community has been largely ignored by historians of British Fascism. When assessing the importance of Fascist and racist groups in British society this is a serious shortcoming. Although to some, particularly the younger Jewish population, the fight against Mosley added excitement to a dreary area in a depressed decade, to the majority of the East End Jewish population the Fascist campaign created terror, as Metropolitan police reports clearly indicate. Fascist violence and the fear of such violence was a major feature of Jewish, and particularly working-class Jewish life in the 1930s, and it was a threat that continued throughout the war.[14]

Yet there was also a wider impact on society from political anti-semitic groups, although again it is important to stress that care is needed in assessing its effect. The gutter-style racist anti-semitism of the Britons and the Imperial Fascist League influenced few in the inter-war period. Nevertheless, the Britons were important in introducing *The Protocols of the Elders of Zion* into this country. Briefly, in the immediate post-war years this forgery gained some success in the Tory diehard world, including *The Times*, the *Morning Post* and the *Spectator*. In society as a whole, there was a much wider belief in the canard of the Jewish responsibility for Bolshevism. It is true that when *The Times* exposed *The Protocols* as a forgery in 1921 the document itself thereafter made little impact on British society.[15] However, if belief in a total Jewish conspiracy was rare, concern over Jewish power in society, which had nourished the belief in *The Protocols* in the first place, did not disappear in inter-war Britain. The British Union of Fascists, social credit, distributist and British Israelite groups all helped to maintain the fear of Jewish influence. This fear was articulated particularly in the 1930s in the idea that Jews were trying to create another world war. It was a major part of Mosley's propaganda but it was also popularly believed by the British public. Lord Beaverbrook, a man who, in the words of his biographer A.J.P. Taylor, 'had no sympathy with anti-semitism', could write in 1938 that the Jews were dragging Britain into war. He commented: 'They do not mean to do it. But unconsciously they are drawing us into war. Their political influence is moving us in that direction'.[16]

---

[14] Thurlow, *Fascism in Britain*, particularly ignores the impact of the BUF's anti-semitic campaign. For an indication of its effect on the East End Jewish community see PRO MEPO (Metropolitan Police Files) 2/3109–3127.

[15] See Lebzelter, *Political Anti-Semitism in England*, pp. 26–7; and Holmes, *Anti-Semitism in British Society*, pp. 141–60.

[16] A.J.P. Taylor, *Beaverbrook* (London, 1972), p. 387.

A poll taken in November 1939 found that 17 per cent of the population thought they were fighting for cynical reasons, mainly 'for the Jews'.[17] It was fear of the 'Jews' War' lie taking hold amongst the British public that was responsible for the failure to appoint one of Britain's ablest communicators, Leslie Hore-Belisha, to the position of Minister of Information in 1940. In the words of the Permanent Under-Secretary for State in the Foreign Office: 'Jew-control of our propaganda would be a major disaster.' This fear also restricted propaganda on behalf of the Jews of Europe. Again anti-semitism, or the need to appease anti-semitism, was responsible for the failure to attack the enemy's most brutal aspect.[18]

There is bitter irony in the fact that in the war, when the essential feebleness of world Jewry was exposed with such tragic consequences, fear of Jewish power continued and was possibly intensified in Britain. An analysis of a Mass-Observation survey on attitudes to Jews in 1940 reveals that 17 per cent of the sample expressed concern over Jewish power in society. The extent of this concern is underlined when we consider that most of the Mass-Observers were liberal or left-wing in their world outlook.[19]

Whilst the 'Jews' War' myth by no means dominated British thinking in the war, a diluted form of it did gain widespread credence. This was in the dual accusation that on the one hand Jews were avoiding their military and civil duties, and on the other profiteering from the war as black marketeers. The black market itself was assumed to be an organized conspiracy, and it was common to believe that the Jews were behind it all. Some Fascists tried to orchestrate a campaign against Jewish black marketeers in 1943, and this met with a good deal of public support. However, the Fascists and anti-semites were only reinforcing stereotypes of Jewish power already well entrenched in the British public.[20]

Fascism and organized anti-semitism also had an indirect impact in the 1930s and 1940s. The threat of such extremism pushed the state onto the defensive on Jewish matters, and rather than attack anti-semitism itself, the British government was happier to appease those who were hostile to Jews. This was seen in its cautious attitude to helping Nazi refugees in the 1930s and in World War II itself. The government believed that a more positive response could lead to a stronger anti-semitic movement in Britain. Only under the severe threat of a Nazi invasion in 1940 was action taken against the British Union of Fascists, although the police had been requesting that this organization,

---

[17] Mass-Observation, *War Begins at Home* (London, 1940), pp. 421–2.

[18] See D. Dilks (ed.), *The Diaries of Sir Alexander Cadogan, 1938–1945* (London, 1971), pp. 241–2; or J. Colville, *The Fringes of Power: Downing Street Diaries, 1939–1955* (London, 1985), pp. 55–6 for Hore-Belisha; and M. Penkower, *The Jews Were Expendable: Free World Diplomacy and the Holocaust* (Chicago, 1983), p. 295 for Allied propaganda and the need to avoid the 'Jewish war' accusation.

[19] See Mass-Observation Archive (M-O A) Directive on nationalities, October 1940.

[20] For a thorough treatment of the issue of Jews and the black market in Britain in the war see T. Kushner, *The Persistence of Prejudice: Antisemitism in British Society during the Second World War* (Manchester, 1989), pp. 62–3, 102–3, 119–22, 127–8, 148–9, 194 and 201.

or at least political anti-semitism, be outlawed since 1934. The internment of Britain's leading Fascists and anti-semites is a complex matter. It is only necessary to say here that the case for Mosley acting as a collaborator had the Nazis invaded has not been disproved – as Diana Mosley hoped it would be by the recent release of the Home Office Mosley papers. Had the Nazis overtaken Britain as they did the rest of Europe, then the British Fascists could well have become very significant.[21]

When Mosley was being interrogated by the government in 1940, Lord Birkett, Chairman of the tribunal, suggested to him that 'you could not hope, in this country of ours, to succeed in any policy which had, as a fundamental ingredient, brutality to the Jews. The British people would not stand for it at all.'[22] Birkett was assuming that anti-semitism in Britain was unrespectable. However, whilst it is true that some extreme British anti-semites such as Joseph Banister have been confined to a 'feverish impotence', it is dangerous to assume that this is always the case.[23] The examples of John Hooper Harvey and Douglas Reed will indicate that even extreme anti-semitism can become respectable in British society. In the late 1930s Harvey was associated with the Nazi-orientated Imperial Fascist League, a tiny organization whose activities were divided between circulating gutter anti-semitic literature, including the ritual murder charge, and anti-semitic violence in the East End of London.[24] It might be assumed that the anti-semitic publications of the Imperial Fascist League made no impact, but through Harvey's skills they reached a wider public. Hooper Harvey was an individual who could operate on many levels, as an author of an obscure Aryan history of England, but also as a well-respected architectural historian. Indeed his book *The Plantagenets* has been a school bestseller for three decades. Yet even in this book Harvey not only praised Edward I for expelling the Jews in 1290, but also accused the Jews of carrying out ritual murder in medieval England. Thus extremist anti-semitism could reach a mainstream audience.[25]

The career of Douglas Reed tells a similar story. Reed was central European correspondent for *The Times* in the 1930s, and his books *Insanity Fair* and *Disgrace Abounding* in 1938 and 1939 were possibly the bestselling non-fiction works of that time and were important in revitalizing his publishers, Jonathan Cape.[26] Yet Reed was also a profound anti-semite, who blamed the Jews for the rise of Nazism and the decline of Britain. In the war his anti-semitism

---

[21] See particularly Thurlow, *Fascism in Britain*, pp. 163–219 for a detailed description of the events leading up to the internment of the British Fascists.

[22] Birkett, 15 July 1940 in PRO HO283/15/10.

[23] This description of Banister is in Holmes, *Anti-Semitism in British Society*, p. 42.

[24] Harvey's association with the Literary Board of the Imperial Fascist League can be found in the Board of Deputies' Defence Committee files on this organization.

[25] For Harvey's 'careers' see C. Holmes and T. Kushner, 'The Charge is Ritual Murder', *Jewish Chronicle*, 29 March 1985.

[26] For Reed see R. Thurlow, 'Anti-Nazi Antisemite: The Case of Douglas Reed', *Patterns of Prejudice*, 18: 1 (1984), pp. 23–34. His importance for Cape is covered in Michael Howard, *Jonathan Cape, Publisher* (London, 1971), pp. 172–3, 189.

intensified. He denied that the Nazis were persecuting the Jews and claimed that Hitler was controlled by the Jews, a view influenced by social credit ideas. Nevertheless, Reed remained an eminently publishable author – indeed Cape made little or no effort to suppress his anti-semitism. He remained a well-known and well-liked journalist and commentator throughout the war. Again, although Reed believed in a most peculiar Jewish conspiracy theory, it was no barrier to his remaining a respectable figure.[27]

These examples taken together indicate that political anti-semitism in the period 1918–45 must not be seen as having a marginal impact. In the 1930s, the BUF and smaller anti-semitic groups created terror in Jewish areas, and throughout the period they helped to reinforce stereotypes of Jewish power in British society. Moreover, as the cases of John Hooper Harvey and Douglas Reed illustrate, even extreme anti-semites could operate at different levels in society and influence a wider public.

However, it is important to keep these groups in perspective. They were often very small, and some of their ideas, such as genetically based racist anti-semitism, failed to influence any but the most pathologically prejudiced individuals.[28] There was also a major difference between their solution to what they saw as the Jewish problem and that of the British public. In his government interrogation in 1940, Mosley told the Advisory Committee that he would remove all Jews from Britain, along with all other 'foreigners'.[29] I would suggest that whilst Mosley's belief that Jews in Britain were essentially foreigners was widely accepted amongst the public, most British people, as George Orwell pointed out, did not actually want to do anything to them.[30] So in terms of policy, the Fascists and anti-semites were separated from public opinion. However, the idea that Jews were not British, an anti-semitism of exclusion (which can be termed conservative anti-semitism) is a vital aspect of the first of two powerful traditions of British anti-semitism examined in the rest of this essay.

The belief that Jews were not, and could never be, British was not confined to those of conservative tendencies. Another survey carried out by Mass-Observation in 1943 on attitudes to foreigners included the category 'Jews'. It brought the response 'I cannot understand the inclusion of Jews' from one man, but it was one of only two out of a sample of sixty-eight.[31] The belief that Jews were essentially 'un-British' was well illustrated in the Bethnal Green Underground disaster in 1943. Here is a contemporary, and not untypical, quote: 'They're saying it was all the fault of the Jews. They lost their nerve. You know like they did in the blitz. They haven't got steadiness like we have. We may be

---

[27] Reed's conspiracy theory was fully developed in his book *All Our Tomorrows* (London, 1942). For Cape's attitude to his anti-semitism, see Guy Chapman, *A Kind of Survivor* (London, 1975), pp. 174–6.

[28] Government figures suggest that some had membership in the hundreds and not even in the thousands. See the MI5 report on the Imperial Fascist League in PRO HO 45/24967.

[29] PRO HO 283/13/40–2.

[30] George Orwell, *Partisan Review*, March–April 1942.

[31] M-O A, DR 3257 March 1943.

slow but we are sure. But the Jews are different, they're like foreigners; in fact, you might say they are foreigners.'[32]

If such views were widespread, one must nevertheless agree with Orwell, who wrote in 1945: 'Antisemitism comes more naturally to people of Conservative tendency, who suspect Jews of weakening national morale and diluting the national culture.'[33] A group of Conservative MPs, who claimed to be representative of the Party, wrote to the Prime Minister in 1940, illustrating this point. They wrote hoping that the refugees present in Britain would not be naturalized as it would 'result in a permanent increase of our already over-large Jewish population. Most of us feel that we would rather hand down to posterity a slowly denuding number of people of British stock than provide new material for increasing the stock of Jewish or Jew-British population', which was already 'a most unhealthy symptom in the body politic'.[34]

Such hostility was not simply theoretical: it had a significant effect on the Jewish community in Britain, particularly on those who had not been naturalized. The anti-alien feeling in Britain, which was inseparable from anti-semitism and had resulted in the 1905 Aliens Act, did not disappear with this legislation. Indeed, it appears to have increased in the period up to 1914 and became intensified to the point of hysteria in World War I. The 1919 Aliens Act was a result of the new confidence of the anti-aliens, and apart from drastically restricting immigration into this country, it also increased Home Office powers over deportation. In some years in the 1920s, more aliens were deported than admitted.[35]

The power of deportation was to be used particularly against Britain's small black population in the inter-war period, the state attempting to make it impossible to be black and British.[36] But it also had a drastic impact on the Jewish community. In 1919, with the Russian Revolution in mind, the authorities deported large numbers of Jewish aliens.[37] This pattern continued throughout the 1920s. Even the Board of Deputies, who had remained silent during the aliens agitation at the turn of the century, was forced to take note of the misery the deportations were causing in the East End. A Board deputation in 1923 told the Home Office that the fear of deportation 'hangs over the whole alien community'. Recently released Home Office files on this issue indicate that the profound anti-alienism of the High Tory Home Secretary Joynson-Hicks and his Home Office officials could easily lapse into anti-semitism.[38]

[32] M-O A, FR 1648 March 1943.

[33] George Orwell, 'Notes on Nationalism' (May 1945) in eds S. Orwell and I. Angus, *The Collected Essays, Journalism and Letters of George Orwell*, vol. III, *As I Please* (London, 1968), pp. 375–6.

[34] Letter to Neville Chamberlain, 21 February 1940, PRO HO 213/44 E 409.

[35] See Paul Foot, *Immigration and Race in British Politics* (Harmondsworth, 1965), p. 105.

[36] Neil Evans, 'Regulating the Reserve Army: Arabs, Blacks and the Local State in Cardiff, 1919–45', *Immigrants and Minorities*, 4 (July 1985), pp. 68–106; Paul Rich, *Race and Empire in British Politics* (Cambridge, 1986), ch. 7.

[37] Julia Bush, *Behind the Lines: East London Labour 1914–1919* (London, 1984), pp. 206–7, covers the departations in 1919.

[38] In HO 45/24765/432156. See also D. Cesarani, 'When Jews Were Deported' *Jewish Socialist*, September 1986, and 'Joynson-Hicks and the Radical Right in England after World War One', in eds Kushner and Lunn, *Traditions of Intolerance*.

Although the deportation of East European Jews continued in the 1930s, more attention was focused on the Central European Jewish refugees from Nazi Europe. Opposition came from many sources. It was most blatant from the BUF with their campaign against the 'refujews'. But there was also widespread hostility from the right–wing popular press, particularly the Beaverbrook, Rothermere and Kemsley empires, which continued their previous anti-alienism.[39] Much of the opposition was on economic grounds, with the professions, most strongly the medical world, campaigning against an influx of German and Austrian Jews. In addition, the security forces objected to the refugees, believing them to be spies or tools of the Nazis brought to Britain to create anti-semitism. Again, the government appeased such sentiments and it was not until the public revulsion after *Kristallnacht* that policy was relaxed. Even then the refugees were allowed entry only on temporary visas.[40]

The internment of 27,000 enemy aliens in 1940, the vast majority of whom were Jewish, has been regarded as 'a minor blot, the result of momentary panic' or, in Miriam Kochan's words, as 'May Madness'.[41] It will be suggested here that it was neither. Without the crisis in the military situation in spring 1940, internment would not have occurred, but this factor on its own does not explain the nature or extent of alien internment. Rather than a temporary aberration by the normally liberal British, internment marked the climax of an anti-alienism that had been increasing since 1918 and which contained a powerful element of anti-semitism. Those clamouring for internment in 1940 – the right-wing popular press and the security forces – had also objected to the Jewish refugees in the 1930s. To both the fact that the refugees were Jewish made them doubly suspicious – Jews could not be trusted.[42] In addition in April and May 1940, the British public, which had previously objected to the refugees only on economic grounds, now turned against the enemy aliens totally. After the fall of the Netherlands in May 1940 it was reported that anti-semitic anti-alienism 'gushed up into the open and became the currency of respectable talk'.[43] It suddenly became the done thing to express anti-semitic sentiments, while opposition to internment melted away. The previously pro-refugee *Manchester Guardian*, *The Spectator*, *Time and Tide* and even the *Jewish Chronicle* all supported the government's measures. Only one per cent of the public disagreed with internment. The independent 'liberal' factor as a barrier against anti-semitic forces in Britain had simply disappeared – almost overnight.[44]

[39] For the British press and the refugees, see A. Sharf, *Nazi Racialism and the British Press* (London, 1963), pp. 157–78.

[40] This is well covered by A. Sherman, *Island Refuge: Britain and Refugees from the Third Reich, 1933–1939* (London, 1973), pp. 175–80.

[41] The first quote is from Howard Brotz, 'The Position of the Jews in English Society', *Jewish Journal of Sociology*, 1:1 (1959), p. 101. The 'May Madness' description is in Miriam Kochan, *Britain's Internees in the Second World War* (London, 1983), ch. 4.

[42] A full discussion of the processes at work in the internment episode can be found in T. Kushner, *Persistence of Prejudice*, pp. 143–50, 173–4.

[43] M-O A, FR 107, 'Feeling About Aliens', 14 May 1940.

[44] See *Manchester Guardian*, 13 May 1940; *The Spectator*, 17 May 1940; *Time and Tide*, 25 May 1940; *JC*, 24 May 1940. For the near total decline in public opposition to internment, see the

The internment episode is another indication of the dangers of assuming anti-semitism in Britain to be unrespectable. It also indicates the intense difficulties of being a foreign Jew in this country prior to 1945. Yet the anti-semitism of exclusion also operated against Jews who were born in this country, or who had been naturalized in it – what the Conservative MPs previously quoted referred to as the 'Jew-British population'.

The pressures on the Jewish community to assimilate will be examined shortly. Before these pressures are analysed it will be necessary to study what happened to Jews in Britain when they attempted to move out of a specifically Jewish milieu. The East European Jewish immigrants who had come in increasing numbers throughout the second half of the nineteenth century had congregated together in districts such as Whitechapel, Cheetham, Leylands and the Gorbals partly out of religious and ethnic solidarity. But it was also because of Gentile hostility, including discrimination from non-Jewish land-lords which meant that the Jewish quarters were clearly delineated, to the extent sometimes of dividing a street in half. Disputes over housing territory could lead to anti-semitic riots, as happened in St Georges and Bethnal Green at the turn of the century.[45] Jewish areas also served an economic purpose and this again reflected non-Jewish discrimination. As Louis Teeman has illustrated for Leeds, many trades and industries were simply barred to Jews, and thus the immigrants were left at the mercy of Jewish employers. Anti-semitism, and the fear of anti-semitism, reinforced Jewish solidarity, and up to 1914 the East European immigrants could live in a sufficiently closed world to avoid such hostility.[46]

After World War I, which had acted as a catalyst in integrating the immigrants and their children, and with increasing Jewish mobility, contact with the non-Jewish world could no longer be avoided. Before then it was the assimilated Jewish population that had had to face social discrimination, whether at the public schools, universities or other privileged Gentile preserves. In the inter-war years, and intensifying in World War II, economic and social discrimination against Jews broadened to encompass all sections of Anglo-Jewry. In Leeds, Jews advancing into the middle classes found themselves excluded from important sources of social contact such as the golf courses and clubs.[47] Thus in 1923 the first Jewish golf course was created as a direct response to discrimination. In the housing sphere Jews moved out of the original immigrant areas but, faced with discrimination from estate agents and hostility from neighbours, went to secondary settlement areas such as Chapel-

---

British Institute of Public Opinion poll in May 1940 quoted in ed. H. Cantril, *Public Opinion 1935–1946* (Princeton, NJ, 1951), p. 12.

[45] These riots are covered in J. J. Bennett, 'East End Newspaper Opinion and Jewish Immigration 1885–1905', M. Phil dissertation (University of Sheffield, 1979), pp. 43–75.

[46] L. Teeman, *Footprints in the Sand* (Leeds, 1986), pp. 167–8. See also H. Pollins, *Economic History of the Jews in England* (London, 1982), pp. 141–6, which discusses the impact of discrimination on Jewish economic structure.

[47] See R. O'Brien, 'The Establishment of a Jewish Minority in Leeds', Ph.D thesis (Bristol University, 1975), pp. 246, 401–2.

town, Hightown or the north London working-class suburbs which, although less intensely, were still generally Jewish.[48]

In the employment sphere, Jews attempting to leave the traditional trades such as tailoring or furniture manufacture were to face a similar reception. Apart from the violence of the BUF in the 1930s, physical attacks on Jews, which had been a feature of the period up to 1914, and then more intensely in the 1917 riots, gave way to anti-semitism in the job and housing markets in the years after 1918. With the prospect of discrimination, many Jews opted for avoidance. The inter-war years witnessed growth in the number of Jews seeking economic independence in the form of retailing, taxi-driving, etc.[49] The children of immigrants attempting to enter the professions in the late 1930s and during World War II found that formal and informal barriers were placed in their way. Whilst not so pronounced as in the United States, there was a *numerus clausus* operating against Jews in legal and medical schools. In 1945 for example, the Leeds School of Medicine was found to be blatantly discriminating against Jews.[50] The increasing movement of the Jewish population out of the working class in the 1930s and 1940s was met with developing hostility from the non-Jewish world in a period of severe economic tension. The Trades Advisory Council of the Board of Deputies was formed in 1940 partly to deal with the growing problem of job discrimination, which it believed reached a peak during and after the war.[51]

The anti-semitism of exclusion also peaked in the political sphere at this stage. The Conservative Party had tolerated a few well-heeled and well-established Jews as MPs up to the 1930s, but as the constituency parties gained power in this decade, Jewish candidates, such as Daniel Lipson, were removed.[52] Tory anti-semitism was largely responsible for the removal of the upstart *nouveau riche* Jew Leslie Hore-Belisha as Minister for War in 1940. Similar pressure was put on the Jewish Lord Mayor of Leeds in 1943. It is no accident that there were so few Jews standing as Conservative candidates in the 1945 election, and that no Conservative Jews were elected.[53]

Thus we see that conservative anti-semitism, or the anti-semitism of exclusion, was a powerful force against all Jews in Britain, whether recent immigrants or long-established members of the Jewish 'aristocracy'. Exclusion shaped the economic and social development of Anglo-Jewry, as well as its

[48] For Leeds see ibid., pp. 242–315 or J. Connell, 'The Gilded Ghetto', *Bloomsbury Geographer* (1970), pp. 50–4; for Hightown see T. Kushner, 'Magnolia Street', *Immigrants and Minorities*, 5: 2 (July 1985), pp. 218–19; for North London see Pollins, *Economic History of Jews*, p. 166.

[49] Pollins, *Economic History of Jews*, p. 217; B. Kosmin, 'Exclusion and Opportunity', in ed. S. Wallman, *Ethnicity at Work* (London, 1977), pp. 48–9.

[50] See BDA C6/4/2/16.

[51] For the formation of the TAC see ed. M. Freedman, *A Minority in Britain* (London, 1955), pp. 213–19 and BDA Cb/10/43/2 File 1 for evidence of increasing job discrimination in the war.

[52] See G. Alderman, *The Jewish Community in British Politics* (Oxford, 1983), pp. 120–1 and W. Rubinstein, 'Jews Among Top British Wealth Holders, 1857–1969', *Jewish Social Studies*, 24 (January 1972), pp. 80–1.

[53] Alderman, *Jewish Community in British Politics*, pp. 119–21; for Leeds in 1943 see the Brodetsky papers in the Anglo-Jewish Archive, AJ3 letter from I. Greenberg, 22 February 1943.

psychological make-up. There is bitter irony in this, for the second powerful force of British anti-semitism pressuring Anglo-Jewry has been the anti-semitism of liberalism, or what Bill Williams has called 'the anti-semitism of tolerence'.[54]

It has been suggested by Colin Holmes that 'the liberal compromise offered emancipation in the expectation that Jews would cease to be Jewish and move closer to British society'.[55] The liberal creed, as embodied in this emancipation contract, theoretically allowed room neither for anti-semitism nor for a distinctively Jewish population. Within the liberal critique of Jewishness was the belief that anti-semitism would only end when society started to tolerate Jews and the Jews in turn gave up their distinctiveness. And the corollary of the liberal critique was that the survival of anti-semitism in a tolerant society such as Britain was due to the Jews themselves. The premise that, by refusing to integrate fully into society, the Jews were responsible for the hostility towards themselves is an example of the theory of 'well-earned' anti-semitism. This itself is a part of liberal anti-semitism.

From social surveys, diaries and literature of the 1930s and World War II, it appears that the most dominant feelings about Jews were not of their being an unassimilable foreign body in British society, but of the reverse. Jews were attacked for refusing to integrate, for being clannish and for ultimately creating anti-semitism. A survey carried out in April 1943 on 'the means of overcoming anti-semitism' found that all the replies amounted 'to a statement that it was up to the Jews themselves to combat anti-semitism'. Most of the suggestions to the Jewish community were that they should 'mix freely with the inhabitants of the country of their adoption'.[56] In these attacks on Jewish exclusivity, the ideas of H. G. Wells were often cited.[57] Wells had no time for Nazi anti-semitism, but then regarded it as a response to the Jews' claim to be the Chosen Race. Although Wells's influence as a socialist was on the wane by World War II, his attitude to the Jews appears to have gained popular support. Furthermore, when the government considered giving physical or propaganda aid to the Jews of Europe in the war, and when General Sikorski quoted Wells in support of his belief that it would be playing the Nazi game in treating Jews as a separate nationality, both Ministry of Information and Foreign Office officials were in full agreement.[58]

The pressure on the Jewish community to remove their religious differences is well illustrated by the campaign against *shechita* (slaughter of animals according to Jewish law) in the 1930s and 1940s and by the experience of Jewish evacuees in World War II. Although a small minority of the population had a genuine

[54] B. Williams, 'The Anti-Semitism of Tolerance', in eds A. Kidd and K. Roberts, *City, Class and Culture* (Manchester, 1985), p. 74.

[55] Holmes, *Anti-Semitism in British Society*, p. 104.

[56] M-O A, FR 1669.

[57] For support of Wells, see M-O A, DR 2356, 2514, 2502 October 1940; M-O A, DR 3163, 1108, 1176, 1372 March 1943.

[58] In PRO FO 371/30917 C7839 minute of G. Lias, 30 August 1942.

interest and admiration for Jewish religious customs, more typical was the reaction of novelist Hamilton Fyfe, who admonished Jews to 'give up their *kosher* meat and their worship of a bloodthirsty, revengeful, anthropomorphic deity'. Fyfe told Anglo-Jewry that its 'troubles [were] due to exclusiveness'.[59]

Opposition to *shechita* was a common cause of anti-semitism in the 1930s and 1940s. Nazi groups in Britain such as the Imperial Fascist League and the Nordic League gained some success amongst the public and animal welfare groups in trying to link *shechita* to the basic evilness and cruelty of the Jews.[60] Thus in a *News Chronicle* debate on Jews in 1943 many of the more 'reasoned' anti-semitic letters were based on a hostility to *shechita*.[61] Organizations such as the RSPCA were not worried about accusations of anti-semitism; in fact they exploited anti-semitism to try to reach their goal of banning *shechita*. In 1939 the chairman of the RSPCA warned the Board of Deputies that 'in the last couple of years there [has been] growing up a very strong feeling of antagonism towards the continuation of the Jewish method of slaughter in the country.'[62] The RSPCA drew up a mini-emancipation contract, telling the Board that if the Jews voluntarily gave up *shechita* it would improve relations with the wider society. During the war the debate continued, and some were more blunt in their threats to the Jewish community. To quote one correspondent: 'Jews have sanctuary and protection in this country and they should therefore be compelled to toe the line, and to adopt British methods of slaughter.' Otherwise, in the words of another, 'a general feeling of resentment is likely to arise against *any* body of aliens who ... do not ... conform to the standard of public opinion.'[63]

The anti-*shechita* campaign then was unsuccessful. However, in the evacuation experiences of Jewish children in the war, the emancipation contract was to have a drastic impact on the religious observancy of Anglo-Jewry. S. S. Levin has suggested that in the years of evacuation 'the damage done to Jewish education is incalcuble'.[64] It is true that many Jewish children were happy to throw off their religious customs. One boy evacuated to Ely with the Jews' Free School from Stepney remembers how unpopular it was when his new school 'found us a "banana-nose" from somewhere to give us a bit of Hebrew-type teaching'. At the other extreme, the Jewish Secondary School's evacuation to Shefford was a model of success, with the Bedfordshire villagers taking a pride in keeping their billeted children strictly orthodox. But the Jewish Secondary School was exceptional in that it was able to monitor its children closely and ease any problems with the hosts.[65]

---

[59] In ed. C. Newman, *Gentile and Jew* (London, 1945), p. 102.

[60] Kushner, *Persistence of Prejudice*, pp. 94–5, 109 and also his 'Stunning Intolerance? Opposition to Religious Slaughter in Twentieth-Century Britain', *Jewish Quarterly* (Spring, 1989).

[61] An analysis of this debate is in the archive of the NCCL, File 41/7.

[62] See BDA E3/53.

[63] F. French, *Northamptonshire Chronicle and Echo*, 3 January 1945; 'Anti-Kosher', *Oxfordshire Times*, 24 December 1943.

[64] S. S. Levin, *A Century of Anglo-Jewish Life, 1870–1970* (London, 1970), p. 69.

[65] For Ely see Spitalfield Books, *Where's Your Horns?* (London, 1979), p. 22; and J. Grunfeld, *Shefford* (Tiptree, 1980) for the Bedfordshire experience.

Elsewhere, with the generally unco-ordinated movement of Jewish children across Britain, such supervision was impossible for the Jewish community. In many cases, the price of being accepted into a family was to abandon Jewish ritual and to join the Sunday school. This was particularly unfortunate with evacuated refugee children. These children were generally in need of strong emotional support and thus were unwilling to risk conflict with their hosts over Jewish religious observance. To other Jewish evacuees, being forced to eat rabbit or pork was a greater grievance than any physical maltreatment, and consequently many had a totally miserable evacuation experience.[66]

Evacuation in World War II acted as an integrative force on Anglo-Jewry. Nevertheless, it illustrated that toleration had its price, the cost being a breakdown in religious observance from which in many ways the Jewish community in Britain has never recovered.

One aspect of liberal anti-semitism is the pressure on the Jewish community to assimilate, to the extent that Anglo-Jewish identity is made difficult or impossible. The other aspect of this control is to blame the Jews for the existence of anti-semitism. This is particularly evident in the case of the government's response to the crisis of European Jewry in World War II, and especially that of the Home Secretary, Herbert Morrison. Bernard Wasserstein, who has carried out a major survey of the British government's policies towards European Jewry has concluded that although 'there was a tinge of anti-Semitism in the words of some British officials and politicians ... anti-Semitism does not by itself explain British conduct'. More important, in Wasserstein's opinion, was bureaucratic indifference to the Jewish fate, where helping 'the Jews of Europe was seen as a low priority'.[67] Furthermore, Herbert Morrison has been described by his biographers as being 'favourably inclined to Jews', a man, according to Neville Laski, without a 'tinge of antisemitism'.[68] It is necessary to challenge both Wasserstein's conclusions about the importance of anti-semitism in the British government's response and this positive image of Herbert Morrison.

In 1942, Morrison was approached by a pro-refugee deputation. With news of the fast deteriorating situation of European Jewry, the deputation wanted action to be taken by the British government, specifically for help to be given to Jewish refugees in unoccupied France. Morrison was reluctant to agree and warned the deputation that there was a 'body of opinion [in Britain] which was potentially antisemitic' and thus should not be ignored. A figure of 1,000 visas for entry into Britain was suggested, but Morrison wished to restrict it firstly to 300 Jews and then to not more than 20. This caused delays and in November

---

[66] See *JC*, 13 February 1942 or B. Steinberg, 'Jewish Education in Great Britain during World War II', *Jewish Social Studies*, 29 (1967), p. 53 for the impact on refugee children.

[67] B. Wasserstein, *Britain and the Jews of Europe 1939–1945* (Oxford, 1979), p. 351.

[68] B. Donoughue and G. Jones, *Herbert Morrison: Portrait of a Politician* (London, 1973), p. 55; and N. Laski, after a meeting with Morrison in October 1936 in the Laski papers AJ33/90.

1942 the issue became academic as the Germans occupied the area previously administered by the Vichy government.[69]

In December 1942 Morrison repeated his warnings about anti-semitism to a Cabinet Committee. 'There were,' according to Morrison 'already 100,000 refugees, mainly Jews, in this country' and 'there was considerable antisemitism under the surface ... If there were any substantial increase in the number of Jewish refugees ... we should be in for serious trouble'.[70] It was a warning to be repeated many times by Morrison and his government colleagues, especially in the Allies' Bermuda Conference on refugees in April 1943. The British government was only prepared to deal with a 'token entry of Jews' – one or two thousand, according to Morrison. At Bermuda, Britain and the United States effectively decided against any measures that would have facilitated a mass exodus, and thus the Conference was doomed. As a Foreign Office official wrote several months after the Conference: 'From our point of view, fortunately, the German Government appear to be intending to persist to the last in their refusal to allow Jews to leave Germany.'[71]

The fear of domestic anti-semitism was at the bottom of the government's refusal to allow anything other than a trickle of refugees into Britain. It was partly based on the distrust of the British people. Morrison himself admitted that 'the general body of public opinion in this country was humanitarian and deeply sympathetic to the plight of the refugees'.[72] But no effort was made to satisfy this sentiment apart from empty gestures such as the Bermuda Conference. Instead, the priority was to appease anti-semitic or potentially anti-semitic British feeling. In addition this fear of anti-semitism was based on the government's distrust of the Jewish refugees themselves, with Herbert Morrison being the worst offender.

There is no doubting Morrison's disgust with political anti-semitism either in Germany or in Britain. Moreover, his approval of Socialist Zionist experiments in Palestine cannot be questioned.[73] Nevertheless, his analysis of the causes of anti-semitism reveals a less favourable picture. In a meeting in October 1936 with Neville Laski and Harry Pollitt to discuss the threat of the BUF in the East End, Morrison suggested the way to end that threat was for Jews to stop their activities as sweated employers and bad landlords; they should be '100 per cent economically clean'. Furthermore, they should avoid being too prominent in local politics, which was, as Geoffrey Alderman has pointed out, close to demanding that Jews should 'accept second class status'.[74] It was an indication of Morrison's belief in a theory of 'well-earned' anti-semitism, which he was to

[69] Morrison, 28 October 1942, in PRO FO 371/32681 W14673 and CAB 66/29 WP (42) 427, 28 September 1942 and 444, 2 October 1942.

[70] PRO CAB 95–15 JR (43) 1st meeting, Committee on the Reception and Accommodation of Jewish Refugees, 31 December 1942.

[71] A. Walker minute, 17 September 1943 in PRO FO 371/36666.

[72] Morrison to a Christian delegation on 28 October 1942 in PRO FO 371/32681 W14673.

[73] Donoughue and Jones, *Herbert Morrison*, pp. 249–58 for details.

[74] Alderman, *Jewish Community in British Politics*, p. 116.

develop further as Home Secretary in the war. In 1941 Morrison launched an inquiry into Jewish refugees' involvement in the black market. The survey produced disappointing results for Morrison, but there had been objections from his Under-Secretary for it taking place at all. The Under-Secretary claimed that singling out the Jewish refugee offenders would only strengthen anti-semitism in Britain. Morrison was unimpressed and revealed his analysis of the situation. It was 'these [foreign Jewish black market offenders who were] creating the anti-alien feeling,' stated Morrison. It was this attitude that led him to restrict entry of Jews in the war and to urge the removal of refugees from Britain after it, so as not to provoke what Morrison regarded as justified anti-semitism.[75]

Wasserstein is right to suggest that direct anti-semitism was rare in government circles in the war. But he ignores the more subtle liberal variety of hostility that blamed the Jews for their own misfortune. This approach was not confined to Herbert Morrison. One of his Home Office colleagues noted late in the war that many more Jewish refugees could have been accepted into Britain 'if they were not so gregarious and not so assertive'.[76] More blatantly, J. Bennett of the Foreign Office gave his reasons for not helping European Jewry: 'Why should the Jews be spared distress and humiliation when they have earned it?'[77] Here again, we have the full implications of what could happen when the emancipation contract was put into action. Liberal anti-semitism not only put pressure on Anglo-Jewry to conform, it also restricted any limited help that could be given to the Jews of Europe in their direst moment.

To conclude, Barnett Litvinoff has suggested that 'If it were possible to analyse the collective psyche of the Anglo-Jewish community, one deep-rooted hypochondria would be exposed; the fear of antisemitism.'[78] Litvinoff is right to suggest that the fear of anti-semitism has been central to the Anglo-Jewish experience in the twentieth century. He is wrong when he calls it hypochondria for, as has been illustrated, that fear was based on very real grounds. In the period from 1918 to the end of World War II, Anglo-Jewry was caught in a vice, between those who insisted that Jews could never be British and should be excluded from society, and those who wanted Jews to assimilate totally. It was an atmosphere more likely to produce Jewish neuroses, particularly the belief that Jews were responsible for anti-semitism, rather than a positive Anglo-Jewish identity.

This essay has concentrated on the period up to the end of World War II and it is thus appropriate to analyse a symposium on Jews published in Britain in 1945.[79] Contributors were generally agreed that Jews were responsible for anti-

---

[75] Morrison note p. 2 on Under Secretary of State's report, 13 December 1941 in PRO HO 213/14.

[76] H. Prestige minute, 7 August 1944 in PRO HO 213/1009.

[77] J. Bennett minute quoted in Rex Bloomstein's 'Auschwitz and the Allies', BBC 2 documentary, 16 September 1982 and reported in *The Listener*, 16 September 1982.

[78] B. Litvinoff, *A Peculiar People: Inside the Jewish World Today* (London, 1969), p. 70.

[79] C. Newman, *Gentile and Jew*. The 'symposium' was actually a collection of essays and articles, some specially written.

semitism, but they differed over what the Jews should do to combat it. Some demanded that the Jews simply cease being Jews, others demanded a system of apartheid. In despair, the editor, Chaim Newman, made a plea for a solution 'in which the Jew can face the world with pride, confidence, peace of mind and remain a Jew'.[80] Since Newman wrote in 1945, the dual forms of anti-semitism have not disappeared in Britain. Comments about Gerald Kaufman's limited British ancestry and the antipathy revealed at the time of the sacking of Leon Brittan – especially the comments made about the need to replace him with 'a red-blooded Englishman' – indicate that the anti-semitism of exclusion, which sees being Jewish and British as a contradictions in terms, still exists.[81] The Brittan affair is also an indication that those who see themselves as totally assimilated can suffere even more when confronted with anti-semitism. Leon Brittan, like Hore-Belisha half a century earlier, was devastated to find that such hostility could be directed towards him.[82]

But liberal anti-semitism has not disappeared: in fact the pressure to assimilate has been even stronger since 1945. Recent opposition to *shechita* and to ultra-Orthodox Jewish schools highlights how the theory of 'well-earned' anti-semitism is also still strong. The National Secular Society has suggested that separate Jewish schools are divisive and 'inevitably exacerbate the existing prejudice and discrimination against immigrants'.[83] Similarly the organization Compassion in World Farming has argued that by banning ritual slaughter 'Britain would be excluding one activity which tends to invoke racial prejudice'.[84] Again, the liberal logic is the less Jewishness, the less anti-semitism.

To summarize, British anti-semitism in the period 1918–45 was not marginal, 'one of the many freak details that made up the normal background of everyday life', in Robert Kee's words, or comparable in eccentricity to the aspidistra cult, as Mass-Observation believed.[85] Its impact, most blatantly in the form of Fascist violence, or more subtly, through pressure on Anglo-Jewry both to assimilate and to remain apart from British society, was powerful. Nor must it be assumed that British anti-semitism was simply unrespectable. It has been shown how extreme anti-semites could successfully operate through all levels of British society, and how in times of severe crisis, such as the invasion panic in the summer of 1940, expressions of overt anti-semitism could become not only respectable, but actually the done thing. Nor has the state been

[80] Ibid., pp. 304–5 and 340.
[81] For Kaufman, see D. Rosenberg, 'Racism and Antisemitism in Contemporary Britain', *Jewish Quarterly*, 32 (1985), pp. 23–4; and on Brittan, *Jewish Chronicle*, 31 January 1986.
[82] For the impact on Hore-Helisha see his talks with the editor of the *Manchester Guardian* in ed. A. J. P. Taylor, *W. P. Crozier: Off the Record. Political Interviews 1933–1943* (London, 1973), p. 132, and for Brittan, *JC*, 31 January 1986, comments by his wife.
[83] *Guardian*, 25 March 1987.
[84] Ibid., 28 August 1985, letter from Carol Long.
[85] Robert Kee, *The World We Left Behind: A Chronicle of 1939* (London, 1984), p. 248. For Mass-Observation's response, see eds A. Calder and D. Sheridan, *Speak for Yourself: A Mass-Observation Anthology, 1937–1949* (London, 1984), pp. 3–4.

immune from anti-semitism, as the internment episode and the failure to help the Jews of Europe illustrate. Simply because Britain, in the modern period, has avoided the horrors of Tsarist and Nazi persecution of Jews is no reason to dismiss British anti-semitism as unimportant. British society, which prides itself on its liberalism, its decency and its humanitarianism, has failed to produce an environment for the healthy existence of a positive Anglo-Jewish identity. This failure reflects the strength and impact of British anti-semitism.

Glossary

The following are non-English words not directly explained in the text.

Ashkenazi	Jew or form of Jewish ritual and liturgy from northern or eastern Europe (Heb)
bagel/baigel	circular bread roll (Yid)
barmitzvah	coming-of-age ceremony for 13-year-old Jewish males (Heb)
Beth Din	court of Jewish religious law (Heb)
Bund/Bundists	Jewish Workers Association of Russia and Poland, founded 1897. Term describing members. (Yid)
chazan	reader of the liturgy during synagogue services (Heb)
chevra/hevra chevroth/hebroth (pl)	association of immigrant Jews with a mutual aid function, sometimes forming the basis of a synagogue. Often used to describe a small congregation (Heb/Yid)
cheder	traditional Jewish elementary school, usually supplementary teaching (Heb)
Chossid/Chassid/Hassid	member of orthodox Russo-Polish religious sect (Heb)
ein horre	lit. evil eye (Yid)
esse	eat (imperative) (Yid)
goyim	gentiles (Heb/Yid)
heim	lit. home – the old country, i.e. Russia–Poland (Yid)
in drerd	lit. in the earth. Expletive – 'Go to Hell' (Yid)
Jewishkeit	corruption of 'Yiddishkeit' (Yid) – Jewishness or Jewish way of life

kashrut	Jewish dietary laws (Heb)
landsleit	Jews from the same town or district in the old country (Yid)
melammed	teacher in cheder (Heb)
Pesach	Jewish festival celebrating exodus from Egypt (Heb)
Rebbe	learned man and semi-official Rabbi. Colloquial.
red nisht a goyish	lit. don't speak gentile i.e. English (Yid)
Roumanishe	Romanian (Yid)
shnorroring	begging (Yid)
Sephardi	Jew or form of Jewish ritual and liturgy originally from Middle East and Spain, later northern Africa and Mediterranean countries (Heb)
Shabbos	sabbath (Heb/Yid)
Shavuos	Jewish festival celebrating the giving of the Law at Sinai (Heb)
shechita	regulations or practice of slaughter of animals according to Jewish religious law (Heb)
sheitel	wig worn by religiously orthodox Jewish women (Heb)
shiva	period and practice of mourning for the dead (Heb)
shochet/shochtim (pl)	licensed animal slaughterer trained to slaughter according to Jewish religious law (Heb)
shtetl	small town in the old country (Yid)
shul	synagogue (Yid)
Sukkos	Jewish festival celebrating the harvest (Heb)
treife	food not conforming to the Jewish dietary laws (Heb/Yid)
yeshiva	academy for advanced study of Judaism (Heb)
Yom Tovim	Festival Days. Colloquial. (Heb/Yid)

Index

DATE D